IN SEARCH OF THE REAL:
The Origins and Originality
of D. W. Winnicott

Dodi Goldman, Ph.D.

JASON ARONSON INC.
Northvale, New Jersey
London

This book was set in 11½ point Garamond by Lind Graphics of Upper Saddle River, New Jersey, and printed and bound by Haddon Craftsmen of Scranton, Pennsylvania.

Copyright © 1993 by Jason Aronson Inc.

10 9 8 7 6 5 4 3 2 1

Library of Congress Cataloging-in-Publication Data

Goldman, Dodi.
    In search of the real : the origins and originality of D. W.
  Winnicott / Dodi Goldman.
      p. cm.
  Includes bibliographical references and index.
  ISBN 0-87668-006-6 (hard cover)
    1. Winnicott, D. W. (Donald Woods), 1896–1971. 2. Psychotherapy.
  3. Psychoanalysis. 4. Winnicott, D. W. (Donald Woods), 1896–1971.
  5. Psychoanalysis—biography. I. Title.
    [DNLM: 1. Psychoanalytic Therapy—in infancy & childhood.
  2. Pediatrics—biography. WZ 100 G619i 1993]
  RC438.6.W56G65 1993
  618.92′8917—dc20
  DNLM/DLC
  for Library of Congress   93-10233

Manufactured in the United States of America. Jason Aronson Inc. offers books and cassettes. For information and catalog write to Jason Aronson Inc., 230 Livingston Street, Northvale, New Jersey 07647.

To Harriet, Noa, Liat, and Micah—with love

Contents

v

Foreword

This is the first book in a projected series that investigates the relationship between Freudian and object relations theory. Although this comparison takes place in the present volume, it happens so seamlessly that the reader might not notice its occurrence. For once this book is begun, the reader is moved into the world of Winnicott; other theorists, even Freud, have to accommodate themselves to this world. Dodi Goldman has managed to blend elements of Winnicott's life, his theoretical and clinical writings, and his place in the psychoanalytic world into an amalgam that is best characterized as a Winnicottian creation. In this book readers are facilitated to produce their own creations of Winnicott. Goldman allows us to utilize him to enhance our understanding of a variety of processes in infancy and early childhood.

It is difficult to discuss any aspect of Winnicott without being able literally to visualize his developmental concepts. Goldman provides this visualization for us and shows how these concepts grew from Winnicott's lifetime concerns and interests. Winnicott's life is used almost as a case illustration of the theoretical concepts that he has introduced. Given that Goldman has done all this in one volume, how could he also fit in any aspect of Freud's writings?

Goldman shows us that Winnicott's frequent citation of Freudian text is not simply a result of psychoanalytic tradition or of political considerations, as other writers have suggested. Rather, Winnicott was organically concerned with utilizing Freudian and Kleinian concepts in a manner that would make these ideas real and clinically relevant to him and his students. Thus Goldman's comparison of Winnicott and Freud takes us even deeper into "Winni's" vision of the mother–infant dyad and the infant's earliest moments. It is not an academic exercise but rather a theoreical adventure to see the points of convergence and divergence that bind these two incredibly different psychoanalysts. It is exactly through the divergences that Goldman shows the limitations and the possibilities of expanding both theoretical realms without either being torn asunder. In this era of multiple models Goldman is able to look at two wonderfully complex writers and perform a Winnicottian task; he shows us what is missing in each without destroying the integrity of either.

This is a remarkable task in a remarkable book and we are indebted to him for sharing these insights with us and for beginning our project in a way that will be hard to equal. As with all things we cherish there is some ambivalence. It will be harder to write and to edit the volumes to come when we begin in the elegant, erudite, and lucid tone that Goldman has provided for us.

—Steven J. Ellman, Ph.D.

Acknowledgment

Writing is a lonely task. The nagging doubt about whether one really has anything to offer that is worth writing makes the task that much more difficult. I therefore owe a great deal to those whose encouragement helped lift my isolation.

To Steve Ellman, who introduced me to a new way of understanding Freud and object relations theory and whose trenchant perspective reverberates in portions of this book. Winnicott once wrote that to do therapeutic work one needs to have in one's bones a theory of emotional development. Psychoanalytic theory is in Steve's bones and I benefited greatly from both his incisive wisdom and his willingness to support my need to go about things in my own way.

To Michael Moskowitz, whose accessibility and critical judgment were important to me both personally and intellectually.

To Larry Gould, who helped me think about why it is that so many people tend to idealize Winnicott today.

To Arnold Wilson, who alerted me to some of the potential dangers of my own methodology.

To Anni Bergman, Phil Bromberg, Carol Kaye, and Michael Lipson, whose thoughtful comments on an earlier draft of this work encouraged me to forge ahead.

To F. Robert Rodman, Christopher Bollas, Katharine Rees, Charollete Riley, Enid Balint, and Eric Trist who, in various ways, shared with me their personal versions of Winnicott's vision.

To Kenneth Eisold, whose presence was felt and appreciated.

To Jason Aronson, whose active encouragement helped energize me for the long haul. To Judy Cohen, production editor at Jason Aronson Inc., and Laura Daly, copy editor, for rescuing me from some of my own tendencies.

And to my family, who collectively had to tolerate a variety of my moods, especially my extended absences even while physically present. I am grateful that you saw me through this with unfailing support.

Introduction

WHY STUDY WINNICOTT NOW?

Donald Woods Winnicott, the renowned British pediatrician and psychoanalyst, was a quixotic figure within the psychoanalytic movement. Only during the last years of his life did he cease being somewhat of an outsider and loner and achieve full recognition within the British Psycho-Analytic Society. It took decades before his writings began to be widely circulated in the United States. His work was concerned primarily with the nature of relationships, beginning with that of mother and infant, which he described in great subtlety. Today, there is an upsurge of interest in his contribution. The many books and papers that make reference to his ideas attest to their capacity to enrich and facilitate others. "The ultimate compliment," Winnicott once averred, "is to be found and used" (1968e, p. 103). This book is an attempt to both find and use him.

Why the sudden interest in Winnicott? Simon Grolnick (1990) has argued that it is because Winnicott was the "master of the middle, the in-between," who "turned compromise and conflict into paradox, paradox that dances between the polarities" within modern thought (p. 3). Contemporary psychoanalysis, poised as it is between phenomenological and mechanistically tinged visions of the psyche, is naturally drawn to Winnicott's account of man as both an innovative symbol maker and a constitutionally and biologically driven organism. Winnicott takes up a position midpoint between controversies. He talks about the maturational drive *and* the facilitating environment. He acknowledges the importance of instincts but refuses to assign them the singular role that classical theory assumed. He develops a notion of Self somewhere between ego psychology, which relegates "the self" to the status of a content of mental apparatus, and self psychology, for which the self is an overarching construct. Within the current psychoanalytic schools—classical, object relations, interpersonal, and self psychological—Winnicott cannot be easily classified. Winnicott speaks to all of Fred Pine's (1990) "four psychologies."

It seems as if many are beginning to recognize the power of someone like Winnicott who is, in Jonathan Miller's (1987) phrase, "neither fish nor fowl nor good red herring" (p. 4). This is the mysterious power inherent in many notions, people, occupations, positions, and times of day that are interstitial by virtue of their falling between the traditional and easy to label divisions of life. Charismatic healers, magicians, and mischief makers, for example, often occupy their position because of some blemish or virtue of their personality, which is seen as unclassifiable. There is also something obscure about their practices and procedures. They work at times and in places that have an interstitial quality: on thresholds, doorways, edges of forests, between midday and midnight. This is the world that, according to Levi Strauss, "lies between the official world of culture on the one hand, and the ferocious world of nature on the other" (quoted in Miller 1987, p. 12).

Doesn't Winnicott possess some of the power and awe of the mischief maker and healer? Don't his "therapeutic consultations" (Winnicott 1971f) often have a near-magical, inimitable quality about them? Winnicott came to occupy an interstitial role because he was preoccupied with what was interstitial in human experience. The starting point of his paper, "The Location of Cultural Experience" (Winnicott 1971a), is Tagore's image of "the sea-shore of endless worlds" (p. 112). Later, in the same paper, referring to a drawing by Marion Milner, he speaks about the "tremendous significance that there can be in the interplay of the edges of two curtains, or of the surface of a jug that is placed in front of another jug" (p. 115). One of his own pencil sketches shows a mother holding her infant in such a way that her breast and the infant's behind are one and the same (reproduced in Rodman 1987). The "interplay of edges" led Winnicott to his interstitial notion of illusion and his seminal concept of the transitional phenomena that are halfway between inner and outer and between total reliance on a self-object for soothing and the soothing of one's self.

The growing interest in Winnicott is also the result of the powerful metaphors he fashioned, such as *holding environment, good-enough mother, transitional object,* and *True and False Self.* Winnicott's ideas were rarely expressed as exact logical concepts; rather, they were, in Guntrip's (1975) words, "imaginative hypotheses that challenged one to explore further" (p. 155). Metaphors are a form of symbolization that bridges the known and the unknown, the conscious and unconscious, the personal and the universal. The imaginative act of metaphor making is one of the ways in which we construct reality (Siegelman 1990). Winnicott's "imaginative hypotheses" seem strikingly apt for the kind of patients seen by the majority of clinicians today. These patients do not come to treatment ready to freely associate and overcome resistances through a therapeutic alliance dedicated to self-understanding. As more and more clinicians are faced with the reality of treating individuals who do not fit the classical neurotic mold, Winnicott's metaphors become increasingly appealing as a way of understanding clinical material.

The danger of such an appeal, however, particularly within our commercial culture, is that Winnicott's metaphors can become quickly fashionable—a cheap intellectual currency, so to speak—and the complex substance of his ideas subsequently lost. Ours is an era with potent anti-intellectual trends. At times Winnicott's deceptively simple, compressed, intuitive, and evocative style creates the illusion of understanding in the absence of concerted intellectual effort.

Winnicott's theoretical and clinical contributions have also increased in relevance over time because of the acceleration of sociological and economic trends that are destroying the ability of many families to provide an appropriate facilitating environment for healthy infant development. "It should be noted," he wrote "that mothers who have it in them to provide good-enough care can be enabled to do better by being cared for themselves in a way that acknowledges the essential nature of their task" (1960h, p. 49).

The deteriorating urban environment fails to provide parents with the necessary security that would enable them to promote the emotional well-being of their children. Despite the fact that one would search in vain through Winnicott's writings for a language that helps explore social injustice, his passionate and uncompromising belief in the importance for mental well-being of a stable, reliable, devoted, responsive, and loving caretaker, supported by a containing familial network, offers a vision of what is necessary to set things right. Winnicott's legacy can serve to guide us toward models of effective prevention.

THE NOTION OF THE REAL

A unifying theme of this book is the search for a sort of experiencing that feels real. Winnicott believed deeply that the individual possesses a unique and innate authenticity. He or she feels most alive and free when in touch with this sense of real self. But the root of inner genuineness—which is always to some extent incommunicable—can be driven inordinately underground. The individual's inner world feels unreal, and he or she is thus unable to communicate spontaneously with the outer world. Put another way, Winnicott celebrates the distinction between existing and aliveness. Existing, which implies a compliant relationship to external reality, creates an experience of unreality for the individual. To be truly alive one must be oneself.

The notion of the real is rooted in Winnicott's unique vision of how an individual deals simultaneously with internal and external reality. The individual is in a constant struggle, he believed, to distinguish fantasy from fact, external from psychic reality, the world from the dream. As Michael Eigen (1991) has noted, Winnicott's problem was "how to develop an account of experience that was not boxed in by inner and outer" (p. 70). Winnicott did not want to be trapped by either solipsistic subjectivity or the claims of objective perception. "I am implying," he wrote to Victor Smirnoff,

> that actual experiencing does not stem directly either from the individual's psychic reality [or] from the individual's external relationships. This sounds rather startling but you can perhaps get my meaning if you think of a Van Gogh experiencing, that is to say, feeling real, when painting one of his pictures, but feeling unreal in his relationships with external reality and in his private withdrawn inner life. [quoted in Rodman 1987, p. 124]

That is why it was so crucial for Winnicott to propose a paradoxical category of experience that is "between" or "intermediate."

Winnicott repeatedly asks a question that he feels psychoanalysis tends to avoid: What is life about? Perhaps the
notion of the real was Winnicott's visceral reaction to the
"nothing but" quality of certain strands of psychology
where human nature is portrayed as nothing but the concat-
enation of conditioned reflexes or the vicissitudes of transformed animal drives. He believed there must be more.
Feeling real, or the meaningfulness of experience, supple-
ments the Freudian emphasis on physical gratification as the
primary criterion for satisfaction. As Winnicott (1971a)
wrote in his essay "The Location of Cultural Experience,"

> You may cure your patient and not know what it is that
> makes him or her go on living. It is of first importance for
> us to acknowledge openly that absence of psychoneurotic
> illness may be health, but it is not life. Psychotic patients
> who are all the time hovering between living and not living
> force us to look at this problem, one that really belongs not
> to psychoneurotics but to all human beings. [p. 117]

The notion of the real is about being alive, creative, spontaneous, and playful; cherishing one's uniqueness; accepting
one's insignificance; tolerating one's own destructive impulses; living with one's own insanity; feeling integrated
while retaining the capacity for unintegration; being receptive and open and knowing how to make use of the world
without needing to react to it; finding and contributing to
the inherited cultural tradition; tolerating one's essential
isolation without fleeing to false relationships or retreating
into deleterious insulation. A healthy individual, in Winnicott's (1967a) mind, was one who felt real and whole
without denying the potential to come undone and feel
unreal:

> Being and feeling real belong essentially to health. . . . I
> contend that this is not just a value judgement, but that
> there is a link between individual emotional health and a

sense of feeling real. No doubt the vast majority of people take feeling real for granted, but at what cost? To what extent are they denying a fact, namely, that there could be a danger for them of feeling unreal, of feeling possessed, of feeling they are not themselves, of falling for ever, of having no orientation, of being detached from their bodies, of being annihilated, of being nothing, nowhere? Health is not associated with *denial* of anything. [p. 35]

Winnicott's primary concern is with the developmental origins of the capacity to feel real. He finds its archaic roots in the subtle interactions between mother and infant. In a beautiful paper written in 1967 he observed:

What does the baby see when he or she looks at the mother's face? I am suggesting that ordinarily, what the baby sees is himself or herself. In other words, the mother is looking at the baby, and what she looks like is related to what she sees there. [1967c, p. 131]

For Winnicott, the precursor of the mirror is the mother's face. Baby looks at mother's face and sees a reflection of his or her own self and aliveness. Mother's face as mirror offers the infant the first opportunity to feel real. But what happens if mother fails to provide the necessary affirmation? If she is too preoccupied, inconsistent, rigid, depressed, or fragile? In such a case, Winnicott argues, baby looks but sees only mother's face instead of a reflection of his or her sense of realness. "Perception," he writes, "takes the place of that which might have been the beginning of a significant exchange with the world, a two-way process in which self-enrichment alternates with the discovery of meaning in the world of seen things" (1967c, p. 132). Winnicott implies that premature perception of insufficiently affirming objective reality produces a distorted sense of inner deadness. Primary creativity atrophies.

It is, therefore, in the very earliest stages of development that mother facilitates, through her dependability, the capacity to feel real. Certain degrees of failure or chaotic adaptation to the child's needs will undermine the potential to feel real. Mother is internalized by the infant not only as an object, but as a total environment. The confidence to feel real is evidence of the dependability of that environment. What is more, mother must allow the infant to bask in the naive belief that the world is personally created. Winnicott goes beyond the Freudian notion of sublimation and posits a primary creativity or absolute originality that is the psychological root which enables an individual, given good-enough maternal care, to have a sense of the reality of any experience or object.

Winnicott's search for an experience of life that is real began with himself but included his way of approaching psychoanalytic theory and understanding his patients' experiences. A prominent trend in his character was the consistent concern that whatever he was doing be a genuine expression of his own spontaneous gestures. Throughout his life, he attempted to approach things as if from scratch.

Psychoanalytic theory, too, had to feel real to him, or else it was intolerable. He therefore dreaded official or dogmatic notions and often had difficulty reading metapsychological works. He asked his colleagues to allow people to discover theory in their own way and to deter from transforming psychoanalysis into a dead language. He pleaded with Melanie Klein, whose presence dominated the British Psycho-Analytic Society, to "destroy this language called the Kleinian doctrine and Kleinism" (Rodman 1987, p. 35), which, in his view, was becoming an impediment to open discussion of scientific ideas. And he applied his uncompromising antidogmatism to himself as well. He strove to avoid being tied down even by his own terms.

Winnicott's work with patients also focused on the experience of what is real in living. Six months before his death, a group of Anglican priests asked for his guidance on how to differentiate between a person who needs psychiatric treatment and one who is capable of helping himself by talking with them. After pausing a long while, Winnicott (1972) replied:

> If a person comes and talks to you and, listening to him, you feel he is boring you, then he is sick, and needs psychiatric treatment. But if he sustains your interest, no matter how grave his distress or conflict, then you can help him alright. [p. 1]

Winnicott based his advice on his observation that many of his more disturbed patients suffered from a sense of futility about their own lives. His approach to treatment was such that he aimed to facilitate the creation of an internal space in which the patient could learn to play so that life would begin to feel real. For him, this was both a modest and substantial goal of treatment that raised questions about the singular role of interpretations as a curative factor. It is precisely for this reason that there has been a certain misunderstanding about whether Winnicott actually engaged in "classical" analysis; he has been accused of substituting "holding" for "interpretation." There can be no doubt that Winnicott remained deeply suspicious of descriptions of analytic work that give credit to the interpretations for all that happens, especially for certain kinds of severely disturbed patients. He was far more attuned to the process that develops within the patient and the patient's capacity to make use of that process. Although interpretive work is essential, more than just interpretation is involved in cure.

Still, from Winnicott's perspective, holding was not an alternative to interpretation in the sense of something the analyst does instead of analyzing. He introduced the term "holding environment" as a metaphor for certain aspects of the analytic situation and process *including* interpretation. The holding environment provides a sense of safety and trust that depends upon the reliability of the caretaker and the affective communication between caretaker and child.

Since reliability and affective communication express themselves in myriad ways, Winnicott was perfectly comfortable in believing that it in no way contradicted the interpretive function.

From Winnicott's perspective, it is always a question of what the patient needs and when and how the analyst offers what is offered. Like many other analysts, he assumes there may be a long initial phase of treatment in which the articulation of unconscious meaning of the patient's associations is not primary (Ellman 1991). Similarly, during phases of regression to dependence, understanding might go beyond the explication of unconscious wishes. At no point does Winnicott deny the crucial importance of the interpretive method. What he does caution against, however, is what he calls the "making of interpretations" which, in his mind, disrupts the "natural evolution of the transference." The analyst preoccupied with "making" interpretations cannot be in a truly receptive frame of mind.

For Winnicott, psychotherapy was essentially a complex derivative of mother's face, affording the opportunity to experience oneself as alive and real. "Psychotherapy," Winnicott (1967c) writes,

> is not making clever and apt interpretations; by and large it is a long term giving the patient back what the patient brings. It is a complex derivative of the face that reflects what is there to be seen. I like to think of my work this way, and to think that if I do this well enough the patient will find his or her own self, and will be able to exist and to feel real. Feeling real is more than existing; it is finding a way to exist as oneself, and to relate to objects as oneself, and to have a self into which to retreat for relaxation. [pp. 137–138]

Or, as he explained once to some of his colleagues:

> Our patients, more and more, turn out to be needing to feel real, and if they don't then understanding is of ex-

tremely secondary importance. The awkward thing is if
they're going to be analysts: they want a bit of understanding then. But the vast majority of my patients haven't
been analysts, and I've had to be contented if they went
away feeling more real than they came. [Winnicott 1967b,
p. 582]

This book explores the way in which the unifying
theme of a search for what is real is evident in both
Winnicott's life and work.

A WORD ON METHOD

A fundamental assumption of this book is that Winnicott's theory in some way mirrors the pattern of his own
subjectivity. He creates and discovers his theory because it in
some way speaks to his own condition. As Kenneth Wright
(1991) argues, theory forms an externalized symbolic structure that mirrors the structure of the theorist's own self.

This is not to say that the truth or heuristic value of
Winnicott's ideas cannot be assessed, evaluated, or analyzed
on their own merits. Ideas, once expressed in a form that
becomes part of shared reality, can be judged by the logic of
that reality. The scientific status of certain ideas can be
evaluated by weighing evidence, seeking parsimony of explanation, assessing internal consistency, and scrutinizing
compatibility with accumulating facts. But the argument
advanced here is that the objective face of theory is not its
only face. The method employed, in other words, is not to
offer an introduction to Winnicott's theory or to evaluate its
scientific status, but to demonstrate what that theory has to
do with Winnicott. Ideas can sometimes be more fully
appreciated when the subjective aspect of theory formation
is taken into account. One way of understanding Winnicott's
theory is to see it as part of his personal struggle to discover
what feels real to him.

WINNICOTT'S WAY

Donald Woods Winnicott was fond of making lists. When invited to give a talk about children's thinking, he noted thirteen different ways the word "think" could be employed (Winnicott 1965c, p. 153). When discussing psychosomatic disorders, he listed all the "natural splits within the medical profession" ranging from surgery to faith healing (Winnicott 1964d, p. 105). In his 1947 paper "Hate in the Countertransference," Winnicott gave eighteen different reasons why a mother naturally hates her baby.

"Habit a second nature! Habit is ten times nature," the duke of Wellington is said to have exclaimed. Wellington was a veteran soldier, and he recognized the way daily drills and discipline could alter a man's natural endowment. But Winnicott's habit of list making, more than it reflects what nurture had done to alter his nature, amplifies that very nature. What does Winnicott's habit of list making reveal about the habits of his mind? One could mistakenly conclude, given his love of lists, that Winnicott was a systematic schematizer. But the key is not so much in the fact of his making lists as in his idiosyncratic *use* of the lists he made. Winnicott used these lists like a child uses a playground—as a contained area enticing one to explore. They were invitations to amplification. His lists represented not so much the rules by which a game is to be played, as the actual playing of the game itself. Rather than being the end product of organized thought, they were the jumping off point from which chaos could be given form. Lists were intended as fluid openings rather than final dictums. Although he enjoyed feeling that his ideas made an impact, Winnicott abhorred dogmatic closures—including his own. That is why at some public lectures he would provide his listeners with a list of topics he would cover, leaving spaces to be filled in as the audience deemed appropriate.

When Winnicott made a list, he was often playing with

words. "We get so used to words through using them and become so dulled to their usage," he once asserted,

> that we need from time to time to take each one and to look at it, and to determine in so far as we are able not only how the word came into being through the poetry of etymology, but also the ways in which we are using the word now. [1968a, p. 233]

Winnicott frequently preferred the gerund form of a word to emphasize the process of an event. "Playing," for example, was more important to him than the content of "play." He also reframed words to arrive at innovative concepts, often turning old ones upside-down. Winnicott turned around the well-known psychiatric diagnostic and descriptive term "de-personalization" to fashion his concept of "personalization." "Integration" suggested to him the idea of "uninte-gration." "Ruthlessness," in Winnicott's hands, was contrasted with a "stage of ruth." Winnicott loved standing classical ideas on their head! Where Freud saw psychoanalysis as a way of freeing people from illusions, Winnicott emphasized the freedom to create and enjoy illusions. Whereas classical technique centered on the value of inter-pretations, Winnicott pointed to the value of not interpret-ing. Where classical theory had explored the infantile fear of being alone, Winnicott spoke of the mature capacity to be alone. Regression, rather than being pathological in that it provides a surfeit of infantile gratification, becomes, in Winnicott's hands, a process of healing through a search for missing experiences. Psychosomatic illness was not a with-drawal of interest from the outside world, as classical theory claimed, but an attempt to rediscover one's own body.

It was Winnicott's character, however, to present these playfully defiant innovations in such a way as to be both creative and orthodox at one and the same time. That is why many psychoanalysts looked upon him with a sense of bewilderment. Many felt that his creativity was too idiosyncratically ambiguous or unnecessary. Others, seeking revisions of classical theory, yearned for him to stake out a more clearly divergent position. In the polarized atmosphere of the British Psycho-Analytic Society, Winnicott chose to remain fiercely independent, even refusing to assume leadership of the Independent Group.

These aspects of Winnicott's character—his staunch insistence on independence, his desire to playfully transform classical concepts, his reticence toward closure and dogma and need to maintain conceptual ambiguity and fluidity—all affected the content of his theory. They were part of his way of making his theory feel real to him. In fact, as Chapter 1 of this book argues, Winnicott's theoretical ideas are inextricably interwoven with his character. The originality of his thought and his originality as a person are virtually inseparable. One cannot easily disentangle Winnicott's creative concepts from the person that he was. His ideas about playing, primary creativity, devoted mothering, withdrawal, spontaneous gestures, communicating and not communicating, and transitional phenomena can all be linked to aspects of his character.

HOME IS WHERE HE STARTS FROM

The struggle to feel real begins, Winnicott argues, in earliest childhood. Winnicott was to advance the psychoanalytic notion that the earliest years of life are of crucial significance in the formation of character. He placed particular emphasis on the way in which the environment facilitated the maturational processes. As T. S. Eliot said: "Home is where one starts from." For this reason, it is worthwhile to investigate the home from which Winnicott started. In particular, this book argues that there is a connection between Winnicott's personal origins and the origins of his ideas. Winnicott was born into a prosperous Methodist family in provincial England. As the youngest child and only son of a local merchant and politician who was frequently away from home, Winnicott was raised by a mother, two older sisters, a nanny, and a governess. This "maternal environment" was to have a profound impact on him. Drawing on autobiographical fragments, reminiscences, interviews, and personal correspondences, Chapter 2 traces the association between Winnicott's theory and his biography.

In a sense, this is an attempt to elucidate Winnicott's ideas in other than just a purely abstract way. Too often, psychoanalytic theory can degenerate into schizoidlike abstractions divorced from human experience. It is particularly important that this not happen in discussing someone like Winnicott for whom staying close to experience, in all its ambiguity, was of paramount importance, and for whom theorizing was quite a personal matter. At the same time, an examination of the biographical roots of Winnicott's theorizing runs the risk of degenerating into a form of psychobiography in which the objective significance of Winnicott's ideas becomes lost in the speculative search for motivations behind the ideas. This book, however, is not a psychobiography. Its main purpose is to demonstrate the centrality of certain themes that are present in both his life and work, not to make vague speculations about Winnicott's psychological motivations for formulating certain ideas.

PEDIATRICS AND PSYCHOANALYSIS

Professionally, Winnicott was unique in pursuing the dual track of pediatrics and psychoanalysis throughout his career. Over the years, he was to handle more than 60,000 cases. This fact alone is testimony to the vitality of his professional involvement. It remains a mystery how, in addition to his twice serving as president of the British

Psycho-Analytic Society, his writing, and frequent public appearances, he was ever able to manage such an extensive caseload. No doubt, the sustained counterpoint Winnicott maintained between pediatrics and psychoanalysis greatly influenced his clinical understanding. Nevertheless, this book argues that psychoanalysis had a more profound impact on Winnicott's developmental thinking than did his training in pediatrics. It is a myth that Winnicott went *from* pediatrics *to* psychoanalysis in the course of his professional development. As Chapter 3 demonstrates, his interest in the latter actually predated his commitment to the former. And it was to the clinical data obtained through analysis to which Winnicott turned when he constructed his theory of early childhood experiences. From his point of view, the analytic material was the only real data from which subjective experience could be understood scientifically. At the same time, however, the concrete observations gleaned from pediatrics served as useful metaphors for the working of the mind.

The analytic material Winnicott relied upon in constructing his theory included his own analyses. Winnicott undertook two: one with James Strachey, which lasted for ten years beginning in 1923, and one with Joan Riviere from 1933 to 1938. Winnicott emerged from these experiences with mixed feelings. As Chapter 3 demonstrates, Winnicott deeply appreciated what he received from his analyses but felt that both were significantly lacking in important ways. Much of Winnicott's later theorizing can be understood as an attempt to fill the gaps in his analyses. He continued his efforts at self-cure through his psychoanalytic research.

THE ORIGINS OF WINNICOTT'S ORIGINALITY

For Winnicott, originality was possible only on the basis of tradition. One of the ways in which he knew his own ideas were real was that they had been articulated long before him by philosophers, theologians, and poets. This did not relieve him, however, from the painstaking task of building a theory of development based on accumulated scientific evidence. Still, Winnicott's dialogue with his intellectual precursors was one in which he was influenced by those whose writings resonated with his own aesthetic sensibilities. In much the same way as he was to describe the infant creating in imagination the very breast presented in reality, Winnicott was to creatively apperceive his intellectual precursors. As Chapter 4 demonstrates, these sources were as diverse as the Romantic poets such as Wordsworth and Keats, the British empiricists, Lewis Carroll, Darwin, the fourteenth-century Lollards, and John Wesley.

Like most thinkers, Winnicott simply took his worldview for granted. An investigation of some of the origins of his originality illuminates the nature of his solitude and connection with his environment. Establishing what constitutes an "influence" in the life of a thinker, however, can be a difficult task. The thinker himself is not always aware of what has shaped his own view of things. Are we to take Winnicott's own word at face value? Is it not also possible that perceived parallels between precursors and Winnicott might be mistaken for direct influence?

Despite these inherent difficulties, Chapter 4 argues that an understanding of Winnicott is enhanced by a recognition of the diverse cultural sources from which he was nourished. One of the legitimate criticisms frequently levied against psychoanalysis is that it tends to be ahistorical. Chapter 4 aims to go beyond an essentially ahistorical and "internalist" historiography whereby only the conceptual ideas of previous psychoanalysts are understood as relevant. Yet it attempts to do so without falling prey to a purely "externalist" account, which denies both the centrality of the clinically derived inferential process and the specificity that sometimes marks genuinely creative developments within psychoanalysis. The nonpsychoanalytic origins of

Winnicott's originality are examined without diminishing the centrality of his psychoanalytic roots.

WINNICOTT: A RADICAL
DEVELOPMENTALIST

Winnicott's search for the real is, above all, a developmental one. Winnicott was a radical developmentalist. His primary theoretical aim was to map out the territory traversed by the developing infant and to observe the gradual formation of a self capable of an experience that is real. It is central to his theory that the caretaker plays an instrumental role in this journey.

As Chapter 5 argues, the developmental theory Winnicott constructed was the result of his ongoing dialogue with Freud's clinical work. Adam Limentani (1989) recalled an interview he had with Winnicott when he went to the London Institute for training. "What kind of analysis do you wish to have?" Winnicott asked him. Limentani, expressing his disgust with political extremism, told Winnicott that he was "hoping for something different," but that he "certainly did not wish for anything not quite Freudian." To this Winnicott replied, "with ill-concealed impatience": "But we are all Freudians," adding after a brief pause, "more or less" (p. 6).

The "more or less" quality of Winnicott's allegiance to Freud has been the bone of contention among critics of Winnicott's work. Did Winnicott introduce modifications that make his way of thinking incompatible with Freud? Did he believe himself to be "Freudian" when, in fact, his innovative formulations are inconsistent with Freud's instinct theory? Which "Freud" is the one taken in by Winnicott? Greenberg and Mitchell (1983), for example, claim that Winnicott was fundamentally disingenuous in his attitude toward Freud, purposely refusing to acknowledge the extent to which he was actually altering the Freudian schema.

Another frequent complaint levied against Winnicott is that his personal language is too difficult to integrate with the conceptual language of Freudian psychoanalysis. His maddening proclivity for inventing terms and staking a claim for a certain degree of ambiguity makes theoretical integration difficult. That is why no attempt has been made, to date, to coordinate Winnicott's theory with that of Freud's.

Chapter 5 examines Winnicott's dialogue with the Freudian corpus. In particular, it demonstrates what aspects of Freudian thought Winnicott internalized and how he made Freud's theory real for himself. It shows how Freud was the theoretical luminary around whom Winnicott orbited and the founding father against whom he struggled to authentically differentiate himself. Winnicott was enormously devoted to Freud, but he needed to constantly defend his own sensitive imagination. Unlike many other psychoanalytic thinkers, Winnicott frequently dared to assess Freud from a subjective point of view. Still, in the end, in terms of method of inquiry, views regarding internal and external sources of stimulation, and developmental paths toward object love, Winnicott was essentially justified in his belief that his theory was a natural extension of Freud. In particular, Winnicott was attuned to, and influenced by, Freud's clinical work prior to World War I. His developmental schema was sufficiently consistent with that of Freud's own to render unwarranted the accusation that he was in any way purposely disingenuous.

SURVIVAL OF THE REAL

The theme of survival was inherent in all of Winnicott's writings. The closer he came to the end of his life, the more explicitly he focused on the issue. His proposition regarding the survival of the analyst was an important element in the controversial talk he gave before the New York Psychoanalytic Society a little more than a year before his death. Once again, Winnicott's subjectivity and his theoretical ideas converged. The "Use of an Object" paper was his last attempt to make public his obscure sense of what enabled him to survive as both a scientist and a dreamer. The epilogue of this book traces the development of the theme of the survival of the real in Winnicott's final paper and last year of life.

D. W. W.:
Winnicott's Presence

DWWinnicott: That is the way Donald Winnicott signed his personal letters. His scribbled signature resembled one of his squiggle games, a technique he developed to facilitate his therapeutic consultations with children. The letters ran together, blurring the boundaries between them, flowing on the page in a whimsical way. Part signature, part doodle, it invites one's own projections. One can barely make out the name, yet it can't be mistaken for another. It was as if he were presenting himself while wishing to remain anonymous—communicating and not communicating at the same time—a theme he was to develop theoretically later in his career.

The scribbled signature was Winnicott's unique way of representing himself to the world, his way of leaving a mark. So it was in all his endeavors—from the Christmas cards he hand drew and painted to the clinical treatment of severely disturbed psychotic patients: he needed to ensure that each act was a spontaneous expression of his inner being. Once

Clare Winnicott, his second wife, suggested that a card he
was drawing looked better left as it was in black and white.
"Yes," Winnicott replied, "I know, but I like painting," and
went on to add color to the card (quoted in Clancier and
Kalmanovitch 1987, p. 160). Following his own internal
impulse was more important than abiding by external crite-
ria.

No wonder Ann Clancier, a French psychoanalyst, and
Jeannine Kalmanovitch, a close friend who translated most
of Winnicott's work into French, entitled an essay about him
"A Splash of Paint in His Style" (Clancier and Kalmanovitch
1990). The phrase is actually taken from Winnicott's 1935
essay "The Manic Defense," in which he recalls the objec-
tion of some of his colleagues to his unconventional use of
the word "fantasy." "The invention of a new word,"
Winnicott replied, "would have been less easily justified
than the treatment of an already existing word with a splash
of paint" (p. 129).

Winnicott was well aware of this bent in his character,
his need to approach things in a personal way that felt
original and real to him. It was one of the reasons he was
reluctant to employ traditional metapsychological terms. In
a private letter to David Rapaport dated October 9, 1953, for
example, he wrote:

> I am one of those people who feel compelled to work in
> my own way and to express myself in my own language
> first; by a struggle I sometimes come around to rewording
> what I am saying to bring it in line with other work, in
> which case I usually find that my own "original" ideas
> were not so original as I had to think they were when they
> were emerging. [cited in Rodman 1987, pp. 53–54]

It is as if theory were a transitional phenomenon for
Winnicott: it offered him concepts that he then reinvented
in accordance with his own sensibilities. As M. Gerard
Fromm (1989) notes, Winnicott seems to "ignore serious

inquiry as to whether his use of a particular concept is something he made or something he found" (p. 5). This tendency, what F. Robert Rodman (1987) has called his "insistence on being himself," (p. xix) and what Masud Khan (1975) refers to as his "inviolable me-ness that enabled him to be so many different persons to such diverse people" (p. xi), helps explain why Winnicott is both enormously appealing to some and ignored, if not mistrusted, by others. Winnicott's personal strivings were so consistently echoed in his theoretical conceptualizations that one cannot easily disentangle his creative concepts from the person that he was. One senses a basic congruity between what he espoused—the ideas he articulated—and the way he was in the world. As Khan, who was both a former patient of Winnicott's and the driving impetus behind the publication of many of his writings noted: "His theories are abstractions of that constant happening which was Winnicott the living person and clinician" (p. xi). Clare Winnicott (1978), too, recognized the intimate connection between Winnicott's creative ideas and his way of being when she wrote:

> What was it about D.W.W. that made the exploration of this transitional area inevitable, and made his use of it clinically productive? I suggest that answers to these questions have to be looked for not simply in a study of the development of his ideas as he went along, but essentially in the kind of personality that was functioning behind them. [p. 17]

Andre Green, the former director of the Institut de Psychanalyse de Paris and holder of the Freud Memorial Chair at University College, London, also acknowledged the bond between thought and thinker. He described how he encountered Winnicott at an international congress of psychoanalysts in Edinburgh in 1961. During the days prior to the congress, the British psychoanalysts organized a series of small working groups with foreign colleagues to familiarize them with the way in which they worked:

In these groups, which were made up of fifteen or so individuals, there was a presentation of clinical material, followed by a discussion. I chose Winnicott's group, because I already knew something of his work. I had heard him four years before, in 1957, at the Paris Congress. He had read a paper on regression and withdrawal that I found very striking, but I had not seen him in action, so to speak, until London, during the little seminar, where I heard him speak for the first time of the squiggle technique. I was greatly struck by the man. Indeed Winnicott's originality of thought and his originality as a person were inseparable: his authenticity, the direct nature of his human contacts, the way in which he immediately became involved in the material that he was presenting. . . . [Clancier and Kalmanovitch 1987, p. 119]

But, it is precisely because Winnicott's "originality of thought and his originality as a person were so inseparable" that he appears, at times, too "idiosyncratic," "obtuse," or "difficult to link with other approaches" (quoted in Davis and Wallbridge 1981, p. xi). It is the reason, for example, that Raymond Cahn has argued that Winnicott's "theoretical neologisms" and "neo-concepts" have a "specificity that cannot be integrated into other theories" (Clancier and Kalmanovitch 1987, p. 114). His reluctance to employ terms in a conventional way, his proclivity for using language in a personal way to arrive at innovative concepts, his failure to clearly acknowledge modifications in theory or the sources from which some of his own ideas derived, all contributed to the reservations many psychoanalysts have about him. Winnicott's ideas, many believe, cannot be easily coordinated with the conceptual language of traditional theory. Masud Khan (1975) recalls calling on Winnicott one Sunday morning and urging him to read Lionel Trilling's "Freud and the Crisis of Our Culture":

He hid his face in his hand, paused, convulsed himself into visibility and said: "It's no use, Masud, asking me to read anything! If it bores me I shall fall asleep in the middle of the first page, and if it interests me I will start re-writing it by the end of that page." [p. xvi]

In a similar vein, Winnicott was reluctant to read the works of Ferenczi, lest he discover that he had actually stolen ideas from him (F. Robert Rodman, personal communication, February 14, 1992). The pride he took in his own inventiveness and the concomitant fear of any unauthentic ventriloquism were both core features of his character.

Winnicott (1970e) showed some recognition of the impact his fierce personalism might have on others in a talk he gave before the Progressive League in the last year of his life. "I have this need to talk," he said, "as though no one had ever examined the subject before, and of course this can make my words ridiculous. But I think you can see in this my own need to make sure I am not buried by my theme. . . . Evidently, I must be always fighting to feel creative . . ." (p. 41).

Not only did Winnicott feel compelled to "fight to feel creative," but he strove to guard against what he perceived as threats to his unique sensitivity. A poignant example of this occurred in the 1920s when, after having been an outpatient physician at Paddington Green, he was finally assigned inpatient bed privileges. At first, Winnicott was excited by his newly won status. But soon, he began to avoid the inpatient unit, handing over the inpatients to a junior associate. In a private letter to Margaret Torrie he explained why:

I knew at the time why I was doing this. I said to myself: the distress of babies and small children in a hospital ward, even a very nice one, adds up to something terrific. Going into the ward disturbs me very much. If I become an in-patient doctor I shall develop the capacity not to be disturbed by the distress of the children, otherwise I shall not be able to be an effective doctor. I will therefore

concentrate on my O.P. work and avoid becoming callous
in order to be efficient. So I lost the status symbol but that
didn't matter somehow. [quoted in Rodman 1987, p. 168]

Winnicott was consistently cautious in choosing his
caseload so as to maximize his strengths and preserve his
receptivity. For years, he deliberately avoided taking on
cases of delinquents because he feared being sidetracked into
a time-consuming endeavor promising little benefit. When
he worked with severely regressed patients, he was careful
to take on only one at a time.

Winnicott's need to defend his own sensitivity helps
explain why Charles Rycroft, for example, described him as
a "crypto-prima donna" (quoted in Grosskurth 1986, p.
399). It was inevitable, given such a temperament, that he
would be ignored by some and alienate others along the
way. Michael Balint, feeling slighted, voiced in a private
letter to him what many felt:

> Perhaps I ought to say here that this has happened several
> times during our friendship. You emphasized on more
> than one occasion that "though"—(I quote here from
> memory)—"Ferenczi and Dr. Balint have said all these
> many years ago, here I am not concerned with what they
> said," or, "I have not had time to read that but I shall ask
> the Honorary Librarian to fill this gap," etc. Of course, in
> this way you always have the audience laughing and on
> your side—no-one among us likes to read boring scientific
> literature and if somebody of your stature admits it in
> public, he can be certain of his success. . . . Your way of
> expressing your ideas forces one into the position of either
> saying "this is splendid and entirely new" or of remaining
> silent. [quoted in Rudnytsky 1991, p. 86]

What Winnicott experienced as his own need "not to be
buried" was seen by others as an obstinate refusal to acknowledge predecessors. The narcissistic need to be

splendid and original had its cost. It is also possible that Winnicott actually gravitated toward situations in which he could actively defend his own spontaneity against perceived encroachments.

Still, because Winnicott's ideas were so clearly an expression of his own way of being in the world, they can be better appreciated by a consideration of his personal style. In a sense, this is not unlike Winnicott's own theoretical distinction between "being" and "doing." Creativity, Winnicott argues (1970), is the "doing that arises out of being" (p. 39). His ideas, concepts, and theories are the "doings" that arose out of his own "going-on-being." These "doings" can, of course, be assessed, evaluated, and analyzed on their own merits. Their truth, or heuristic value, can be determined in and of their own right. Ideas, once expressed in a form that becomes part of shared reality, ought to be judged by the criterion and logic of that reality. But these same ideas can be more fully *understood* as "creative apperceptions," the coloring of shared reality in an individual way, a way that can give, according to Winnicott, a feeling of great significance and make life feel real and worth living.

What was it, then, about Winnicott's "going-on-being," his relationship with himself, others, ideas, and things that compelled him to the psychoanalytic view that he came to hold? Which trends in his own character show up as themes in his theorizing? What was it about *his* nature that brought him to view *human* nature the way he did? How is Winnicott's subjectivity mirrored in his theory? And what tools do we have to assess how his apperceptions became perceptions and conceptions? In a sense, psychoanalysis itself was designed as such a tool. But, in the absence of any clinical data on Winnicott, we are left to rely on the subjective experiences he made public and the personal recollections of those who knew him.

Those closest to Winnicott referred to him affectionately in an elliptical, condensed way: D. W. W. When Clare

Winnicott (1978) was asked by the editors of a book on transitional objects to write something of a personal nature about him, she must have felt she was capturing something of his essence when she chose to refer to him simply by these initials.

What the use of simple letters to represent Winnicott's being captures about him is precisely those qualities that make him such a deceptive writer and theoretician. He quite naturally strove to remove trappings of pretension. It was as if he preferred the risk of being ignored over the dread of feeling he was making false or insincere claims. He was free from ostentation or showy extravagance. As a result, he often expressed his ideas in such a highly compressed way that the reader is not always aware of the complexity of what is being articulated. The ease with which one reads Winnicott's evocative passages must be matched with concerted intellectual effort; seemingly vague passages mask astonishingly precise nuances. As Arnold Modell (1983) points out:

> He was a successful lecturer to lay audiences but behind his simple statements (which at times appear almost banal when taken out of context) stands a hidden subtlety and complexity which is at times quasi-poetic in its form and is indeed difficult to grasp. [p. 111]

Winnicott's public talks before diverse lay audiences reveal another fundamental element in his character: his humility. In his talk (1968b) before the Association of Teachers of Mathematics, for example, he opens by acknowledging:

> In the areas of mathematics and of teaching I am a greenhorn. Your newest student knows more than I do. Certainly I would not have accepted Mr. Tahta's and your invitation, except that in his initial letter he seemed to know that I belong to an alien speciality, and that he could

only expect from me a comment on the ecology of the
particular garden that I happen to cultivate. [p. 55]

Similarly, in an address (1967e) before representatives of
schools for delinquent boys he willingly conceded that

> I know I could not do your job. By temperament I am not
> fitted for the work that you do; and in any case I am not
> tall enough or big enough. I have certain skills and a certain
> kind of experience, and it remains to be seen whether
> there can be some pathway found between the things that
> I know something about and the work that you are doing.
> It might happen that nothing that I say will have any effect
> at all on what you do when you go back to your work. [pp.
> 90–91]

Winnicott's professed humility was offset, however, by
other trends in his character, such as the delight he took in
being observed by others and a certain subtle or implied
arrogance he displayed at times. Winnicott was a graceful
narcissist and a natural performer. He loved being surrounded by people watching him conduct therapeutic consultations or listening to his case presentations. From his
personal correspondences it is evident that he thrived on the
opportunity to present his ideas to audiences of all kinds.

At the same time, he allowed himself latitude with
patients that would not have been tolerated in less prominent clinicians. The license he took was part of a pattern of
making the therapeutic enterprise feel real for him, personally. He refused to define psychoanalysis based on frequency
or regularity of sessions. Instead, he believed in a form of
"psychoanalysis on demand" (Winnicott 1977, p. xv), in
which his motto was often "How little need be done?"
(Winnicott 1962f, p. 166). He saw the actual person of the
therapist, and a personal technique, as essential ingredients
in therapy. At times, he went so far as to imply that
psychoanalysis was not *what* was done but *who* was doing it
(Winnicott 1958b).

Winnicott offered tea to patients, sought one out in a public restaurant to change an appointment, held another's hands for a long period of the analysis, and even gently rocked a patient's head. He was frequently late to his appointments at Paddington Green, which he nicknamed his "psychiatric snack-bar." Eric Trist recalls seeing him shout advice across a crowded room to a mother whom he had merely overheard having a discussion with another woman (Eric Trist, personal communication, March 1, 1992). Winnicott often agreed to see children on an irregular basis, rather than transfer them to more available colleagues. As Katharine Rees, a psychiatric social worker who worked with him at Paddington Green, remarked: "It is as if he felt that an ounce of Winnicott was worth a pound of pedestrian psychotherapy." As a result, at least some of the children were sorely "short-changed" (Katharine Rees, personal communication, September 23, 1991). He obviously felt special or unique such that he allowed himself to do whatever felt right to him at the very moment.

The narcissistic trend in his character appeared as a central theme in his theory as well. Healthy emotional development was contingent, in Winnicott's view, on a primary experience of what could be called healthy narcissism, in which the infant is allowed to feel itself to be the creator of the world. Without this archaic experience—which, for Winnicott, is both a developmental and potential aspect of all experience—life would feel futile and unreal.

Winnicott's own narcissism remained "healthy" in the sense that it did not preclude a capacity to enter imaginatively into other people's lives. It did not have the dead-end quality of more pathological forms of narcissism. Although his overt behavior might have appeared, at times, to be narcissistic, he genuinely enjoyed being used by others and not exploiting them. As much as he wanted to be himself, he wanted others to be themselves. As he wrote once to Augusta Bonnard: "Let's enjoy being ourselves and enjoy seeing what we do when we meet it in the work of others"

(Rodman 1987, p. 117). If anything, Winnicott's narcissism caused him to *underestimate* the difference between himself and others (Charollete Riley, personal communication, November 5, 1991). He was obviously blessed with a genius for quickly and intuitively grasping another person's core conflicts and communicating this in a way that the person could take in. He took it for granted that others were equally competent. As a result, he was not particularly concerned with how the formal structure of analysis might serve as a safeguard against potential abuses.

Winnicott did recognize, however, the inherent limitations of his own tendency to perceive intuitively. What served him well clinically—the ability to grasp intuitively the rhythm of each individual—needed, at times, to be offset by a capacity to "think." As Winnicott (1945b) wrote in an article that he contributed to the *Liberal Magazine*: "I think we would always rather hear the thinkers talking about what they are thinking out than hear the intuitive people talking about what they know" (p. 170).

Still, Winnicott's belief in unconscious processes kept him fundamentally suspicious of the deceptive appeal of structured thought. As he elaborated in the same article:

> The danger is partly that the thinkers make plans that look marvelous. Each flaw as it appears is dealt with by a still more brilliant piece of thinking out, and in the end the masterpiece of rational construction is overthrown by a little detail like GREED that has been left out of account— the net result being a new victory for unreason, with its consequence: an increase in the public distrust of logic. [p. 170]

One senses, therefore, in Winnicott's writings the concerted struggles of an intuitive man, suspicious of the deceptive appeal of structured thought, to present his ideas as thought through rather than solely personal expressions of what he knows.

Furthermore, the narcissistic aspect of Winnicott's temperament, his subtle displays of entitlement, never diminished the genuine respect he expressed toward those with whom he worked. Clare Winnicott said that he frequently would come bounding up the stairs exclaiming, "I have learned so much from my patients today!" (quoted in Grosskurth 1986, p. 399). At the end of supervision he would often thank a student for helping him. Jean Marc Alby, Professor of Psychiatry and Medical Psychology at the Faculté de Médecin Saint-Antoine in Paris, had come to know Winnicott during a series of Anglo-French psychoanalytic meetings. Reflecting on Winnicott's modesty, he commented:

> He did not believe himself to be omnipotent with his patients. He did not ask of them what they were not capable of giving. Thus he did not expect mothers to be very good or even good, but simply good enough; he sustained those who had difficulties with their children, telling them to do at least what they could, whereas Freud said that whatever mothers do it will be bad in any case. [Clancier and Kalmanovitch 1987, pp. 110–111]

In a similar vein, Winnicott (1968c) himself describes how at times he makes interpretations "mainly to let the patient know the limits of my understanding" (p. 219).

The "limits of understanding" was something that Winnicott wrestled with consistently. On the one hand, he assumed that everyone, child or adult, has a primary desire to be understood. He writes very little about "defenses" and a great deal about how patients guide therapists toward what they really need. Winnicott saw patients as more communicative than evasive, more collaborative than antagonistic. Playful self-revelation was far more curative, he believed, than "clever" interpretations.

At the same time, however, he theorized about an

essentially isolated and noncommunicative core to the personality. And, personally, he tended to fear being insufficiently understood or appreciated, even when this was not the case. He felt, for example, that Anna Freud never adequately acknowledged his notion of the transitional object, when, in fact, she was known to have spoken with great respect about it (Katharine Rees, personal communication, September 23, 1991). Winnicott was also often surprised when he was able to express an idea in clear and simple language that other people understood (Clancier and Kalmanovitch 1987). He seemed to have a profound sense that he just didn't understand enough and that, therefore, others wouldn't understand him. Yet he also had an unyielding desire to put that which he was vaguely becoming aware of into words. That is probably why his manner of speech has been described as "both daring and timid, the hesitant search for the right words, and the failure to find them. . . ." (Clancier and Kalmanovitch 1987, p. 138). His style of writing often has the quality of talking to himself out loud. And, in his therapeutic work, he knew how to make clinical use of not-knowing. As one of his students observed, Winnicott's competence as a therapist included a "capacity to tolerate feeling ignorant or incompetent and a willingness to wait until something genuinely relevant and meaningful emerged" (Casement 1985, p. 9).

His tendency to be skeptical about his own understanding contributed to his mistrust of the language of psychoanalysis as well. In a private letter to Anna Freud, dated March 18, 1954, Winnicott voiced his doubts about the psychoanalytic lexicon. Characteristically, he began by acknowledging that he has an "irritating way of saying things in my own language instead of learning how to use the terms of psycho-analytic metapsychology." He went on, however, to "try to find out why it is that I am so deeply suspicious of these terms. Is it because they can give the appearance of a common understanding when such understanding does not exist? Or is it because of something in myself? It can, of course, be both" (Rodman 1987, p. 58).

This is vintage Winnicott. On the one hand, he showed a willingness to look candidly inward at the obstacles within himself while, at the same time, gently chiding his colleagues for their hubris. What is more, Winnicott was far less concerned about theoretical ideas being "true" than he was about things that felt real to him being useful to others. He evaluated theoretical ideas using the same criterion that he elevated into a primary value and a goal of therapy: the feeling that something is real. And for theoretical ideas to be real, they had to have a personal and subjective foundation; acquired jargon would not suffice. The world of ideas was a dead letter unless animated by one's own subjective stance.

A poignant example of Winnicott's way of animating technical discussions and questioning presumed knowledge appears in a private letter he wrote to Gabriel Casuso, a Cuban psychoanalyst, in 1956. Casuso had written a paper in which he discussed his year-old son's discovery of his penis. In response, Winnicott playfully and defiantly turned conventional wisdom on its head by amusing himself with the question: "What is the penis symbolical of?" Winnicott wondered if, perhaps, to some extent the penis might be symbolical of "a snake or of a baby's bottle or of the baby's body as it moved in the womb before the arms and legs became significant. . . . Or, of other more fundamental objects as, for instance, the toothbrush, or some toy or . . . of the fish or reptile" (Rodman 1987, pp. 99–100). This was Winnicott's way of letting his colleagues know that he felt one should never presume one knows these things for certain.

Winnicott's capacity to look inward, to be in touch with his internal world, contributed to making him such an astonishing clinician. As Peter Rudnytsky (1991) commented: "Beneath his vitality and self-confidence, Winnicott must have had a tenaciously regressed ego of his own to tolerate his stressful work with patients'' (p. 140). Or, as Anne Clancier (Clancier and Kalmanovitch 1987) noted, he was "perhaps above all a man who allowed his unconscious to function, who knew how to identify with others at a deep level" (p. 109). In his paper "Hate in the Countertransference," Winnicott (1947) states quite explicitly that an analyst must be in touch with his or her own primitive nature. One cannot deny hate that really exists in oneself. He writes,

> If we are to become able to be the analysts of psychotic patients, we must have reached down to very primitive things in ourselves, and this is but another example of the fact that the answer to many obscure problems of psychoanalytic practice lies in further analysis of the analyst. [p. 196]

It was precisely his ability to experience the ebb and flow of his own unconscious processes that also allowed Winnicott to respond genuinely and creatively to shared reality. As Marion Milner (1978) put it: "Whatever it means to say that someone is a genius, I do wish to make clear that I believe Winnicott was on excellent terms with his primary process; it was an inner marriage to which there was very little impediment" (p. 42).

This "inner marriage," however, was not without its external strains. It was probably this very same quality that led many who knew him to describe him as basically a loner and sometimes quite difficult (Grolnick 1990). He frequently gave the impression that he was asleep when he was listening, "waking up" only to ask a most pertinent question that seemed to come out of nowhere (Clancier and Kalmanovitch 1987). Serge Lebovici describes how during an International Congress of Psychoanalysis, Winnicott chaired a session. Someone was reading a paper when he noticed that Winnicott had put his head down on his hands on the table, his eyes shut. When the speaker finished, Winnicott did not move. Lebovici remembers thinking at the time that Winni-

cott was dead. Then, suddenly, he sat up as if nothing at all
had happened (Clancier and Kalmanovitch 1987, p. 133).

To some, this undoubtedly appeared odd, if not down-
right eccentric. Evelyne Kestemberg, for example, met Winnicott in Stockholm in 1963. He appeared to her to have an
"unconventional side" that sometimes seemed "strange."
And she recalls her sense of fright watching him cross a
street when nobody else would do so, feeling certain that he
would certainly be run over. "I think the drivers saw that he
was not looking," she writes, "for indeed he gave the
impression that he was not looking, as if he were moving in
a world of his own" (p. 127).

Was this a form of retreat? Withdrawal? Recourse to
inner resources? He was obviously, among other things,
drawing on his own personal experience when he described
(Winnicott 1962a) the special psychological condition of
mothers in the weeks before and after giving birth by saying:

> In concentrating or in becoming preoccupied, we can be
> said to become withdrawn, moody, anti-social, or just
> irritable, according to our pattern. I think that this is a pale
> reflection of the thing that happens to mothers, if they are
> well enough to surrender to motherhood. [pp. 69–70]

Kestemberg believed that Winnicott distanced himself
from whatever might distract him with "total contempt for
the outside world" (Clancier and Kalmanovitch 1987, p.
127). This is not unlike Winnicott's own description of the
"ruthlessness" of the artist. It may also help explain why he
became preoccupied with the theme of communicating and
not communicating, which emerged quite naturally from his
own "frightening fantasy of being infinitely exploited"
(Winnicott 1963h, p. 179). Clancier (Clancier and Kalmanovitch 1987) on the other hand, felt that it was thanks to this
same "auto-erotic capacity" that Winnicott was able to
struggle against disease and emerge after each of his numerous coronary attacks. Whatever the case may be, there

was obviously a quality of his experience that made him particularly attuned to the themes of withdrawal that he was to develop later in his career (Winnicott 1954c, pp. 255–261).

As fruitful and potentially eccentric as his self-absorbed preoccupation might have been, public expression generally remained within the bounds for the English gentleman he was reared to be. Public decorum was maintained. He was playful but never frivolous or irresponsible. His childlike qualities usually appeared charming and whimsical rather than inappropriate. The boundaries of his ideas and concepts might have been fluid, but he consistently kept his mischievous and self-disclosing impulses checked. Although quite forthcoming about his own limitations—no other analyst allowed such detailed public scrutiny of analytic work—his candor was never such that it spoiled by being confessional or overintimate.

If Winnicott's dialogue with his own inner processes did not give rise to confessional utterances, it did express itself in the unique quality of his presence. Many who came in contact with him commented on his "poised somatic stillness" in one way or another (Khan 1975). Drawing on his experience as Winnicott's patient, for example, M. Khan wrote in the introduction to the French version of Winnicott's *Therapeutic Consultations* about

> the extraordinary tranquility emanating from that somatic presence, at once balanced and sparkling, that he possessed when he was sitting and "holding" the regressed patient in the clinical situation. Only those of us who have had the privilege to be his patients and were the object of his care can testify to his unique quality of attention, psychical as well as somatic. [quoted in Clancier and Kalmanovitch 1987, pp. 74–75]

Khan was mistaken to believe, however, that only Winnicott's patients were aware of there being something

special about the quality of his presence and attention. Eva
Rosenblum, the French psychoanalyst, recalls how on the
occasion of a conference she was standing on the platform of
a London station. Suddenly, Winnicott appeared on the
platform. She barely knew him, having met him only casu-
ally, "glass in hand," at a party. What surprised her most
was her own reaction. She found herself approaching him on
the platform saying, "Oh! When I see you the sun comes
out." "I could never remember," she added, "whether I felt
shy at going up to a gentleman I knew so little and saying
something like that!" (Clancier and Kalmanovitch 1987, pp.
75–76). And Anne Clancier has recounted her personal
impressions of a seminar given at the Institut E. Claparède:

> What struck me most about the little man was his eyes,
> which, although they looked shut, nevertheless shone
> brightly. He questioned us, but they were not at all the
> same questions as those posed by Mme L.—they were
> rather odd questions and one didn't know what he was
> getting at. At the same time, one felt a kind of empathy—
> it was really very strange. [p. 74]

"One didn't know what he was getting at." That is a
common experience of many who encounter some of Winnicott's work—and this despite the fact that he is really a
quite precise thinker. There is a frequent sense that he is
"getting at something," that he is close to an experience that
is difficult to grasp intellectually. Partly, this is because he
had an obvious fascination with that which is barely percep-
tible. Winnicott was drawn naturally to that which is preverbal and, perhaps, that which is impossible to ever put into
words. He tended to work more from his body than from his
mind. As he repeatedly acknowledged about himself: "I am
not an intellectual and in fact I personally do my work very
much from the body-ego" (Winnicott 1960a, p. 161). He
challenged himself to put those bodily experiences into
words. The process begins with muddle. This is not unlike

the way the self comes into being, according to Winnicott: from desultory formless activity reflected back. An infant, Winnicott claimed, gradually drifted from unintegrated to integrated states and back again. Winnicott had a unique capacity to tolerate and even enjoy both formless quiescence and the restive search for form. As he testified about himself in a lecture before students: "What you get out of me, you will have to pick out of chaos" (quoted in Grolnick and Barkin 1978, p. 37).

Marion Milner (1978), in a memorial meeting of the British Institute of Psycho-analysis held after Winnicott's death, described this feature of his in vivid detail:

> Over the years, when we had a gap in time and we had arranged to meet and discuss some theoretical problem, he would open the door and then be all over the place, whistling, forgetting something, running upstairs, a general sort of clatter, so that I would be impatient for him to settle down. But, gradually, I came to see this as a necessary preliminary for the fiery flashes of intuition that would follow, when he did finally settle down. [p. 37]

Eventually, Winnicott was to elevate this personal characteristic into a principle of psychoanalytic technique: allowing for phases of "nonsense," when no thread of material should be analyzed because what is happening is the preliminary chaos that precedes the creative process. Muddle is not necessarily the expression of conflict, but the necessary formlessness out of which the self creates something real.

There was, as Serge Lebovici notes, a "great air of freedom" about Winnicott (Clancier and Kalmanovitch 1987, p. 133). He loved life and lived wholeheartedly. As Madeleine Davis (Davis and Wallbridge 1981) has pointed out, perhaps the most important temperamental influence affecting Winnicott's work was his "belief that life is worth living" (p. 3). Many who knew him used the word "pixie" to describe him. Betty Joseph called him "a bit of a Peter Pan" (Grosskurth 1986, p. 399). Until very late in his life, he would ride his bicycle with his feet on the handlebars and drive his car with his head through the roof and a walking stick on the accelerator. In fact, when he was 71 years old, his cycling behavior brought a warning from the police about his infringements of important traffic regulations (Rudnytsky 1989).

Clare Winnicott, in a visit to New York before her death in 1984, enjoyed telling Simon Grolnick (1990) how she and Donald would often end up playing on the floor together. She also recalls how he would present her with a new squiggle every morning at breakfast. If they were separated, she would receive one in the mail (Clancier and Kalmano-vitch 1987). He had an English sense of humor that included lightness on serious occasions (James 1982). What capti-vated Marion Milner (1978), the first time she heard him speak in public, was the "mixture in him of deep seriousness and his love of little jokes" (p. 39). He loved playing piano, singing, dancing, writing poems, as well as physical activi-ties. As a student he was a champion runner. He has been described as having had an "inexhaustible vitality" (Khan 1975, p. xxxvi) and an "immense capacity to enter into things and enjoy himself" (Winnicott 1983, p. 4). Fragments of what was intended to be his autobiography, discovered after his death, were entitled "Not Less Than Everything" (Grolnick and Barkin 1978).

Clare Winnicott (1983) recalls that somebody stayed at their house one weekend and said to her:

> "You and Donald play, don't you?" So I said, "Do we? I have not thought of it in that way." He said: "Oh, yes you do. You play with me. You play with all kinds of things. My wife and I, we don't play." And I thought a lot about it, and I could see what he meant. We *did* play with arranging our furniture—chucking this out or—with books, with reading. . . . We had our Saturdays *always* for play. . . . [p. 5]

Is it any wonder, then, that Winnicott was to turn "playing" into a central theoretical concept, a sign of health, maturity, and mental well-being? That he was to assert that the capacity to play was testimony that the individual was developing "a personal way of life . . . of becoming a whole human being, wanted as such, and welcomed by the world at large" (Winnicott 1964a, p. 130)? Or that psychoanalysis could only really begin once a patient was helped to acquire the capacity to play? Play was, after all, Winnicott's own personal idiom. And it was an idiom more sensual than sexual. He apparently never lost that sense of wonder and terror that a child feels in the face of the universe, what Khan (1975) calls his "naive and wayward innocence" (p. xii). Clare Winnicott (1978) even drew the specific connection between his capacity to play and the content of his theoretical writings when she said:

> The essential clue to D.W.W.'s work on transitional objects and phenomena is to be found in his own personality, in his way of relating and being related to, and in his whole life style. What I mean is that it was his capacity to play which never deserted him, that led him inevitably into the area of research that he conceptualized in terms of the transitional objects and phenomena. [p. 18]

Yet, for all his natural ability to play, Winnicott (1965a) always respected the fact that "spontaneity only makes sense in a controlled setting" (p. 213). Self-imposed controls make pleasures and feelings serve the expression of ideas, giving them form and, therefore, meaning (Davis and Wallbridge 1981, p. 140). This is why Martin James (1982) says of Winnicott: "Egregious, he was happy to be, but never a silly sheep; playful, but never irresponsible" (p. 493). He was relaxed, but not careless.

In a typically English manner, he deeply respected institutions. His two terms of office as president of the British Psycho-Analytic Society, his forty-year affiliation with Paddington Green Children's Hospital, his participation as a member of the special committee appointed in 1953 by the International Psychoanalytical Association to investigate the crisis in the Paris Psychoanalytic Society, and the stream of papers he read before his own society are all testimony that he was devoted to and worked well through existing structures. He was devoted to his patients, his organization, and to his wife. His capacity for devotion carried over to his general belief that it was the task of the healthy individuals in society to carry the ill members (Winnicott 1967a, p. 37). It is not surprising, therefore, that so central to Winnicott's theory were his ideas about ordinary devoted mothers.

Winnicott was the inspiration behind the committee set up to erect a statue of Freud in Swiss Cottage. His secretary, Joyce Coles, recalled how Winnicott was particularly delighted with the thought that children would clamber up on the great man's head while playing (Clancier and Kalmanovitch 1987). That was Winnicott: playfully irreverent and deeply respectful.

Winnicott's fantasy about the Freud statue also reveals the indirect manner in which he sometimes expressed opposition. He stayed within the existing establishment while simultaneously knocking at it all the time. As Katharine Rees observed: "He didn't like head-on arguments . . . Instead, he would throw the gauntlet from the sidelines" (Katharine Rees, personal communication, September 23, 1991). He may have had some problem with his own aggression. It was definitely important for him to feel that his aggression was tolerated. Although not afraid of stating his own opinions, he defused confrontations with disarming charm. Throughout the tumultuous years of activity in the British Psycho-Analytic Society, he distanced himself from the sectarian squabbles, even refusing to assume the leadership of the so-called Independent Group.

Still, periodic expression of defiance was crucial for his

sense of himself as real. As he said once (Winnicott 1960b) in response to Joseph Sandler's paper on the superego:

> The capacity for object-relationships having become established, the child can now proceed to such things as obedience, defiance and identification. I note that Mr. Sandler leaves out defiance. He speaks of the child's need to feel loved, but the child must also feel real, and if defiance is omitted from the scheme and the child only obeys or identifies, then the child sooner or later complains of lack of feeling real. [p. 472]

Without defiance, Winnicott would have felt disconnected from himself.

F. Robert Rodman, who edited some of Winnicott's personal letters, believes that Winnicott's available aggression actually grew over time (F. R. Rodman, personal communication, February 14, 1992). It is doubtful whether Winnicott could have been as truly useful to his patients as he was had he not been sufficiently in touch with his own aggression. In fact, on two occasions at the memorial meeting in his honor at the British Psycho-Analytic Society the word "ruthless" was even linked to his name (Milner and Gillespie 1972). This was the same word Winnicott employed to describe a stage of infant development and an important element in the analysis of severely disturbed patients. He saw ruthlessness as an aspect of the primitive love impulse, rather than as an inherently destructive force. Winnicott (1968c) viewed inborn aggression as "variable in a quantitative sense" (p. 226). Even after sublimation and displacement, a certain amount is still "left over" (Rodman 1987, p. 108). Aggression, therefore, had to be tolerated in oneself and received by others. Winnicott's private letters are permeated with a sense of how he could be unflinchingly forward while struggling to harness his own aggression for constructive purposes.

Winnicott's capacity to tolerate his own aggression was perhaps best conveyed by the absence of any naive sentimentalism in his thinking. He wrote openly about how analysts can hate their patients. He purposely coined the term "good-enough" mother to convey his belief that motherhood cannot be reduced to mawkish sentiments alone. Winnicott was sensitive to the importance of mother's role, but he never sentimentalized it. "Any kind of sentimentality," he wrote in a letter to P. D. Scott, "is worse than useless" (Rodman 1987, p. 22). In the first of his broadcast talks (Winnicott 1964a), he discusses a mother's love for her infant in a candid way:

> Let me quickly say that I'm not talking about sentimentality. You all know the kind of person who goes about saying, "I simply *adore* babies." But you wonder, do they love them? A mother's love is a pretty crude affair. There's possessiveness in it, there's appetite in it, there's a "drat the kid" element in it, there's generosity in it, there's power in it, as well as humility. But sentimentality is outside it altogether and is repugnant to mothers. [p. 17]

Sentimentality was repugnant to Winnicott because it entailed a denial of unconscious reservoirs of cruder emotions. He believed that any sentimental swing in attitude would invariably be followed sooner or later by a reaction. As he wrote once in a letter to the editor of the London Times:

> The sentimentalist in regard to crime is using the criminal for the expression of his own hidden criminality. . . . The practice of the Courts must be founded on something more sure than sentimentalism, either on the deep feelings of unsentimental people who can reach to the criminal in themselves, or else on the thinking-out of those who can take into account the unconscious. [quoted in Rodman 1987, p. 15]

Winnicott might have made original contributions toward understanding the antisocial tendency, but he was never naive about its consequences.

Winnicott's understanding, care, and devotion to people and institutions, in other words, was always tempered by an unsentimental appraisal of unconscious factors, a proclivity for defiance, an effort to make his own aggression tolerable, a willingness to be frontal, and an aversion to direct confrontation. At the same time, he never spoiled his connection by the wish to impose his beliefs on others. He was not an evangelist and never proselytized. Although he undoubtedly had the wish to influence others, he preferred to be found rather than try to convert. By temperament and upbringing, he was virtually incapable of zealous enthusiasm for his cause. In part, this is due to the deep respect he had for the individual's own spontaneous gestures on which he was reluctant to intrude or impinge. But it is also the expression of what Khan (1975) has called his "militant incapacity to accept dogma" (p. xi).

Winnicott's antipathy to dogma placed him in a sensitive position, however, when it came to his proclivity for inventing new theoretical terms. He had to balance his aversion to transforming his own ideas into a new canon with both the pleasure he took in his inventiveness and the strength of his convictions. In his paper "The Development of the Capacity for Concern," for example, just before he postulates the existence of a separate "object mother" and "environment-mother" in the immature infant's mind, Winnicott (1963a) qualifies his own theoretical innovation by saying: "I have no wish to invent names that become stuck and eventually develop a rigidity and an obstructive quality . . ." (p. 75). No wonder Arnold Modell (1983) commented once that Winnicott was a "psychoanalytic revolutionary without the temperament or personality with which to make a revolution" (p. 112).

This aversion to dogma, the persistent wish that boundaries, although containing, remain fluid, helps explain why Winnicott failed to develop a truly systematic, comprehensive, or coherent theory. This is not to say that he was lacking in strong convictions, for Winnicott certainly had his share. But, rather than develop a grand scheme, he articulates a point of view. As J. B. Pontalis remarks, Winnicott failed to provide a "theoretical grid" (Clancier and Kalmanovitch 1987, p. 140). In part, this is attributable to what Winnicott recognized as his own intellectual limitations. As he confessed once to Charles Rycroft: "It is one thing to come at a problem through clinical work and to formulate something in one's own language, and another thing to take ideas and interrelate them, thus contributing to the building of theory" (quoted in Rodman 1987, p. 87).

Although many of Winnicott's ideas may resonate with the clinical experience of others, it is unlikely that they will be transformed into a new psychoanalytic orthodoxy. As Pontalis remarked: "One might say that there are 'Kleinian' patients. I don't think there are 'Winnicottian' ones" (Clancier and Kalmanovitch 1987, p. 140).

Winnicott's reluctance to engage in systematic theory building is also very much rooted in the practical side of his character. As Davis and Wallbridge (1981) have noted, he was far too down-to-earth for the word "intellectual" ever to be applied to him. He was always concerned with the practical aims of child care and development. It is not a coincidence that the actual paraphernalia of infant care—the bath, the blanket, the teddy bear, the bottle—all figure prominently in his writing. The environment is always considered in terms of the actual lives and attitudes of the caretakers. The logical or formal consistency of theory, on the other hand, was never of paramount importance to him. By being intimately involved with the care and management of children, he was fully cognizant of the limitations of theory. As he once said:

> The nearer a worker is to the child the more difficult it will be for him or her to discuss theory without being over-whelmed by a sense of the unreal. Theory seems futile to someone who wants to know now what to do with a

problem of management. [quoted in Davis and Wallbridge 1981, p. 8]

It was as if Winnicott, despite his scientific bent, related to his own ideas more as "regulative fictions" than as truth (Khan 1975). He was acutely aware that belief systems were relative and that the views he held were a product of the times in which he lived (Winnicott 1971b). This might help explain why he refrained from polemics, either to defend the positions he took or to dispute those taken by others. This, of course, left him open to criticism, especially in the charged atmosphere of the rival camps within the British Psycho-Analytic Society. The personal price he had to pay— and it was a bitter one for him—was to be denied teaching positions within the society as long as these were predicated on allegiance to one or the other of the factions (Rodman 1987). He would not be frightened into conformity, and he consistently preferred an atmosphere of openmindedness to one of opinionated and intolerant beliefs. As he indicated in a private letter to Roger Money-Kyrle in 1954, for example: "I think what irritated me was that I faintly detected in your attitude this matter of the party line, a matter to which I am allergic" (quoted in Rodman 1987, p. 79).

Or, as he wrote in a dramatic joint letter to Melanie Klein and Anna Freud on June 3, 1954, urging them to dissolve the double training program in the British Psycho-Analytic Society: "If we in the present try to set up rigid patterns we thereby create iconoclasts or claustrophobics (perhaps I am one of them) who can no more stand the falsity of a rigid system in psychology than they can tolerate it in religion" (quoted in Rodman 1987, p. 72).

One can infer from this letter how important it was for Winnicott to defend his own sensibilities against pressure to react. What the iconoclast and the claustrophobic have in common is that they are both reacting rather than being themselves. Sensitive to the pressure this was exerting on him, he hoped to facilitate more "breathing space" for himself and others. This was Winnicott's private adult version of what he described theoretically in terms of the infant's experiencing impingements that preclude potential space.

Perhaps another way of understanding Winnicott's aversion to dogma is to say that he was endowed with a certain naive certainty. It is a certainty born of basic trust rather than a compulsion to defend against doubt. In his poised, dignified, idiosyncratic, and playful manner, he was, fundamentally, what could be called a believer in "grace." He related to the world in a self-effacing way as if there was an order beyond all immediate situations and conflicts. As Evelyn Kestemberg said about him: "It was as if Winnicott had found a sort of grace in living" (Clancier and Kalmanovitch 1987, p. 128). Perhaps this is what Anne Clancier meant when, after hearing him for the first time, she said:

> [Winnicott] possessed that self-confidence that characterizes certain discoverers, who are convinced that they have nothing to lose by expounding their observations and hypotheses in all honesty; he also possessed that other kind of self-confidence, which, as Freud said, characterizes the child who knows that he was his parents' favourite, especially his mother's favourite. [p. xii]

Whatever the source of Winnicott's confidence, or belief, in grace, it provided him with a certain moral strength, allowed him to be profoundly available to other people's needs, and enabled him to "accept fallibility as a fact of human endearment" (Winnicott 1970a, p. 114). Winnicott entered the clinical situation relatively unburdened by his own theory, waiting, patiently, for what he called the "sacred moments." He felt comfortable asking people to accept paradoxes without trying to resolve them. Khan (1975) put it this way:

> He sensed a mystery, only he called it paradox, and tried to define it, instead of explaining it away. This is what gave

his work with children its unique quality of wonder and surprise. One can claim for Winnicott that he was of Montaigne's persuasion: "Wonder is the foundation of philosophy, enquiry its progress, ignorance its end." [p. xxxxiii]

Winnicott appreciated the wonder of life, but he was never sentimental, even about his own sense of wonder.

2

Home Is Where
He Starts From

History deals with the teasing gap separating a lived event
and its subsequent narration.

> (Simon Schama, "Dead Certainties")

For years before his death in 1971, Clare Winnicott had
been urging her husband to write an autobiography. She felt
that his style of writing would lend itself naturally to the
task. Unfortunately, he managed to write only a few pages,
keeping the notebook to himself all the time. After his death,
Clare Winnicott discovered the fragments.

The text of this autobiographical fragment is reminiscent of the literary style Winnicott preferred most: stream
of consciousness writing (C. Winnicott 1983). For a title, he
had chosen "Not Less Than Everything," a quote from T. S.
Eliot. The inner flap of his notebook read:

T. S. Eliot   "Costing not less than everything"
T. S. Eliot   "What we call the beginning is often the end
               And to make an end is to make a beginning.
               The end is where we start from."

               Prayer
D. W. W.   Oh God! May I be alive when I die.

Winnicott's prayer is paradoxical in both content and form. Not only is he requesting the seemingly impossible—to be alive when dead—but he appears to be asking a question and making a demand at the same time. The prayer is also an elaboration of Eliot's thought that "the end is where we start from," a paradoxical twist on a theme Winnicott was to devote his entire professional life to elucidating: the crucial significance of our beginnings for what we will become.

When focusing on the earliest beginnings, Winnicott placed his emphasis not only on how the mother's presence was experienced by the infant, but also on the meaning of her absence. Winnicott (1962b) describes how these earliest absences could be experienced as a form of "unthinkable anxiety" or, what he later came to call, primitive psychic agony (p. 57). The intolerable absence was beyond the infant's capacity to encompass or integrate. In one of his last papers, published posthumously, Winnicott (1963b) was to link this "anti-experience" with the clinical fear of break-down and the specific fear of death. A person who had suffered the primitive agony as an infant might be driven in the future to pursue the events he was unable to comprehend in the past. What had been registered as an interruption in the infant's existence would have to be made sense of so that development could continue. In his autobiographical fragments, Winnicott wrestles with his own fear of death, which includes the intolerable thought of absence, by contemplating the experience of his own presence during that absence.

Winnicott's prayer is followed by an imaginative description of his own death. It read as follows:

I died.

It was not very nice, and it took quite a long time as it seemed (but it was only a moment in eternity).

There had been rehearsals (that's a difficult word to spell. I found I had left out the 'a'.) The hearse was cold and unfriendly.

When the time came I knew all about the lung heavy with water that the heart could not negotiate, so that not enough blood circulated in the alveoli, and there was oxygen starvation as well as drowning. But fair enough, I had had a good innings: mustn't grumble as our old gardener used to say. . . . .

Let me see. What was happening when I died? My prayer had been answered. I was alive when I died. That was all I had asked and I had got it. (This makes me feel awful because so many of my friends and contemporaries died in the first World War, and I have never been free from the feeling that my being alive is a facet of some one thing of which their deaths can be seen as other facets: some huge crystal, a body with integrity and shape intrinsical in it). [C. Winnicott 1989, p..4]

Clare Winnicott (1989) says that Winnicott was using this notebook as an "exercise to deal with his immediate problem of living, which was that of dying" (p. 3). He did so through imaginative elaborations. One can sense, from this intimate fragment, the extent to which Winnicott experienced himself as an isolate. His prayer was for his own aliveness, even if all there was to experience was the cold emptiness of the hearse and the inside of his own dead body. It was a solitude free of resentments, yet tinged with the guilt of the survivor. Still, there was, as always for Winnicott, an element of connection—connection through some higher religious order where life and death are transcended. This is the realm of basic trust, or grace, described in the previous chapter. It is quite possibly a transformation of some of those crucial experiences that Winnicott himself describes as features of the infant's earliest moments of being with mother.

No information is available about Winnicott's own early infancy, but some sense of the quality of his childhood can be gleaned both from what he has written about it and from what has been recalled by others.

Donald Woods Winnicott was born on April 7, 1896, in the provincial area of Plymouth, Devon, to Frederick and Elizabeth Winnicott. He was named after his maternal grandfather and was the youngest and only boy of three children. His older sisters, Violet and Cathleen, were five and six years older than he.

Winnicott's father, who was 41 years old when Donald was born, was a prosperous merchant who traded in diverse goods. Adam Phillips (1988) claims he dealt in women's corsets. Other sources say he sold hardware for the British navy (Clare Winnicott 1983). He was a successful public man, twice elected mayor of Plymouth, and was knighted in 1924. Among other honors, he was chairman of the local Chamber of Commerce, was manager of the Plymouth Hospital Committee, and, in 1934, was given the freedom of the city. Clare Winnicott (1989) describes him as a tall and slim man with an "old-fashioned quiet dignity and poise about him, and a deep sense of fun" (p. 5). He was apparently a person of high intelligence and sound judgment. Still, he was, according to Winnicott, burdened by learning difficulties and "sensitive about his lack of education. . . . He always said that because of this he had not aspired to Parliament, but had kept to local politics—lively enough in those days in faraway Plymouth" (C. Winnicott 1989, p. 8).

One can only speculate as to the extent to which this might have contributed to Donald's own modest style of writing: his feeling uncomfortable with specialized technical language, distrust of intellectual formalism, and reluctance to make scholarly references to authoritative texts. Perhaps it also helps explain why for every one lecture that Winnicott was asked to give before professional societies he gave at least a dozen to gatherings of less elitist audiences and why it gave him particular pleasure to speak before ordinary people who were involved in the care of others (Khan 1975).

Little is known about Winnicott's mother, Elizabeth, although Clare Winnicott (1989) describes her in vague terms as being a vivacious and outgoing woman who was "able to show and express her feelings easily" (p. 5). A sense of vitality and stability flowed from her, and she was known to have a sense of humor and to be musical. The household itself was a lively one, bustling with activity. There was a large garden, an orchard, a croquet lawn, a tennis court, a pond, and high trees enclosing the whole estate. There was one special tree to whose branches Donald would retreat to do homework and perhaps to fantasize. He also apparently spent much time as a child frequenting the kitchen. His mother complained that he spent more time with the cook than with the rest of the family. It is interesting to speculate what drew Donald, as a child, to the place that symbolized the maternal center of the family establishment. Interestingly enough, even as an adult, whenever Winnicott would travel to strange places he would invariably be drawn to seek out and spend time in the local kitchen.

Across the road was a second Winnicott household belonging to his paternal uncle Richard, his wife, and five children. The eight cousins would spend the endless hours of childhood together. Vitality and imagination were in the air. As one of Winnicott's sisters reported, the question "What can I do?" was never uttered in their extended household. There was always an abundance of playmates, something to do, and space in which to do it. No less important was that there was always room for one to be alone, secret hiding places in which a child's imagination could soar and to which he or she could withdraw. It was an unobtrusive setting that facilitated solitude and escape, no less than gregarious encounters.

The extended Winnicott household was blessed with what appears to have been a generally cheerful disposition.

They were all endowed with an irrepressible sense of humor. This was a family in which, according to Clare Winnicott (1989), "there were no 'tragedies' . . . there were only amusing episodes" (p. 7). Is it any wonder, then, that Winnicott as an adult was able to graciously "accept fallibility as a fact of human endearment" (Winnicott 1970a, p. 114)? A consistent line can be drawn from this relatively benign and nonintrusive setting to Winnicott's capacity for belief and faith in natural processes.

When the Winnicott trust decided, in 1986, to gather together for publication the transcripts of talks and lectures Winnicott had given before a variety of diverse groups, they chose as their title "Home Is Where We Start From." The words are taken from a poem of T. S. Eliot's that apparently spoke to Winnicott's heart:

> Home is where one starts from. As we grow
>   older
> The world becomes stranger, the pattern more
>   complicated
> Of dead and living. Not the intense moment
> Isolated, with no before and after,
> But a lifetime burning in every moment.

Home *is* where Winnicott started from. And his home was such that it provided him with an elemental sense of security in the world. From his earliest years, he could always take for granted that he was loved. As Clare Winnicott reported to Phyllis Grosskurth (1986), she "used to tell him that he knew from the moment he opened his eyes on the world that he was loved, and she teased him that he suffered from 'benignity'" (p. 399).

Peter Rudnytsky (1989) points out that Winnicott's position within the family resembled Freud's description of the son who "has been his mother's undisputed darling" and "retains throughout his life the triumphant feeling, the confidence in success, which not seldom brings actual success along with it" (p. 334). Wrote Clare Winnicott (1989),

[He] was . . . free to explore all the available spaces in the house and garden around him and to fill the spaces with bits of himself and so gradually to make his world his own. This capacity *to be at home* served him well throughout his life. There is a pop song which goes, "Home is in my heart." That is certainly how Donald experienced it and this gave him an immense freedom which enabled him to feel at home anywhere. [p. 6]

Winnicott's basic sense of security, which was at the root of what he was to describe theoretically as the "capacity for faith," was born in the web of loving relationships that he encountered in his early childhood. This was a household whose capacity for communication was strengthened by its inherent rootedness in its own surroundings. The family was proud of being Devonian, and they were so much an integral part of the land and community that a village was eventually named for them. Although Winnicott never had the opportunity to actually find the village, it gave him great pleasure just to know that it was there.

One cannot overestimate the significance for Winnicott's upbringing and character to have been a part of this wider network of familial identification. The Winnicotts were people whose confidence was rooted in relative prosperity and a sense of belonging to the very soil upon which they stood. These social circumstances liberated Winnicott from the poor boy's struggle for success and acclaim. Unlike many psychoanalysts, Winnicott was never an outsider within his culture. He displays neither the determined struggle of the self-made man extricating himself from a social class nor the anxious longings or willful assimilation characteristic of the immigrant.

For the Winnicotts, there were no threats, or impingements, from without. They felt protected by being part of what was beyond them. The continuity of the family existence—one could say, borrowing Winnicott's terminology, the "going-on-being" of the family—was ensured by an "environmental mother," which, in this case, took the form of a social setting that the Winnicotts perceived as a natural extension of themselves. Or, to put it another way, the wider social circle enabled the Winnicott family to feel safe, just as the father, in Winnicott's developmental model, allows the mother to feel secure so that she can be preoccupied with her maternal functions.

It will be left to the future biographer to paint a more detailed, differentiated, and perhaps more realistic picture of Winnicott's earliest years than is possible from the sources currently available. The picture of nearly idyllic family life needs to be given greater depth through an assessment of the complexities of the interrelationships. Despite the fact that greater clarity and differentiation could emerge from a detailed biographical study, it is likely that the family contours outlined here will remain basically intact. When Clare Winnicott (1978) wrote her own abbreviated account of Winnicott's early life she already anticipated that some readers might feel their credulity was being taxed. For this reason she responded in advance by saying:

> Some . . . may be inclined to think that it sounds too good to be true. But the truth is that it *was* good, and try as I will I cannot present it in any other light. Essentially he was a deeply happy person whose capacity for enjoyment never failed to triumph over the setbacks and disappointments that came his way. [pp. 9–10]

Winnicott obviously drew on his own experience when, in his essay "On Security" (1960c), he described how "children find in security a sort of challenge, a challenge to them to prove that they can break out" (p. 30). Elsewhere, he (1960d) claimed that healthy development requires "a steady progression, that is to say, a well-graduated series of iconoclastic actions, each in the series being compatible with the retention of an unconscious bond with the central figures or figure, the parents or the mother" (p. 92). According to Winnicott, the developing child is motivated by two tendencies. The first is to get away from the family, "each step giving increased freedom of ideas and of functioning." The second "works in the opposite direction and it is the need to retain or to be able to regain the relationship with the actual father and mother." Winnicott believed that "it is this second tendency which makes the first tendency a part of growth instead of a disruption of the individual's personality" (p. 91).

Clare Winnicott (1989), despite her one-dimensional representation of Winnicott's childhood, did acknowledge that

> there is a sense in which the quality of his early life and his appreciation of it did in itself present him with a major problem, that of freeing himself from the family, and of establishing his own separate life and identity without sacrificing the early richness. It took him a long time to do this. [p.10]

Winnicott's autobiographical notes and private letters indicate some of the milestones in his struggle to differentiate and separate "without sacrificing the early richness." These recorded incidents help illuminate some of the tendencies in his character, tendencies that were to leave their mark in his theoretical conceptualizations as well. It is impossible, however, to discern the extent to which Winnicott's recollections, although presented as veridical, are, in fact, reconstructions influenced by his own adult notions of development.

At the age of 3, for example, Winnicott experienced an incident with his father that he describes in a way that has both oedipal and reparative features. According to his autobiographical fragment (C. Winnicott 1989), his father used to irritate and taunt him with one of his sister's wax dolls, parodying a popular song with the words:

> Rosie said to Donald
> I love you
> Donald said to Rosie
> I don't believe you do.

Winnicott couldn't precisely recall whether his father sang it this way or turned the words the other way around. Whatever the case, he vividly remembered feeling that "the doll had to be altered for the worse." One day, therefore, while he was playing on one of the slopes in the family garden, he took his own private croquet mallet and "bashed flat the nose of the wax doll." "I was perhaps somewhat relieved," wrote Winnicott,

> when my father took a series of matches and, warming up the wax nose enough, remoulded it so that the face once more became a face. This early demonstration of the restitutive and reparative act certainly made an impression on me, and perhaps made me able to accept the fact that I myself, dear innocent child, had actually become violent directly with a doll, but indirectly with my good-tempered father who was just then entering my conscious life. [quoted in C. Winnicott 1978, p. 8]

Winnicott's portrayal of his father here is perhaps disingenuously benign. It was, after all, his father's taunting and Donald's sensitivity to it that constitute the backdrop of the story. This fact, coupled with Clare Winnicott's comment that Donald suffered from excess "benignity," may be an indication that within the Winnicott household there was not much room for the direct expression of anger. Michael Eigen (1981b) points out that any expression of anger would have seemed out of place in this family. That is why, he presumes, the angry moments Winnicott did experience "made a great impression on him and played a crucial role in his later theorizing" (p. 110).

An argument can be made, however, that the "benign" family atmosphere, more than it impacted on his theorizing about aggression per se, had a more indirect impact in that it generated in his character that profound interest in, and propensity for, ambiguity. Much of Winnicott's work is concerned with elucidating the basic quality of ambiguity that is inherent in all experience. That is why he places such special emphasis on accepting, without resolving, paradoxes and on avoiding polemical disputes. On some level, this predilection to the ambiguous, and the reluctance to engage in confrontations, can be seen as ways in which Winnicott deals with his own aggressive impulses.

Adam Phillips (1988) also points out that Winnicott's interpretation of the doll incident was narrowly oedipal, not fully acknowledging the degree to which Sir Frederick was threatening Donald's burgeoning masculinity. As Phillips writes: "His possible and ordinary confusion, as a child, about his sexual identity is temporarily resolved by a violent but paradoxical act in which it could not have been clear to him what it was that he was actually trying to destroy" (p. 27).

What Phillips seems to be suggesting is that Winnicott, by aggressively asserting his masculinity through the destructive act against the doll, was also, paradoxically, crushing symbolically his own nascent and confusing masculinity as well. In his own developmental theory, Winnicott places great emphasis on the self as constituted through aggressive action, but he writes very little about masculinity or femininity as qualities central to the way the self experiences itself.

This, of course, links up with the criticism, frequently leveled against Winnicott, that he tends to "ignore" the role of the father in development. This criticism is, at times, somewhat overstated, given the nature of the particular material Winnicott chose to elucidate. After all, Winnicott was struggling to make a genuine contribution regarding the importance of earliest infancy. At the time of his writing, the real mother's significance was often denied, either by an exclusive focus on the technique of bodily care, which could be performed by good nurses as well as by mothers, or by singular emphasis on intrapsychic libidinal gratifications. Winnicott wished to shift the focus to the emotional development of the infant as it evolved through the facilitating gestures of the caretaker. His emphasis is really more on the maternal *function* than on the woman as mother. Furthermore, he was writing in a cultural setting wherein infant care was assumed to be a woman's prerogative. In his mind, the father, at the earliest stage, was a duplicate mother.

Still, there is definitely what could be called a maternal bias that permeates Winnicott's writings. Fathers and sexual identity are but small sideshows in development. The father's main function is to enable the mother to be the best mother she can possibly be. As Phillips (1988) points out, the father's coming between the child and the mother is of far less interest to Winnicott than the transitional space from which the father is absent, yet which "initially both joins and separates the baby and the mother" (Winnicott 1971a, p. 121). The real drama is the one dominated by the maternal. In fact, Winnicott possessed such a strong maternal identification that Katherine Whitehorn, in an article in *The Observer* based on an interview with him, went so far as to describe him as a "Madonna" (quoted in Grosskurth 1986, p. 233).

Winnicott was deeply offended by Whitehorn's characterization (Winnicott Correspondence 1949–1970). After receiving an advance copy, he shot off a letter to her in which he confessed having difficulty reading the material "because the whole thing is highly charged emotionally for me." He was reacting, nevertheless, before having "cooled down." What gave him the "worst shock" was her introducing the word "Madonna." "As part of general mythology," he writes,

> they have a very real place, but you are talking about actual mothers and babies, and the word madonna connotes a miracle and the elimination of sex and the whole concept of the husband and what he means to his wife. I think that whoever put this word in . . . made a big mistake. [Winnicott to Whitehorn, September 23, 1966]

The issue, however, was not purely academic. He felt misunderstood and was insulted. "I want to say," he continued,

> that while I recognise a maternal identification in myself I
> think the word female identification is not something I
> would ever say about myself. At any rate it starts people
> thinking along the wrong lines; possibly it does not feel
> like this to you but from my point of view there is an
> immense difference. [Winnicott to Whitehorn, September
> 23, 1966]

Winnicott was quite insistent on distinguishing between the maternal and the feminine; the issue of homosexuality obviously loomed large. Throughout his writings, he struggled to differentiate homosexual tendencies from a healthy individual's capacity to identify with the opposite sex. When consulted by a male confidant, for example, who, after the arrival of a new baby, felt confused about his own sexual identity, he replied:

> Everybody is bisexual in the sense of the capacity to
> identify with man and woman. There is a great difference,
> however, between a unified personality such as that of a
> man with a capacity for identification with a woman, and
> a similar but different thing, a male man with a split off
> woman self. . . . I think that the study of man's identifica-
> tion with woman has been very much complicated by a
> persistent attempt on the part of psychoanalysts to call
> everything that is not male in a man homosexuality,
> whereas in fact homosexuality is a secondary matter or less
> fundamental and rather a nuisance when one is trying to
> get at man's woman identification. [quoted in Rodman
> 1987, p. 155]

Whitehorn was "amazed and saddened" by Winnicott's intense reaction, and fearful of a libel suit. "It's a sad business" she writes, "that an article in which I meant you

so immensely well should have given you only pain . . . "
(Whitehorn to Winnicott, undated). She was sorry he objected to the word "Madonna" but felt that it was an "image
word" that she had used "interpretively." She went back to
her original interview notes and found that his exact words
had been: "I'm not a very masculine identified person—not
homosexual, it's not the same thing, people don't always
understand that . . . I'd be no good as a mother but I've got
it in me to know what a mother feels."

It is most intriguing that Winnicott felt that he'd be "no
good as a mother" given how the mothering function
became such a central preoccupation for him. He was quite
cognizant that this interest of his must have had roots that
were very deep. As he said in the postscript to his first
collection of broadcast talks (Winnicott 1957e):

> I suppose that everyone has a paramount interest, a deep,
> driving propulsion towards something. If one's life lasts
> long enough, so that looking back becomes allowable, one
> discerns an urgent tendency that has integrated all the
> various and varied activities of one's private life and one's
> professional career. As for me, I can already see what a big
> part has been played in my work by the urge to find and to
> appreciate the ordinary good mother. Fathers, I know, are
> just as important. . . . But for me it has been to mothers
> that I have so deeply needed to speak. [p. 123]

How are we to account for Winnicott's "urgent tendency"? Why was it that he became so preoccupied with the
role of the ordinary mother in human development? How do
we understand his emphasis on the element of the analytic
process with regressed patients that resembles surrogate
maternal care?

As Winnicott suggested, the issue of the centrality of the
maternal went beyond mere professional interest and
touched on some essential integrating force in his private life
as well. The roots of that integrating force are to be found in
the recesses of Winnicott's childhood.

There is some evidence that Winnicott was bound to his mother by a profound depressive tie. At the age of 67, Winnicott wrote a poem about his mother that he sent to his brother-in-law, James Britton. He attached to it a note: "Do you mind seeing this that hurt coming out of me. I think it had some thorns sticking out somehow. It's not happened to me before and I hope it doesn't again" (quoted in Phillips 1988, p. 29).

The name of the poem is "The Tree," which probably refers to the special tree in the Winnicotts' garden that young Donald sat in to do his homework. Part of the poem reads as follows:

Mother below is weeping
      weeping
      weeping
Thus I knew her

Once, stretched out on her lap
  as now on dead tree
I learned to make her smile
  to stem her tears
  to undo her guilt
  to cure her inward death
To enliven her was my living. [p. 29]

It was one of Winnicott's primary interests as a clinician to observe the ways in which children dealt with the psychological unavailability of depressed mothers whose quality of attention was unreliable. A child with a seriously depressed mother could feel, in Winnicott's (1960e) words, "infinitely dropped" (p. 75). Infants and young children with depressed mothers would be compelled to sacrifice their own development to look after the mother's mood. They would, as Winnicott wrote in his poem, make a living out of enlivening her.

Is it possible that Winnicott's striking clinical observa-

tions about these children were based on his own fundamental experience of dealing with his mother's depression?
Was her depression overt, or was there merely an unconscious link between the sensitive boy and Elizabeth's depressive tendencies? When he writes in the poem "Thus I knew
her," was he implying a secret bond between them, as if only
he knew her thus? To what extent can Winnicott's adult
professional work—the living he made for himself—be understood as part of an unconscious attempt to enliven his
mother, or perhaps simply to return her to her ordinarily
good-enough state?

Although it is possible that Winnicott's sensitivity to his
mother's depressive side sheds some light on his "deep
driving propulsion . . . toward finding the ordinary good
mother," there were, undoubtedly, additional familial
forces at work. One of these was, of course, Sir Frederick.
Winnicott writes very little about his father. It is known that
Donald, as the youngest child and only son, had the privilege
of walking home from church with his father on Sundays (C.
Winnicott 1983). A hint of the role Sir Frederick's played in
his life can be gleaned from a brief comment made by
Winnicott while recalling an incident that occurred when he
was 12 years old (C. Winnicott 1989). Young Donald came
home one day and used the curse word "drat." His father
"looked pained as only he could look," then blamed his
mother "for not seeing to it that I had decent friends." It was
there and then that Sir Frederick decided to send Donald
away to boarding school, which he did when Winnicott
turned 13. "So," wrote Winnicott recalling the incident,
"my father was there to kill and be killed, but it is probably
true that in the early years he left me too much to all my
mothers. Things never quite righted themselves" (p. 8).

Winnicott is referring here to the fact that not only was
his father a somewhat distant figure preoccupied with public
affairs, but that he was the only boy with two older sisters,
a nanny to whom he was very attached, a sometime governess in the house, and another aunt living in the house a lot

of the time (Clare Winnicott 1983). This is what led Michael Eigen (1981) to argue that Winnicott's personal sense of identity remained skewed as a result of a "felt deficiency on the father side" (p. 110). It is also possible that Winnicott's unique status as a young male among females might have been an additional contributor to Winnicott's tendency to perceive experiences in terms of their inherent ambiguity. What "never quite righted itself" was the capacity to perceive himself as emotionally and sexually distinct and separate from all his mothers. For, not only was there ambiguity as to the quality of his gender identification, but it was probably a serious question in his childish mind who, precisely, was his mother. Unfortunately, too little information is available about the actual child-rearing practices within the family: How central was the nanny? Did the governess also play a maternal role? Did the older sisters assume, at times, parental functions? How involved was Elizabeth in the day-to-day care of her children? Who nursed Donald as an infant? In the absence of any clear data about these issues, one is left to note the possible connection between Winnicott's having been raised with "multiple mothers" and his later theoretical preoccupation with the importance of the one real devoted mother for emotional well-being.

Clare Winnicott (1989) claims that because he was so very much the youngest member of the household, and because he was so loved by all these women, a deliberate effort was made, particularly by his mother and sisters, not to spoil him. Still, Winnicott was raised in the shadow of what must have seemed to him as a child powerful females to whom he owed an unrepayable debt. As he said in "The Mother's Contribution to Society," "It follows that every man or woman who is sane, every man or woman who has the feeling of being a person in the world, and for whom the world means something, every happy person, is in infinite debt to a woman" (Winnicott 1957e, p. 125). Winnicott's psychological development hinged upon separating out of this female environment without reneging on his "infinite debt."

One way Winnicott handled this challenge, as an adult, was by turning to an objective study of the mother. This allowed him simultaneously to acknowledge, master, and submit to the reality of his feelings of dependence upon women. This is probably the root of the accusation that Winnicott "idolized" mothers. Although this accusation is unfounded, and probably based on a superficial reading of Winnicott, it was perhaps the perceived result of the fact that Winnicott was dealing with his own fear of dependence upon women by becoming an expert on mothers. "Split-off" homosexuality and efforts to cultivate motherliness as a trait were both emotional dead ends. Not able to become an ordinary devoted mother himself, he devoted himself to understanding the crucial significance of her ordinary function. Winnicott virtually acknowledged this internal process when, in the context of discussing man's "fear of WOMAN," he wrote:

> For my part, I happen to have been drawn towards finding out all I can about the meaning of the word "devotion", and towards being able, if possible, to make a fully informed and fully felt acknowledgement to my own mother. Here a man is in a more difficult position than a woman; he obviously cannot come to terms with his mother by becoming a mother. . . . He has no alternative but to go as far as he can towards a consciousness of the mother's achievement. The development of motherliness as a quality in his character does not get far enough, and femininity in a man proves to be a side-track to the main issues. One solution for a man caught up in this problem is to take part in an objective study of the mother's part, especially the part she plays at the beginning. [Winnicott 1957e, p. 126]

Winnicott had his first objective opportunity as a child to separate himself from his maternal environment when, in

1910, his parents sent him to Leys School in Cambridge, where he specialized in the sciences. The whole family came to see him off. Sitting alone on the train, he felt sorry about parting from them until the train entered a long tunnel, just outside Plymouth. As the train entered the tunnel, he could no longer see his family. "All through this tunnel," said Clare Winnicott (1989), recalling what her husband had told her,

> he settled down to the idea of leaving, but then out again the other side he left them behind and looked forward to going on to school. He often blessed that tunnel because he could honestly manage to feel sorry to leave right up to the moment of entering it. [p. 9]

It was as if the tunnel provided a kind of transitional space that enabled him to move from relative dependence to relative independence. Having had earlier experiences of being alone in his family's physical presence, he would now have to rely more fully on his capacity to keep them alive in their physical absence.

At Leys Winnicott was, according to Clare Winnicott, in his element. It was there that he was able to develop to their fullest his athletic and social inclinations. He ran, cycled, swam, played rugby, made friends, and sang in the choir. It was at Leys that he had the opportunity to form intimate ties with other boys. Each night he would read a story aloud to the others in his dormitory. He joined Baden-Powel's Boy Scouts. No doubt the chivalrous codes of the scouting movement reinforced the standards of civility he had brought with him from home. It also gave him the first opportunity to experience his skill at working with younger children.

This was a time when the impulses of puberty burst forth, and with them the romantic confessional yearnings of a young man encountering a new sense of himself. A hint of the intense exuberance of this period is found in a letter he wrote to one of his newfound friends, Stanley Ede:

This afternoon I went an eight mile walk to the Roman
Road with Chandler, and we told each other all we
felt. . . . Oh Stanley!

> Your still sober and true—
> although seemingly intoxicated
> but never-the-less devoted
> friend
>   Donald [C. Winnicott 1989, p. 11]

Winnicott's new awakening included a growing recognition of his own professional ambitions. According to
Winnicott, his decision to study medicine originated in an
experience at Leys that forced him to confront his own
dependency needs. He had broken his collarbone while
playing rugby. "I could see," wrote Winnicott, "that for the
rest of my life I should have to depend on doctors if I
damaged myself or became ill, and the only way out of this
position was to become a doctor myself, and from then on
the idea as a real proposition was always on my mind . . ."
(p. 10).

Although the profound motivations for a vocation are
not reducible to a single explanation, it is highly likely that
this fear of dependence contributed substantially to his
decision. More than any other analyst, Winnicott was to
stress the primacy of dependence, both developmentally
and therapeutically. By becoming a doctor, he could transform a passive situation into an active one. This same fear of
dependence may also be at the root of the passion for
freedom that so characterized him. What Winnicott is probably ignoring, however, in his own description of the gen-
esis of his vocation, is the same profound wish for restitution
and reparation that he had so clearly recognized when
discussing the doll he had chosen to mutilate as a young
child.

Whatever might have been the combination of motivations that contributed to this new turn in Winnicott's search

for a separate and distinct identity, he recognized immediately that it would bring him into conflict with his father. Sir Frederick's business was very much a family affair and he desperately wanted Donald to come on board (Clare Winnicott 1983). The idea of a rift with his father made Donald so anxious that he hoped to deny his own inclinations. He tried to make himself go into the business to please his father. The man who would eventually go on to formulate the seminal idea of the True Self and False Self found himself, at this stage, deluding himself into compliance. As he revealed in a letter to his close friend, Stanley Ede, written when he was 16 years old:

> Father and I have been trying consciously and perhaps unconsciously to find out what the ambition of the other is in regard to my future. From what he had said I was sure that he wanted me more than anything else to go into his business. And so, again consciously and not, I have found every argument for the idea and have not thought much about anything else so that I should not be disappointed. And so I have learned to cherish the business life with all my heart, and had intended to enter it and please my father and myself. [C. Winnicott 1989, p. 10]

So severe were his initial efforts at denial, and so leery was he of confronting his father, that he initially felt a repulsion at the thought of becoming a doctor. His genuine yearnings, however, could not be suppressed for long. As he wrote to Stanley:

> When your letter came yesterday you may have expected it to have disappointed me. But—I tell you all I feel—I was so excited that all the stored up feelings about doctors which I have bottled up for so many years seemed to burst and bubble up at once. Do you know that . . . I have for ever so long wanted to be a doctor. But I have always been afraid that my father did not want it, and so I have never mentioned it. . . . [C. Winnicott 1989, p. 11]

Luckily for Winnicott, and the subsequent history of psychoanalysis, his friend, who was a year older, agreed to speak
with Sir Frederick on Donald's behalf. Only after the way
was paved did Donald find the courage to write his father a
letter that convinced him to accede to his studying medicine. Interestingly, Winnicott displayed similar timidity in
directly confronting authority when he had to inform the
Headmaster at school that he had decided to become a
doctor. In the end, however, Winnicott was off to Jesus
College, Cambridge, where he took his degree in biology and
then medicine.

Winnicott was described by a friend who knew him
well during the years at Cambridge as "a medical student
who liked to sing a comic song on Saturday evenings in the
ward—and sang 'Apple Dumplings' and cheered us all up"
(p. 11).

His room at the college was a popular meeting place.
Winnicott rented a piano and played while singing in his
pleasant tenor voice. In his later years, Winnicott was to say
on more than one occasion that if he hadn't turned to
psychoanalysis as a profession, he would have liked to have
been a comic in a music hall. According to Adam Phillips
(1988), Winnicott's hearty love of life, playful gregarious-
ness, and flair for the dramatic, were all to have an impact on
his later theorizing. As he put it:

> In his own writing Winnicott would occasionally make
> psychoanalysis sound curiously like entertainment. He
> sometimes found it difficult to keep the language of per-
> formance—routine, timing, play, setting and so on—out of
> his theoretical discourse, and the figure of the actor crops
> up consistently in his work as an awkward presence . . .
> his work, in a sense, initiates a comic tradition in psycho-
> analysis. [p. 31]

Winnicott's years as a medical student in Cambridge
were disrupted by World War I. As a medical student, he was

exempt from army service, but the loss of many of his friends in the war was a source of deep regret to him and compelled him to seek a way to serve. Years later, Winnicott (1963a) noted that it was the opportunity for what he called "contributing-in," for giving to the environment, that enabled the infant to hold anxiety and develop the capacity for concern. Winnicott's reaction to the war demonstrated his own felt need to participate, to make sense of events by taking part in them, to contain his anxiety by seeking a reparative gesture. He applied for, and was accepted as a surgeon probationer and was drafted to a navy destroyer. Although he was subject to a great deal of teasing both because he was one of the youngest men on board and because his father was a merchant rather than a naval officer, Winnicott seems to have been able to make the most of his experience. He had much free time, which he spent consuming the novels of Henry James (C. Winnicott 1989).

After the war, in 1918, Winnicott went to St. Bartholomew's Hospital in London, where he continued his medical training. This was a period of intense professional development in which, according to Clare Winnicott (1989), he "literally worked almost all day and night, but he would not have missed the experience for the world" (p. 13). It was at St. Bartholomew's that he was exposed to Lord Horder, a great teacher who taught him the significance of detailed history taking and who repeatedly emphasized that doctors should listen carefully to what the patient said, rather than simply ask questions. This style of professional help, which encouraged both respectful mutuality in the relationship as well as openmindedness of scientific inquiry, resonated well with Winnicott's natural proclivities. It was to become the hallmark of his psychoanalytic technique.

Winnicott had initially intended to become a general medical practitioner somewhere in the countryside. The image of a country doctor had a romantic and heroic quality that appealed to Winnicott's idealistic bent. The country doctor, after all, was a well-known figure from the nineteenth-century novels Winnicott had devoured in his youth. What is more, his future first wife's father was a GP and Winnicott promised her that he intended to go that route as well.

It was at this time, however, that a friend of his lent him a copy of Freud's *Interpretation of Dreams*. According to Clare Winnicott, the book made such a powerful impression on him that he immediately decided to stay in London to undergo a personal analysis. This explanation seems a bit shallow in that it leaves out the more personal difficulties he was experiencing at the time that led him to seek treatment.

A letter he wrote from that time to his sister Violet shows Winnicott consumed by the naive enthusiasm of the novice:

> May I explain to you a little about this method which Freud has so cleverly devised for the cure of mind disorders? . . . Psychoanalysis only gives a man a fair chance to bring his own will against the situation in question. And as a person's will is always sufficient against a realised tendency (as a rough rule) there is great hope for the future. [quoted in Rodman 1987, p. 3]

So great was Winnicott's naivete that he concluded his description of psychoanalysis by saying:

> So now you know a little about a very vast subject which has the great charm of being really useful. It remains for me to put what I am learning to the test. Even if I do not take up any subject which allows of psychotherapy in my work, the knowledge will always be useful as a hobby. [p. 3]

He was not yet ready to acknowledge that the charming hobby was to become his calling.

3

Pediatrics and Psychoanalysis

There is an oft-repeated myth about Winnicott, rein-forced by the title of his own collected works, that in his professional development he moved *through* pediatrics *to* psychoanalysis. In fact, his interest in psychoanalysis pre-ceded his decision to enter pediatrics and, although he began to practice pediatrics before psychoanalysis, his professional interest in these two areas developed together.

In 1919, at the age of 23, Winnicott found himself unable to recall his dreams. While looking for a book that might help him, he came across a work on Freud by a Swiss parson named Oskar Pfister. On or about this time, a friend lent him Freud's *Interpretation of Dreams,* translated in 1913 by A. A. Brill. These books exerted a most powerful influence on him and were the catalyst for the enthusiastic letter to his sister Violet, referred to in the previous chapter. Winnicott obviously felt that Freud's ideas corresponded to or resonated with his own subjectivity. He gravitated toward them because he saw in them a semblance of his own self.

At that time, Winnicott was still studying medicine at St. Bartholomew's Hospital in London and had not yet begun to specialize in pediatrics. In fact, he still had his eye on being a general practitioner in the countryside. But, in a taped interview with Michael Neve in 1983, Clare Winnicott claimed that at that time Winnicott already knew that he wanted a psychoanalysis and that only in London would one be available to him. Being a GP in London, on the other hand, was not in the least appealing to him. So how did he enter pediatrics? According to Clare Winnicott (1983), it was part accident, part the influence of people he admired:

> I think he was impressed by certain people—now I'm not going to remember their names, but they were quite famous people and one of them *was* a pediatrician. And he became his house surgeon for a time and just thought, you know, this is perhaps something I'd like to do. And he applied for two jobs in hospitals—there was no pediatric course to go to any more, then, in those days—and he set up practice as a pediatrician in Harley Street. I think it was really the influence of people, people he admired, who were doing the kind of work that he was interested in. [p. 7]

The pediatrician she refers to might be Leonard George Guthrie, author of the pioneering book *Functional Nervous Disorders in Childhood,* who contributed to the special psychological orientation at Paddington Green Children's Hospital. It was characteristic of Winnicott that rather than pursue some predesignated program, he simply followed his intuition and the admiration he felt for somebody's personal style. One must consider as well, of course, that he was attracted to pediatric work because it came naturally to him. As J. P. Tizard (1971) said about him:

> Donald Winnicott had the most astonishing powers with children. To say that he understood children would to me

sound false and vaguely patronizing; it was rather that children understood him and that he was at one with them. . . . A good example of his acceptance by and communication with children is what happened when he was about to visit a Danish family for the second time after an interval of a few years. The children remembered his playing with them very well and were delighted at the prospect of again meeting an Englishman who could speak Danish. When their father said that Dr. Winnicott could not speak a word of their difficult language his children simply did not believe him. [p. 226]

The same qualities that made Winnicott uniquely accessible to children were at the root of his ability to work successfully with psychotic or regressed adults. Many of the adult analyses he conducted were with highly disturbed individuals who had had unsuccessful analyses with others (Little 1990). Apparently, he was profoundly open to the rawness of human experience; he could tolerate the painful exposure of undiluted impulses, or the chaos of unbridled fantasies. It was to these kinds of experiences, no matter what the age of the patient, to which Winnicott was naturally attuned.

Still, Winnicott's particular genius with children has been noted by nearly everyone who has watched him work (Gillespie 1971). He enjoyed being a hands-on pediatrician. He understood in a deep way that children are able to communicate with some urgency once they feel that there is someone who might possibly understand. His unassuming and direct manner, and his uncanny ability to quickly grasp the core of a child's psychological difficulties, strengthened a child's belief in being understood. Eventually, people were to come from around the world for consultations with him. In the decades of his association with Paddington Green Children's Hospital and The Queen Elizabeth Hospital for Children he was to see over 60,000 cases. During World War II he served as a consultant psychiatrist to the Government Evacuation Scheme, which entailed supervising close to 300 delinquent children being housed in a group of five hostels. After the war, and despite his heavy weekly workload, he even spent many of his Sundays driving to a school for maladjusted children in the countryside (Katharine Rees, personal communication, September 23, 1991). There is probably no other figure in the history of psychoanalysis with such a volume of practical experience with children.

There can be no doubt that the continuity of Winnicott's practical experience with children had a major impact on his theorizing. He began his independent medical practice as a pediatrician and, as he put it, he "never cut loose" (Winnicott 1975, p. ix). As a physician in a children's hospital, he had the valuable experience of having to meet the reality of social pressures. At the Queen Elizabeth Hospital for Children from 1922 to 1933 he was in charge of the rheumatism clinic, which dealt with rheumatic fever, chorea, and concomitant heart disease. Before the advent of penicillin, he dealt with large epidemics of encephalitis lethargica, summer diarrhea, and various polio epidemics.

Pediatrics strengthened Winnicott's conviction that there were natural processes that should not be interrupted. Life's roots (the word "root" appears frequently in his writing) were organic, not something that could be calculated or contrived. Children, he concluded, cannot be made to develop; at best they can be provided with a relatively unintrusive, but supportive, setting in which they may flourish. "We cannot even teach them to walk," he once wrote to an anthropologist working in Tanzania, "but their innate tendency to walk at a certain age needs us as supporting figures" (quoted in Rodman 1987, p. 186). And to a group of midwives he (1957a) proclaimed: "One general idea goes right through what I have to say: that is that there are natural processes which underlie all that is taking place; and we do good work as doctors and nurses only if we respect and facilitate these natural processes" (p. 107). Winnicott had great faith—perhaps exaggerated—in the "silent integrative forces" of natural growth processes.

Unlike some child analysts, Winnicott was as consistently attuned to the practical problems of management as he was to the unconscious processes of the child. His therapeutic consultations were predicated on the assumption that there was "an average expectable environment to meet and to make use of the changes that have taken place in the boy or girl in the interview, changes which indicate a loosening of the knot in the developmental process" (Winnicott 1971f, p. 5).

Winnicott always took into account the child's physical development, the resources of the social class from which the child came, and the availability and capability of the parents to facilitate the maturational process. The evacuation experience brought him into daily contact with the devastation brought by the breakup of families. When he took on the evacuation consultancy, he knew he would have to turn his attention to issues of care and management. The overburdened local staffs were desperate for practical advice (Winnicott 1984).

Winnicott (1941) genuinely believed in the value of an uninterrupted dialogue between the clinical data obtained through pediatrics and the clinical data of psychoanalysis, feeling that "the proper procedure is obviously to get all we can both from observation and from analysis, and to let each help the other" (p. 61). Following his own muse, he straddled both disciplines, frequently seeing himself as a "pediatrician who has swung to psychiatry, and a psychiatrist who has clung to pediatrics" (Winnicott 1948b, p. 157). Winnicott (1942) noted how "odd flashes of insight from parent and child remind the analyst of material patiently acquired in analytic work" (p. 82). Occasionally, he went even further and claimed to have "learned much that is of value in analysis from the therapeutic consultation, and from the study of other non-analytic material" (p. 82).

Pediatric practice allowed Winnicott to observe the somatic processes of children interacting with caretakers. This was the basis of his conclusion that mother and infant were a single unit. "The mother's milk does not flow like an excretion," he said,

> it is a response to a stimulus, and the stimulus is the sight and smell and feel of her baby, and the sound of the baby's cry that indicates need. It is all one thing, the mother's care of her baby and the periodic feeding that develops as if it were a means of communication between the two—a song without words. [Winnicott 1957a, pp. 111–112]

Winnicott creatively transformed many of these concrete observations into potent metaphors for the working of the mind. Watching what mother and baby did together contributed to his understanding of what went on inside the baby's mind. An infant's experience of breathing, which appears to come both from within and without, was seen by Winnicott (1945a) as the basis for the conception of spirit, soul, or anima. "Holding," "handling," "object presenting," and "transitional objects" are all metaphors for psychic processes rooted in concrete phenomena observed in child–parent interactions. His observation that midwives frequently interrupt the delicate initiation of breast feeding by impatiently shoving the breast into the baby's mouth, and that the baby responds by instinctive withdrawal (Winnicott 1957a), was probably the backdrop to his notion that the infant needs to "create" the breast.

Winnicott's transformation of concrete observations into metaphors for psychic processes is consistent with his natural proclivity for working from his own body ego. As he (1963a) once reflected: "To some extent, I always listen with my throat" (p. 83). Winnicott was always elaborating what he believed were the somatic origins of self, fantasy, and abstract ideas. "The basis of a self," writes Winnicott (1970b), "forms on the fact of the body which, being alive, not only has shape, but which also functions" (p. 270). When a patient would reveal fantasy material in regard to the transference, Winnicott (1989) would invariably ask about the "accompanying orgastic bodily functioning" (p. 26).

Nevertheless, psychoanalysis, not pediatrics, was the primary vehicle for both Winnicott's clinical understanding of children and his formal theorizing. Although pediatrics concerns itself with the care of the developing child, it was actually psychoanalysis that provided Winnicott with a developmental point of view.

Nineteen twenty-three, the year Winnicott received his first appointments at The Queen Elizabeth Hospital and Paddington Green, was also the year he undertook a personal analysis with Strachey that was to last for ten years. This analysis enabled Winnicott to see children for the first time as real people rather than as merely anatomic or somatic beings. Analysis enabled Winnicott to see the child through the eyes of the analyzed adult. As he later recalled:

> It was only through analysis that I became gradually able to see a baby as a human being. This was really the chief result of my first five years of analysis, so that I've been extremely sympathetic with any paediatricians or anybody who can't see babies as human, because I absolutely couldn't, however I used to try. [Winnicott 1967b, p. 574]

The crucial intersection of Winnicott's first years in analysis and as a practicing pediatrician imbued him with a sense of wonder and excitement. He felt like a pioneer with two vast worlds opening to him simultaneously. His fertile and creative mind bridged the gap. "I was starting up," he wrote about those years,

> as consultant pediatrician at the time, and you can imagine how exciting it was to be taking innumerable case histories and to be getting from uninstructed hospital-class parents all the confirmation that anyone could need for the psychoanalytic theories that were beginning to have meaning for me through my own analysis. At that time, no other

analyst was also a pediatrician, and so for two or three decades I was an isolated phenomenon. [Winnicott 1962c, p. 172]

In his first published work, *Clinical Notes on Disorders of Childhood*, published in 1931, Winnicott already took the unpopular and revolutionary stand that emotional disturbance could lead to arthritis in children. In another early paper, "Appetite and Emotional Disorder" (Winnicott 1936), he asserted:

> No case of collywobbles in a child, of vomiting or of diarrhoea, or of anorexia or constipation can be fully explained without reference to the child's conscious and unconscious fantasies about the inside of the body. . . . Even if we want to confine our attentions to physical disease within the body we still have to say that no study of a child's reaction to a physical disease could be complete without reference to the child's fantasies about his inside. [p. 35]

Winnicott was acutely aware of how his psychological orientation brought him into conflict with traditional pediatrics. There was, in his mind, a fundamental "difference of emotional attitude" between them (Winnicott 1953, p. 102). The pediatrician, for example, relates to every symptom as a "challenge to his therapeutic armoury." In contrast, the child psychoanalyst believes that symptoms are produced and maintained because of their value; the child "needs the symptom because of some hitch in emotional development." The child psychoanalyst, unlike the pediatrician, therefore, is not a symptom-curer (Winnicott 1944, p. 86).

As a result of this fundamental difference in attitude and clinical approach, Winnicott frequently found himself in the role of advocate for psychoanalysis before pediatric audiences. A characteristic example is the talk he gave before the Eighth International Congress of Paediatrics (Winnicott 1956b):

My contribution must be to make an examination of the difficulty that paediatrics is in. There is something wrong somewhere, and it can be assumed that if something is wrong we would all wish to put it right. It is often said that paediatricians are necessarily good with children. This I believe to be true. Here, however, it is my job to make the further observation that being good with children is not psychology. It is altogether a different subject. . . . I am making it my main point . . . that sooner or later it must be recognized that the science underlying psychological paediatrics already exists in dynamic psychology. . . . I do ask here and now for respect from the physical sciences for psychoanalysis, and I ask this especially from those who dislike it. Disliking it is no argument against it. [p. 320]

Advances in the treatment of physical ailments afflicting children, such as the discovery of antibiotics, made it possible, he thought, for pediatrics to begin to focus on the child's emotional development. In his mind, psychoanalysis deserved respect from pediatricians because it was the most precise instrument available for studying human nature objectively. Winnicott (1952) was absolutely convinced that the elucidation of the earliest stages of emotional development must come chiefly from psychoanalytic treatment, "whether it be used in the analysis of small children or of regressed adults or of psychotics of all ages" (p. 221). These were the main source of data from which Winnicott inferred the subjective life of infants. "If from various analyses certain common factors emerge," he wrote, "then we can make definite claims" (p. 221). Or, as he said in his paper on "The Theory of the Parent–Infant Relationship" (1960h):

Indeed it is not from direct observation of infants so much as from the study of the transference in the analytic setting that it is possible to gain a clear view of what takes place in infancy itself. This work on infantile dependence derives from the study of the transference and countertransference phenomena that belong to the psychoanalyst's involvement with the borderline cases. [p. 54]

Even when he attempted to understand the mental state of infants immediately after birth, Winnicott (1949b) turned to an analysis of the dreams of his adult patients. Psychoanalysis, where regression is a key feature, takes priority over the objective study of infants and the infant–mother relationship when it comes to understanding even the birth traumas of infants. And in his paper "The Observation of Infants in a Set Situation" (1941), which is the closest Winnicott ever comes to a controlled observational study, he writes:

> It is illuminating to observe infants directly, and it is necessary for us to do so. In many respects, however, the analysis of two-year-old children tells us much more about the infant than we can ever get from direct observation of infants. This is not surprising; the uniqueness of psychoanalysis as an instrument of research, as we know, lied in its capacity to discover the unconscious part of the mind and link it up with the conscious part and thus give us something like a full understanding of the individual who is in analysis. [p. 61]

Although Winnicott believed that direct observation would never suffice to construct a psychology of early infancy, it could play an important role as a corrective to misguided inferences. In his paper "On the Contribution of Direct Child Observation to Psycho-Analysis" (1957b), he argues that it is sometimes possible by direct observation to prove that what has been discovered in analysis could not, in fact, have occurred at the age presumed by the analyst. "Direct observation," he writes, "proves that the patients have been antedating certain phenomena and therefore giving the analyst the impression that things were happening at an age when they could not have happened" (p. 112). The importance of direct observation, therefore, is to help analysts distinguish between what is "early" and what is "deep."

But because direct observation of the infant cannot yield information about the inner subjective experiences of the neonate, Winnicott relied on psychoanalytic inferences to build a theory of the earliest years. In discussing the depressive position in normal emotional development, for example, he (1954a) writes:

> We can state the preconditions for the depressive position achievement. We have a great deal of practical experience to draw upon because of the number of times we have watched patients, patients of any age, reach this stage in emotional development under the clear conditions of an analysis that is going well. [p. 264]

Because Winnicott built his theory of emotional development on psychoanalytic inferences, he was reluctant, despite his day-to-day contact with children of all ages, to offer precise timetables for emotional development. He (1962e) firmly believed that health was equivalent to maturity; that is, that there is an appropriate degree of emotional development according to an individual's chronological age. For Winnicott (1967a), premature ego development or self-awareness was no more healthy than delayed awareness. Still, because he was basing his developmental sequence on psychoanalytic inferences, he was cautious not to delineate specific dates for normative growth. As he wrote in the paper on the depressive position (1954a): "If it be eventually proved that a baby had a depressive position moment in the first week of life I shall not feel disturbed. Meanwhile, the depressive position is something placed at six to twelve months . . ." (p. 264).

Winnicott's reluctance to offer precise timetables is all the more striking given the importance he attributes to careful history taking in the therapeutic process. Once he (1963d) even went so far as to assert in a strikingly oversimplified way that "psychoanalysis for me is a vast extension of history-taking, with therapeutics as a by-product" (p. 199).

The psychoanalyst, Winnicott (1959–1964) wrote elsewhere, "can be looked upon as a specialist in history-taking"
(p. 132). He can trace a disorder in a patient from childhood
through late adult life and see the way there has been a
"transmutation all along the line from one type of disorder
to another" (p. 132). But, again, this is psychoanalytically
informed history taking—where descriptions of symptomatic behavior and inferences about unconscious processes go
hand in hand.

Winnicott underwent two extensive analyses: the first,
with James Strachey from 1923 to 1933, and the second with
Joan Riviere from 1933 to 1938. Naturally, little is known
about the actual content or conduct of these analyses. Yet,
from an examination of Strachey's letters to his wife, Alix,
Winnicott's private letters, and allusions made by Winnicott
in some of his public utterances, a hint of Winnicott's
feelings about the analyses can be gleaned. The emerging
picture is a complex one in which elements of gratitude and
appreciation are mixed with a lingering dissatisfaction. At
the same time that he was experiencing obvious benefit from
the process, Winnicott implies that his analyses, rather than
being liberating, were in some ways constricting due to their
theoretical rigidity. As a result, Winnicott became a believer
in the therapeutic endeavor, but he attempted to right what
was wrong with his own analyses through the medium of his
psychoanalytic research and writing.

James Strachey, a writer and member of the Bloomsbury
group, had been analyzed by Freud. Finding himself aimless
and without direction, he had written a personal letter to
Freud asking for treatment. To his surprise, Freud invited
him to Vienna. As Strachey described himself in those days:

> A discreditable academic career with the barest of B.A.
> degrees, no medical qualifications, no knowledge of the
> physical sciences, no experience of anything except third-
> rate journalism. The only thing in my favour was that at
> the age of 30, I wrote a letter out of the blue to Freud,

asking him if he would take me on as a student. For some
reason he replied, almost by return post, that he would.
[quoted in Kohon 1986, p. 47]

Apparently, Freud had been pleased to be solicited by
someone from England just as World War I erupted. Upon
his return to England, Strachey was accepted as an analyst
because of his personal contact with Freud. He then devoted
much of his intellectual energies to producing, together with
his wife Alix, a controversial translation of the Standard
Edition of Freud's writings. Michael Holroyd (1973), who
wrote a biography of Strachey's brother Lytton, inter-
viewed James toward the end of his life. Holroyd describes
him as an isolated man who wore a Sigmund Freud beard
that made him look like an "almost exact replica of Freud
himself" (p. 21). One can only guess how Strachey's strong
transference to Freud played itself out in his own analytic
work.

    What brought Winnicott into treatment with Strachey?
It was obviously not intellectual curiosity alone. Winnicott
(1962c) felt at the time that he "needed help," so he turned
to Ernest Jones, who then put him in contact with Strachey.
In recalling his consultation with Jones, he described himself
as a "rather inhibited young man asking whether anything
could be done about it" (Winnicott Correspondence, undated). One can speculate that "inhibition" was possibly short-
hand for what later became a major theoretical concern:
True Self issues revolving around compliance versus experiences that are real. In his paper "Two Notes on the Use of
Silence" (1963c), Winnicott mentions having suffered from
a "serious symptom" in which his larynx would follow the
sounds that he would hear and particularly the voice of
someone talking to him (p. 83). It is striking that this would
be a symptom of a man who became so preoccupied with the
illusory boundary between inside and outside. One can
certainly speculate that this symptom captures how Winnicott's unique attunement to others might compel him to

struggle to maintain his individual sensibility in the face of perceived impingements. The symptom also brings to mind Clare Winnicott's description of her husband finding it difficult to separate himself from his maternal environment.

Another way of understanding Winnicott's symptom is in terms of what Thomas Ogden (1989) has described as "autistic-contiguous forms of imitation" (pp. 73–75). According to Ogden, in this form of imitation the individual experiences a "change in the shape of his surface as a result of the influence of his relations with external objects" (p. 74). Referring to the work of E. Gaddini (1969), Ogden (1989) believes there are times in which even adults use this form of imitation as a way of holding onto attributes of the object "in the absence of the experience of having an inner space in which the other person's qualities or parts can in phantasy be stored" (p. 74). This is an elaboration of Fenichel's (1945) idea that imitation represents an important aspect of sensory perception and that one can perceive the other by experiencing the other through one's own bodily sensations.

Winnicott entered analysis at the age of 27, the same year he married his first wife, Alice Taylor. The marriage was a troubled one from the outset; the couple was obviously not having sexual relations in their first year of marriage (Meisel and Kendrick 1985). Although not much information is available about her, Alice Taylor was apparently a high-strung and nervous woman who, according to some accounts, suffered from significant psychiatric disturbance (Grolnick 1990). Obviously of artistic temperament, some sources refer to her as a potter (Phillips 1988), while other people recall her as a "beautiful operatic singer" (Clancier and Kalmanovitch 1987, p. xvi). Masud Khan once made the claim that "taking care of her took all of his [Winnicott's] youth" (quoted in Clancier and Kalmanovitch 1987, p. xvi). Despite obvious difficulties, Winnicott stayed with her for many years, refusing to divorce her "until she was strong enough to be able to tolerate it" (Katharine Rees, personal communication, September 23, 1991). This was in 1949, the same year his father passed away. By that time, Winnicott was 53 years old. Two years later, he married Clare. He arranged for Alice to live in a cottage in the countryside and maintained contact with her even after the divorce.

What meaning did it have for Winnicott care so devotedly for a troubled woman? Alice, after all, was not the only disturbed woman he took under his wing. Between 1943 and 1949 a severely regressed schizoid woman treated by Marion Milner (1969) lived at the Winnicott home. It was Winnicott who had brought the patient ("Susan") to Milner and who, as long as she resided at their home, even paid for her treatment. One wonders what strain this might have added to the Winnicotts' marriage. Only after the divorce did "Susan" move out, the breakup of the marriage producing in her a serious regression (Hughes 1989).

The strain in the Winnicott marriage may be the clue to why Winnicott never had any children of his own. Could it be that Winnicott's theoretical views about the "good-enough" mother were rooted in his recognition that his wife was too preoccupied with her own emotional sickness to experience the "illness" of "primary maternal preoccupation"? Or is it possible that it was Winnicott who was too self-absorbed, too much the perpetual child himself, to make room for a real child within his home? It is difficult, after all, for a puer to be a father.

Although in none of his public writings or speeches does Winnicott ever even allude to his thoughts about having children, in his unpublished autobiographical fragment he discusses the difficulty that a man has dying without a son to imaginatively kill and to survive him. Winnicott (1989) describes a son as providing "the only continuity that men know" (p. 4). Obviously, Winnicott in some way grieved not having a child of his own.

Winnicott was probably alluding to his own personal situation when he wrote in his essay "Integrative and Disruptive Factors in Family Life" (1957c) how "married people with no children can and do find all sorts of other ways of in fact having a family; they may be found sometimes to have the largest families of all. But they would have preferred to have had their own born children" (p. 43). The 60,000 cases Winnicott treated was one obvious way he found of "having a family."

Winnicott remained deeply respectful of what he obtained from his analysis with Strachey. He (1969b) once even described Strachey as his "favorite example of a psychoanalyst" (p. 510). In his obituary for Strachey, Winnicott said he thought of him not as a great man, but as one whom he admired for his "unassailable intellectual honesty" and the depth of his cultural life (p. 509). Actually, Strachey's familiarity with literature, music, and ballet filled Winnicott with envy and made him "feel somewhat boorish when in his company" (p. 508). Strachey was erudite and sophisticated—something Winnicott was not.

Strachey, in Winnicott's mind, was also an analyst who was "not blinded by any kind of faith" (Rodman 1987, p. 193). He was a "good analyst" because he was neither dogmatic nor indoctrinating. There was no implicit message that the patient need acquire an absolute faith. This aspect of Strachey's character resonated with Winnicott and probably influenced him as well. The position Strachey took, for example, in regard to the developing split within the British Psycho-Analytic Society was absolutely consistent with Winnicott's own beliefs. A letter sent by Strachey to Edward Glover in 1940 reads as if it could have been penned by Winnicott. "I should rather like you to know," writes Strachey,

> that—if it comes to a showdown—I'm very strongly in favour of compromise at all costs. The trouble seems to me to be with extremism, on *both* sides. My own view is that Mrs K [Melanie Klein] has made some highly important contributions to psychoanalysis, but that it's absurd to make out (a) that they cover the whole subject or (b) that

their validity is axiomatic. On the other hand I think it's equally ludicrous for Miss F [Anna Freud] to maintain that psychoanalysis is a game reserve belonging to the F family and that Mrs K's views are fatally subversive. [quoted in Rayner 1991, p. 18]

Winnicott and Strachey shared the common roots of the independent tradition.

Despite Winnicott's obvious affinity and admiration, his relationship with Strachey—at least in the earliest years of analysis—was strained to a greater degree than Winnicott ever acknowledged in public. Strachey's private letters to his wife Alix, however, offer some indication. Alix Strachey happened to be in Berlin undergoing her own analysis when her husband took Winnicott on as a patient; letters were exchanged on a nearly daily basis. In these correspondences, Winnicott is portrayed as derelict in paying for treatment. One dated October 9, 1924, for example, reads as follows:

I'm beginning to doubt whether Dr. W.'ll ever stump up. He finally sent an order to someone to sell something out. And the reply was that the signature didn't stimm with the original signature when the things were bought. He thinks he vaguely remembers or he imagines it's possible, that his father signed his name for him. But I think he's altered his writing on purpose to make further delays. Meanwhile at any moment the Rates may be due and all lost. [Meisel and Kendrick 1985, pp. 83–84]

In another letter, dated November 3, Strachey refers to Winnicott as being "awfully leisurely" about paying his bill. "Although he got another nice bill on Saturday," writes Strachey, "and though he had a most suitable dream last night, there wasn't a sign today of his intending to pay it. (I told him a month ago that I wanted him to stump up each time)" (pp. 106–107).

One cannot help but be a bit skeptical about the nature

of the therapeutic relationship given Strachey's obvious mistrust of Winnicott's motives in delaying payment. Was this Strachey's way of handling resistance? Or is this simply an example of how the financial dependence of a struggling analyst with a small practice (Strachey had only one other patient at the time) can cloud the analytic space? In one letter to his wife, Strachey provides a rather explicit example of how Winnicott's resistance to paying distracted him during the analytic session. Referring derogatorily to Winnicott as "Winnie," Strachey writes to Alix:

> The buzzer announcing Winnie was followed by a longer pause than usual today; & I rightly guessed that he was writing the cheque on the stairs. He rushed in & pressed it upon me—die Tinte noch nass ["the ink still wet"]; threw himself upon the sofa & started off feverishly with: "There's someone whose name I keep forgetting." And then long talks about why he should forget names—other people whose names he forgets, etc. It flashed into my mind that he'd made some mistake over my name on the cheque, & I nearly risked the coup de theatre of walking over to the writing-table where I'd put it down, & looking at it. However, I restrained myself. When he'd gone, I went and looked at it: he hadn't signed it! [p. 109]

Was Winnicott's "forgetfulness" a way of expressing some specific dissatisfaction with treatment? A form of resistance? Or, perhaps, another example of the narcissistic strain in his character where he feels entitled to a certain latitude? Whatever the case may be, there is some indication that Strachey, at least in the early phases of the analysis, felt dismissive toward Winnicott. He secretly referred to him as "poor little Winnie" (p. 115). What's worse, he derisively labeled him a "Rankschuler"—a term of opprobrium referring to followers of Otto Rank, who deviated from orthodox Freudian psychoanalysis.

Strachey's characterization of Winnicott as someone

who is "cut out to be a Rankschuler" (p. 115) indicates how some of the ideas Winnicott was to later develop theoretically surfaced clinically quite early on in the treatment. Rank's book, *The Trauma of Birth,* created quite a stir in psychoanalytic circles both because of its content and, perhaps more so, because he had displayed the temerity to publish it without the consent of Freud's inner circle. This occurred at a time when cancer had been detected in Freud's jaw and palate and the issue of "defections" from the ranks of orthodoxy threatened Freud's followers. Rank's main argument in the book was that the transition from the security of the womb to the painful stimulations of the postnatal environment generates tremendous fear and anxiety in the infant. This primal anxiety is repressed, but throughout life the individual reacts to subsequent separations with fear and strives to reestablish the state of bliss experienced in the womb. Though unconsciously desiring to return to the safety of the mother's body, the individual is at the same time frightened by such a prospect, especially since it suggests the possibility of a reenactment of the initial birth trauma.

Winnicott, from the outset of his own analysis, was apparently quite preoccupied with "Rankian"-like ideas that centered on his mother. Strachey wrote to Alix that Winnicott was having fantasies that he urinated on his mother at the moment of birth (Meisel and Kendrick 1985). In addition, he saw his mother, rather than his father, as a castrating figure. One night he had a virulent anxiety dream in which his wife, disguised in a bearskin, embraced him, took out a penis, and castrated him. The next night he dreamed of a pleasant encounter with his father. Strachey interpreted Winnicott's dreams as defensive—he preferred to think of his mother as castrater because he didn't want to freely express the murderous wishes he had toward his father. Winnicott's normal Oedipus complex was, Strachey believed, more deeply repressed than the inverted one. Given Winnicott's later theoretical emphases, it is reasonable to conclude that he found Strachey's oedipal interpretations unsatisfactory.

Although Strachey was more of a translator than an innovator, his main psychoanalytic contribution came in a series of lectures in 1933 in which he formulated his ideas about the mutative interpretation. In these lectures he explicated the principle that the crucial instrument of change in psychoanalysis is the interpretation, accurately timed, which gathers together the patient's material and clearly deals with a sample of transference neurosis (Strachey 1934). Winnicott learned from Strachey to appreciate the curative power of interpretations. As he confessed in a private letter in 1952 to Ernest Jones:

> In 10 years' analysis Strachey made practically no mistakes and he adhered to a classical technique in a cold-blooded way for which I have always been grateful. He did, however, say two or three things that were not interpretations at a time when interpretation was needed. Each one of these has bothered me and at some time or other have come out in an unexpected way. [Rodman 1987, p. 33]

Seventeen years later, however, in an obituary for Strachey, Winnicott offered a different version of how he had benefited from analysis. His perception of his own treatment was now filtered through the lens of decades of experience during which his own views of the curative elements in treatment had crystallized. "I would say," writes Winnicott (1969b),

> that Strachey had one thing quite clear in his mind as a result of his visit to Freud: that a process develops in the patient, and that what transpires cannot be produced but it can be made use of. This is what I feel about my own analysis with Strachey, and in my work I have tried to follow the principle through and to emphasize the idea in

its stark simplicity. It is my experience of analysis at the hand of Strachey that has made me suspicious of descriptions of interpretive work in analysis which seem to give credit to the interpretations for all that happens, as if the process in the patient had got lost sight of. [p. 508]

The ambiguity of this passage is startling. What does he really mean when he says that his analysis with Strachey has made him suspicious of interpretations as the mutative factor? Is Winnicott crediting Strachey for nurturing the process in the patient, or is he chastising him for believing that it is interpretations that facilitate change? Is Winnicott's description a veiled way of expressing ambivalence toward his former analyst? By the time Winnicott had written this passage he had come to believe that although interpretive work is essential, more than just interpretation is involved in cure. Orthodoxy in technique was reserved for certain kinds of patients or certain phases of treatment (Little 1990). Was it a lingering transference distortion that caused Winnicott to assess Strachey's work as being like his own, or was Strachey genuinely doing something in the analysis that was different from what he believed he was actually doing?

Winnicott's second analysis with Joan Riviere, which lasted from 1933 to 1938, was no less problematic than had been his first one with Strachey. On the one hand, Winnicott seems to have felt at times that his analysis with Riviere was a liberating experience. He told a supervisee, Jennifer Johns, that having an analysis with Riviere was like "surfacing and seeing the surrounding territory after having been in a ditch for years" (quoted in Riviere 1991, p. 32). On the other hand, however, Winnicott felt hurt and perhaps misunderstood when Riviere remained unreceptive to his theoretical innovations. She apparently displayed intolerance toward his efforts to break new theoretical ground, and his representation of his work as a corrective to their mutual mentor, Melanie Klein.

Riviere, who had been analyzed by Freud, was the first

lay analyst in England. A child of the English upper-class intelligentsia, Riviere was interested in language and, like Strachey, was one of Freud's official translators. A member of the distinguished Verral family, she had, according to Ernest Jones, a "strong complex about being a well-born lady" (quoted in Brome 1983, p. 132). She became one of Melanie Klein's most devoted followers and, as controversies deepened, frequently attacked Freud in print. Riviere staked out an unambiguous and, from Winnicott's point of view, dogmatic position on psychoanalysis. According to her view, psychoanalysis was

> not concerned with the real world, nor with the child's or adult's adaptation to the real world, nor with sickness nor health, nor virtue nor vice. It is concerned simply and solely with the imaginings of the childish mind, the phantasied pleasures and dreaded retributions. [quoted in Grosskurth 1986, p. 170]

In particular, Winnicott was "shocked" (Rodman 1987) by the introduction Riviere had written to a collection of Kleinian papers in which she described Klein's ideas as "a fully integrated theory which . . . takes account of all psychical manifestations, normal and abnormal, from birth to death, and leaves no unbridgeable gulfs and no phenomena outstanding without intelligible relation to the rest" (Klein et al. 1952).

Winnicott was hurt by Riviere's characterization because his own article on transitional phenomena had been rejected for the collection. He was told that he would have to bring his ideas in line with those of Klein if he wanted his paper included, but he refused. Such a demand collided with Winnicott's natural distaste for closed systems. Comments like Riviere's were, he felt, turning Klein's contribution into an "'ism' which becomes a nuisance" (Rodman 1987, p. 37). The Kleinians were too contemptuous of other viewpoints for his taste. He felt it no disgrace that there were many questions psychoanalysis could *not* answer, and he firmly believed in a scientific attitude in which "any advance in scientific work achieves an arrival at a new platform from which a wider range of the unknown can be sensed" (p. 35). In addition, Riviere's dogma constituted a personal threat for Winnicott. Her convictions left no room for creative individuals, like himself, with ideas that are personal and, perhaps, original.

There is substantial evidence that the smugness and certainty of Riviere's theoretical beliefs negatively affected Winnicott's analysis with her. This comes through clearly in a long letter that Winnicott wrote to Melanie Klein on November 17, 1952. The Friday before, Winnicott had read a paper entitled "Anxiety Associated with Insecurity" before the British Psycho-Analytic Society. The paper was criticized and immediately restated in Kleinian terms. This, of course, offended Winnicott, for whom it was so vitally important to say things in his own way. Although Winnicott acknowledged that this need of his might be "annoying" to others, he found it equally disturbing that every idea had to be stated in Kleinian terms. Winnicott wrote to Klein about this incident in a way that echoes his notions of mothers meeting their infant's spontaneous gestures:

> What I was wanting on Friday undoubtedly was that there should be some move from your direction towards the gesture that I make in this paper. It is a creative gesture and I cannot make any relationship through this gesture except if someone come to meet it. [Rodman 1987, p. 34]

He continues by referring directly to his analyses:

> I think that I was wanting something which I have no right to expect from your group, and it is really of the nature of a therapeutic act, something which I could not get in either of my two long analyses, although I got so much else. There is no doubt that my criticism of Mrs. Riviere was not

only a straightforward criticism based on objective observation but also it was coloured by the fact that it was just
exactly here that her analysis failed with me. [p. 34]

Winnicott was obviously hurt, not only by the response
to his paper, but by what he perceived as Riviere's failure to
provide what he terms a "therapeutic act." In his mind, this
entailed a respectful responsiveness to the patient's attempts
to discover and act upon the spontaneous gestures of the
True Self. Instead, what he encountered with Riviere was an
intolerance toward his own efforts at theory building.

In part, this was the result of an unhealthy situation, not
unique to the British Psycho-Analytic Society, in which
personal analyses became tainted by issues of theoretical
loyalty and disloyalty. Winnicott's problematic relationship
with Riviere was indicative of the internal difficulties associated with training analyses. As Limentani (1989) has described it:

> In training there is an unavoidable contamination of the
> analytic relationship by the more complex clan or "ex-
> tended family" relationship of the Institute as well as with
> fellow candidates. Thus there is an actual psychoanalytic
> family situation to be lived out, which causes untold
> repercussions in the transference. [p. 74]

Objective scientific discussions, too, fell prey to what Edward Glover once bitterly referred to as the "phenomenon
of postponed obedience" (quoted in Hughes 1989, p. 8).
Winnicott, of course, was uniquely sensitive to demands for
compliance.

Riviere, it appears, responded quite negatively to Winnicott's efforts to incorporate the environment into a psychoanalytic theory of development. Once, during his analysis, he told her that he was writing a paper on the
classification of the environment and she "just wouldn't

have it" (Winnicott 1967b, p. 576). As he told John Padel (1991) when they met privately for dinner one evening:

> I said to my analyst, "I'm almost ready to write a book on the environment." She said to me, "You write a book on the environment and I'll turn you into a frog!" Of course she didn't use those words, you understand, but that's how what she did say came across to me. [p. 36]

Despite feeling that he had "gained a tremendous amount" from his five years of analysis with Riviere, Winnicott (1967b) had to wait a long time before he "could recover from her reaction" (p. 576).

It is not uncommon in the history of psychoanalytic disputes that the arguments of protagonists are portrayed by their opponents as signs of "incomplete analyses" or "neurotic illness." Scientific disagreements frequently degenerate into attacks on character. From Riviere's point of view, Winnicott's refusal to accept all of Klein's formulations and his insistence on stating theory in his own language were symptomatic of his personal difficulties. She felt he was struggling too hard to be his own real self. She saw this as a "block" in him and did not hesitate to tell him so (Rodman 1987, p. 94). Winnicott was deeply distressed by Riviere's reaction, repeatedly trying to set things right with both her and Klein. He genuinely admired both these women, but found it difficult to tolerate not being accepted by them. As always, he looked for a way to express his hurt and disagreement that would not threaten to sever connections. This often entailed acknowledging his own limitations as a prelude to self-assertive protest. As he wrote privately to Klein:

> This matter which I am discussing touches the very root of my own personal difficulty so that what you see can always be dismissed as Winnicott's illness, but if you dismiss it in this way you may miss something which is in

the end a positive contribution. My illness is something
which I can deal with in my own way and it is not far away
from being the inherent difficulty in regard to human
contact with external reality. [Rodman 1987, p. 37]

Winnicott's final remark, that his personal illness reflects an "inherent difficulty in regard to human contact
with external reality," indicates how his theoretical notions
about feeling real, primary creativity, and illusion are, to
some extent, rooted in his personal subjective experience,
including his own symptoms. His strength as an innovator
became evident as he struggled to continue his analyses
through the medium of his work and research as a clinician.
In fact, much of Winnicott's later theorizing can be understood as an attempt to fill gaps in his analyses. As he (1947)
noted on one occasion: "Psycho-analytic research is perhaps
always to some extent an attempt on the part of an analyst to
carry the work of his own analysis further than the point to
which his own analyst could get him" (p. 196).

The intimacy of the early mother–infant relationship,
which probably remained unexamined in his analyses, became Winnicott's focus. Clinically, he attempted to provide
his patients with precisely what he felt was missing from his
own treatment—an analysis of what allows him to be a
whole human being who feels real. He would reach beyond
putatively mutative oedipal interpretations toward holding
his patients in a way that would restart the natural developmental process. But, by doing so, he was also looking
inward.

Self-cure obviously remained a motive for Winnicott's
psychoanalytic investigations. But self-cure was not a flight
into sanity; sanity, from his point of view, could be as
imprisoning as insanity. As he wrote in "Primitive Emotional
Development" (1945a): "There is . . . much sanity that has a
symptomatic quality, being charged with fear or denial of
madness, fear or denial of the innate capacity of every
human being to become unintegrated, depersonalized, and
to feel that the world is unreal" (p. 150).

Self-cure, therefore, entailed a strengthened ability to tolerate the constant dialectic between inside and outside, objective and subjective, sanity and insanity. What Winnicott wanted was not to feel sane, but to experience in a way that felt free. Involvement in psychoanalysis—as patient, therapist, researcher, theoretician, and self-healer—was part of Winnicott's struggle to feel real, despite the demands of external reality, and to feel whole, while achieving a measure of insanity. As he (1964b) wrote in his review of Carl Jung's autobiography, *Memories, Dreams, and Reflection*:

> If I want to say that Jung was mad, and that he recovered, I am doing nothing worse than I would do in saying of myself that I was sane and that through analysis and self-analysis I achieved some measure of insanity. Freud's flight to sanity could be something we psycho-analysts are trying to recover from. . . . [p. 483]

4

The Origins of Originality

What does a writer need to know? In one word, I'd say, predecessors. I don't know why it is that things become more precious with the awareness that someone else has looked at them, thought about them, written about them. But so I find it to be. There is less originality than we think. There is also a vast amount of solitude. Writers need company. We all need it. It's not the command of knowledge that matters finally, but the company. It's the predecessors. As a writer, I don't know where I'd be without them. [Amy Clampitt, "Predecessors, et Cetera"]

The author is not only himself but his predecessors, and simultaneously he is part of the living tribal fabric, the part that voices what all know, or should know, and need to hear again. [John Updike, *Odd Jobs: Essays and Criticism*, p. 137]

How do we account for the making of such an impressionistic psychoanalytic creator as Donald Winnicott? Can the origins of his original vision be delineated? What were the intellectual roots from which he drew the raw materials for his creative apperceptions?

One of the strongest criticisms levied against psychoanalytic theory is its tendency to be ahistorical. When and where history is admitted into the critical purview of psychoanalysis, it usually takes the form of an "internist" historiography—the only data considered relevant is the conceptual ideas of previous psychoanalysts. Advances in theory are seen as internal "technical" developments. Rarely are these ideas traced to the broader or nonpsychoanalytic cultural milieu. As a result, psychoanalysis often offers a history of ideas about the unconscious without reference to their roots in social reality.

There is a danger, however, in countering this criticism by promoting entirely "externalist" historiographic accounts. Such versions of psychoanalysis tend to deny the specificity and the occasional unpredictability that marks genuinely creative developments within psychoanalysis. Externalist versions fail to give sufficient weight to the inferential process implicit in clinical work; data from unconscious processes are removed from the history of the unconscious. Purely externalist accounts, therefore, run the risk of degenerating into a facile and dangerous sociological reductivism.

Is it possible to avoid the Scylla of internalist historiography without falling prey to the Charybdis of externalist accounts? Can the nonpsychoanalytic origins of Winnicott's originality be discerned without diminishing the centrality of psychoanalytic sources? Can his thinking be linked to precursors without forfeiting or denying that which is truly creative?

"One can only be original," declared Winnicott in his typically dialectical fashion, "on the basis of tradition" (1971c, p. 117). It is well known that he was steeped in Western culture, read and wrote poetry, took an active interest in religion, enjoyed the arts, studied music, medicine, and pediatrics. But Winnicott was never compulsive enough to link his own productions with the important historical, literary, and aesthetic antecedents. In fact, his works are neither annotated nor referenced in a scholarly manner. He was not inclined to check citations or acknowledge sources—certainly not the nonpsychoanalytic ones. Like most thinkers, Winnicott simply took his worldview for granted.

An investigation of some of the origins of this worldview illuminates the nature of Winnicott's solitude and connection with his environment. While such an inquiry may not necessarily explain Winnicott's ideas, it can help elucidate the nature of his thought. Such an examination also highlights that there really is, as Amy Clampitt says, less originality than we think, but also a vast amount of solitude.

It is not easy to assess the impact of precursors on Winnicott's original thinking. Part of the difficulty resides in distinguishing between parallels and influences. The mere discovery of parallels between Winnicott's ideas and those of thinkers who preceded him may tell us virtually nothing about what actually influenced him. Winnicott, after all, dealt in an area that is of universal concern. Humans, quite naturally, find themselves problematic and puzzle over their origins, their motives, their passions, and their creativity. These universal concerns are as much the business of writers, poets, theologians, and philosophers as they are of psychoanalysts. Parallels, therefore, may hint at much, but they guarantee little.

An assessment of the impact of precursors on Winnicott's thinking is further complicated by the nature of his relationship to his own intellectual roots. He displayed varying degrees of benign neglect, respect, irreverence, admiration, disregard, and acceptance. In part, this is due to the unusual mix in his character of humility and the need to remain distinctive, to find his own way of putting things. As he (1949b) wrote in a footnote to his paper "Birth Memories, Birth Trauma, and Anxiety":

> It will be observed that I . . . am making an attempt to state
> my own position in my own words. I am only too happy
> when after making my own statement, I find that what I
> have said has been said previously by others. Often it has
> been said better, but not better for me. [p. 177]

It is also a function of the way in which Winnicott ap-
proached intellectual tasks. As he (1945a) wrote in his paper
"Primitive Emotional Development," which he read before
the British Psycho-Analytic Society:

> I shall not give an historical survey and show the develop-
> ment of my ideas from the theories of others, because my
> mind does not work that way. What happens is that I
> gather this and that, here and there, settle down to clinical
> experience, form my own theories and then, last of all,
> interest myself in looking to see where I stole what.
> Perhaps this is as good a method as any. [p. 145]

What Winnicott describes as his "method" is quite reminiscent of the way in which the infant, according to Winnicott,
gradually encounters the world of objects. At first, the
primitive ego is simply "gathering this and that, here and
there." Later, the infant will learn to make "use" of objects,
as Winnicott did when he interests himself in "looking to see
where I stole what."

What, then, are the sources from which Winnicott drew
intellectual sustenance? Who were the precursors with
whose ideas Winnicott played while creating his own concepts? This chapter will deal with some of the nonpsychoanalytic origins of Winnicott's original ideas. The
next chapter will place Winnicott within a psychoanalytic
context.

THE MIND OF AN ENGLISHMAN

There was something about Winnicott that struck many
people—particularly outside England—as being characteris-

tically English. Martin James, writing in 1961, tried to explain to Winnicott why it was difficult for many European psychoanalysts to digest his contribution. "Your approach," he wrote, came across as "typically British and totally beyond the comprehension of the Teutonic Hartmann style of theorist" (Winnicott Correspondence, Dr. Martin James to D. W. W., December 6, 1961). Charles Rycroft (1985) also observed that Winnicott was "somewhat of an outsider" within the psychoanalytic movement because he was too much of an intuitive Englishman. Central European thinkers had a predominantly intellectual, rationalist style. Winnicott, on the other hand, "had no time for impersonal, mechanical abstractions such as the mental apparatus or cathexes and counter-cathexes . . . " (p. 141).

Just as the Winnicott family was deeply rooted in the physical landscape of Devon, Donald Winnicott's mind was part of the British cultural terrain. He internalized many facets of British intellectual tradition. According to its historical heritage, Britain is insular ("A Nice Little Tight Little Island") and Protestant. The aftermath of the English Civil War of the seventeenth century created a political culture characterized by the flowering of a multitude of original political ideologies. One influential movement at the time was even called "The Independents," the same name adopted by members of the British Psycho-Analytic Society who, like Winnicott, refused to align themselves with either Anna Freud or Melanie Klein. Toward the end of the seventeenth century, a second convulsion—the "Glorious" Revolution of 1688—brought an end to the reign of James II, who was perceived as attempting to restore authoritarianism to England. The outcome of this turbulent period in British history was the creation of a political culture that rejected authoritarianism on the one hand, and the instability of republicanism or the tyrannies of enthusiastic ideologies, on the other. The principle of constitutional monarchy, with its notions of stable parliamentary government and political liberalism, came to dominate British culture.

These fundamental notions about how society is best organized were very much a part of Winnicott's thinking. His allegiance to psychoanalysis included a recognition that there were political implications to unconscious processes. Although temperamentally averse to political activism (his staunch libertarianism, fierce personalism, acute sensitivity to unconscious motivations, and distrust of programmatic ideologies or misguided enthusiasms, all combined to make political engagement difficult), he periodically ventured forth into the realm of applied theory. In doing so, Winnicott, forever the Englishman, staked out a paradoxical position as a democratic monarchist and supporter of the status quo.

Winnicott's forays into applied theory reflected his primary emphasis on the psychology of the individual and the centrality of healthy familial homes in assuring the well-being of all citizens. Democracy, for Winnicott (1950b), was the most "mature" form of social organization. It is an "innate" tendency that becomes actualized when a large enough proportion of a given country's citizenry obtains a level of emotional maturity to make it so. It is a "society well adjusted to its healthy individual members" (p. 240). The secret ballot was essential because it allows for "the *illogical* election and removal of leaders"; it ensures the "freedom of the people to express deep feelings, *apart from conscious thoughts*" (p. 241). The stability of democracy rests with the "ordinary man and woman, and the ordinary, common-place home" (p. 247). By not being burdened by government interference, ordinary good parents can be "creators of the innate democratic factor" (p. 247).

Although Winnicott offers an important and consistent point of view regarding the connection between human development and politics, his position suffers from too narrow a perspective. For example, he fails to take into account that the secret ballot not only serves unconscious processes but protects individuals from political abuse. The stability of democracy, as another example, rests not only on the natural instincts of ordinary good parents but on their economic viability as well. Winnicott has a great deal to say about the environmental conditions that foster emotional well-being, but nothing to say about the connection between economic decline and political regression.

Winnicott's narrow perspective leads him to some questionable conclusions regarding the status of women in political culture. His deep appreciation of unconscious fantasies regarding males and females lapses, at times, into sexist stereotypes. His starting point for any discussion regarding women is the unconscious fear—common to both genders—of WOMAN. This is not an individual's fear of a particular woman, but a basic fantasy rooted in the primary experience of absolute dependence. Winnicott was convinced that the unconscious fear of WOMAN is a "powerful agent in society structure" and is "responsible for the fact that in very few societies does a woman hold the political reins" (p. 252).

Winnicott, however, remains ambiguous as to the practical implication of his insight. On the one hand, he assumes that "men and women have an equal capacity," and that it "would not be possible to say that only men could be suitable for leadership on grounds of intellectual or emotional capacity for the highest political posts" (p. 251). On the other hand, however, since "there is no relation to the father which has such a quality" of absolute dependence, a man who has power politically "can be appreciated much more objectively by the group than a woman can be if she is in a similar position" (p. 253).

In a similar vein, and drawing conclusions that were equally ambiguous, Winnicott extended his unconscious perspective to include a reverence for the monarchy as a collective transitional object. Again, he is drawn to conclusions inherently supportive of the English status quo. In 1970, a year before he died, he (1970c) participated in a debate on the survival of the monarchy in a piece called "The Place of the Monarchy." Although he describes himself

as "not unduly sentimental about royalty and royal families," he does "take the existence of the monarchy seriously," believing that without it, Great Britain "would be quite
a different place to live in" (p. 260). In his article, Winnicott
describes the unconscious use that the public can make of
the monarchy and, in particular, in a way that corresponds
to what he sees as an "axiom" of unconscious object-
relating: what is good is always being destroyed. He sees it as
natural and healthy that people are always putting the
monarchy to test and that the monarchy continues to survive. For Winnicott, the continued existence of the monarchy is an indication that

> there exist here and now the conditions in which democ-
> racy . . . can characterize the political system, and in
> which a benign or a malignant dictatorship . . . is for the
> time being unlikely to appear. Under such conditions,
> individuals, if they are emotionally healthy, can develop a
> sense of being, can realize some of their personal potential,
> and can play. [p. 268]

It is evident from Winnicott's positions that the constitutional monarchy that evolved in seventeenth-century England was perceived by him as the guardian of emotional
well-being. The political system in which he grew up became
normative for healthy development.

English political culture included not only particular
social institutions, but a way of looking at human nature and
conducting public discourse (Rayner 1991). The loathing of
ideological authoritarianism produced a general distrust of
closed systems of theory and thought. The phrase, "Please
to God, no enthusiasm," captured this mindset. There was a
public ideal of quiet debate and civilized discourse that
would inevitably lead to compromise, justice, and fair play.
It was essential that there be no fanaticism.

This was the political expression of what became
known, philosophically, as British empiricism. From the

empirical point of view, as initiated by such thinkers as Locke, Berkeley, and Hume, knowledge was seen as arising from perceptions and experience, not from innate ideas. Conflicting perceptions could be sorted out by discussion and compromise—both within the individual's mind and between social groups. Hypotheses could be evaluated and discarded based on evidence. The empirical tradition was, therefore, one of open-mindedness and a love of trial and error. In this mode of learning, error is as valuable as truth, and doubt can be enjoyed.

In both Winnicott's writing and conduct, it is evident that he was, to a large extent, a product of this philosophic tradition. As Masud Khan (1975) said about him, he was "reared in the tradition of his people, the English. For him facts were the reality, theories were the human stammer towards grasping facts" (p. xi).

The lectures on human growth and development that Winnicott delivered annually at the University of London were published under the title *Human Nature*—a possible reference to David Hume's *Treatise on Human Nature*. As Martin James (1988) points out, Winnicott's work is closely aligned with Hume's attempts to make knowledge available, in Hume's phrase, "for Human Use." Hume's moderate skepticism was consistent with Winnicott's own provisional cast of thinking. Winnicott repeatedly emphasized that his ideas were always tentative and that he learned as much from his mistakes with his patients as he did from his successes. He even emphasized how the analyst's failures play a curative role. Winnicott's fundamental attitude, like that of the British empiricists, was that ideas and concepts could be evaluated and respected for their heuristic and truth value, no matter what their source. Factionalism, ideological dogma, reliance on authority, and zealous evangelicalism were all alien to his spirit (Rayner 1991, p. 9). Winnicott consistently sought open-minded and playful discussion rather than combative or polemical debate. In his private letters he repeatedly asserted the somewhat naive belief that through discussion theoretical disputes would evaporate. Like the empiricists, he preferred empirically derived ideas based on observation of the external world over attempts to build coherent or systematic theories based on a priori thought. In his vision of human nature, the infant's knowledge of the world was the result of his perceptions and experiences in the world and not merely the product of his innate ideas.

Nevertheless, it would be a mistake to describe Winnicott as a strict empiricist—although he probably tended to see himself as one to a greater extent than actually was the case. He was, after all, far more intuitive than he cared to admit. He also did not really accept the empiricist notion that self-knowledge obtained through introspection had a privileged status. His was a two-person psychology, not unlike that of Wittgenstein, who spoke of solitary thinking as internalized dialogue (Cavell 1988). As Winnicott (1966d) once commented: "I *am* means nothing unless *I* at the beginning *am along with another human being* who has not yet been differentiated off" (p. 12).

Most important was Winnicott's rejection of the empiricist notion that reality is "stamped in" through the sense organs. His position on this issue was far more complex and subjective. The empiricists had a theory of knowledge based upon a kind of sensory atomism in which the mind is an agency of discovery viewing its own ideas as "like" the objects that are the sources of the sensations it receives. For Winnicott, on the other hand, the mind is endowed with a capacity for primary creativity. If it merely "discovers" reality, reality does not "feel real." Creative apperception must accompany passive perception. An experiencing self—a notion more akin to existentialism than empiricism—is central to Winnicott's worldview (Ticho 1974). What is more, Winnicott's view of the experiencing self takes into account temperamental variability; the mind is not a tabula rasa, but an active agent that must contend with stimulations originating both within and without.

Still, Winnicott was deeply influenced by the pragmatism of British empiricism. He also displayed what has been called the "playful use of nonsense" characteristic of English writers (Clancier and Kalmanovitch 1987, p. 110). He knew how to treat things lightly and seriously at the same time; his gracious demeanor conveyed what could be called a bearable lightness of being. Winnicott would have been in good company, for example, with a whimsical writer like Lewis Carroll, who, like Winnicott, bridged the gap between the sciences and humanities (Carroll was a writer and a mathematician) and was the only boy in a family surrounded by several sisters. Could it have been his memory of Lewis Carroll that prompted Winnicott in his autobiographical fragments to pray to God that he might be alive after his own death? After all, Carroll's (1960) depiction of Alice shrinking like a telescope in the first chapter of *Alice in Wonderland* reads like this:

> She waited for a few minutes to see if she was going to shrink any further: she felt a little nervous about this; "for it might end, you know," said Alice to herself, "in my going out altogether, like a candle. I wonder what I should be like then?" And she tried to fancy what the flame of a candle looks like after the candle is blown out. . . . [p. 32]

Winnicott's affinity with Carroll is also evident in that both writers are deeply concerned with the radical ambiguity between that which is absolutely subjective and that which is absolutely objective. Perhaps the most poignant example of this appears in *Through the Looking Glass* when Alice, Tweedledum, and Tweedledee, discussing the Red King asleep against a tree, are plunged into murky metaphysical waters:

> —"He's dreaming now," said Tweedledee: "and what do you think he's dreaming about?"
> —Alice said, "Nobody can guess that."

—"Why about you!" Tweedledee exclaimed, clapping his
hands triumphantly. "And if he left off dreaming about
you, where do you suppose you'd be?"

—"Where I am now, of course," said Alice.

—"Not you!" Tweedledee retorted contemptuously.
"You'd be nowhere. Why, you're only a sort of thing in
his dream!"

—"If that there King was to wake," added Tweedledum,
"you'd go out—bang! just like a candle!"

—"I shouldn't!" Alice exclaimed indignantly. "Besides, if
I'm only a sort of thing in his dream, what are you, I
should like to know?"

—"Ditto, ditto!" cried Tweedledee. He shouted this so
loud that Alice couldn't help saying:

—"Hush! You'll be waking him, I'm afraid, if you make so
much noise."

—"Well, it's no use your talking about waking him," said
Tweedledum, "when you're only one of the things in
his dream. You know very well you're not real."

—"I am real!" said Alice, and began to cry.

—"You won't make yourself a bit realler by crying,"
Tweedledee remarked: "there's nothing to cry about."

—"If I wasn't real," Alice said—half-laughing through her
tears, it all seemed so ridiculous—"I shouldn't be able to
cry."

—"I hope you don't suppose those are real tears?"
Tweedledum interrupted in a tone of great contempt.
[p. 238–239]

Carroll has the Tweedle brothers defending the view
that all material objects, including ourselves, are only—in
Berkeley's words—"sorts of things" in the mind of God.
Alice, on the other hand, represents the common-sense
position of Samuel Johnson, who believed that he had
refuted Berkeley by kicking a large stone. Carroll was obviously troubled by the dilemma. As Bertrand Russell once
remarked about the Red King's dream: "If it were not put
humorously, we should find it too painful" (quoted in
Carroll 1960, p. 238). Carroll, it seems, saw no way out.

After all, Alice herself is dreaming about her encounter with the dreaming Red King. Winnicott, too, was intrigued by the conundrum but searched for a way to both preserve the paradox without suffering infinite regress. Eventually, Winnicott tried to bridge the gap between the Red King and Alice by developing his concept of the "third" or "intermediate" area of experiencing.

In a paper entitled "Alice and the Red King: A Psychoanalytical View of Existence," Professor J. C. Solomon (1963) discusses the case of a patient who reported the following dream:

> There is a giant lying on the grass. There is a big round circle above him indicating that he is dreaming (like in the comic strips). I'm in that dream just doing ordinary things. I get the idea that I exist only in his dream. It is important for him to stay asleep, because if he wakes up, I will disappear. This is a tremendous fear. [p. 63]

Solomon, after connecting this dream with the image of the Red King, outlines the way in which an infant achieves a sense of his own existence. "There is a distinct connection," writes Solomon,

> between the feeling of existence on the part of the child and the appreciation of the existence of the mother. The emotional or perceptual experience of the infant/mother union must occur before the awareness of one's own existence is established. . . . The development of the knowledge of one's existence . . . is derived from the introjection of the primary object which had previously incorporated the subject. . . . The child's sense of existence is contingent on internalizing the mother who has internalized him. [pp. 69–72]

Although Solomon never mentions Winnicott by name, the similarity to Winnicott's thinking is more than apparent. In Winnicott's (1967c) own words:

> What does the baby see when he or she looks at the mother's face? I am suggesting that ordinarily, what the baby sees is himself or herself. In other words, the mother is looking at the baby, and what she looks like is related to what she sees there. All this is too easily taken for granted. [p. 131]

Winnicott, in other words, is trying to explicate the developmental origins of the Red King's conundrum. But, rather than develop a well-structured, well-organized theoretical system, Winnicott, like Carroll, prefers to tolerate "nonsense" or paradox. That is what led Anne Clancier (Clancier and Kalmanovitch 1987) to remark: "It is easy to see how people who are too Cartesian, too rationalistic, cannot appreciate Winnicott. There is that pragmatic side of the Anglo-Saxons and the same love of nonsense . . . " (p. 114).

A ROMANTIC AT HEART

In a talk given to the National Association for Mental Health in 1965 entitled "The Price of Disregarding Psychoanalytic Research," Winnicott (1965b) drew a distinction between "two roads to the truth: the poetic and the scientific." The link between these two forms of truth, said Winnicott,

> is surely in the person, in you and me. The poet in me reaches to a whole truth in a flash, and the scientist in me gropes towards a facet of the truth; as the scientist reaches the immediate objective, a new objective presents itself. Poetic truth has certain advantages. For the individual, poetic truth offers deep satisfactions, and in the new expression of an old truth there is opportunity for new creative experience in terms of beauty. It is very difficult, however, to use poetic truth. Poetic truth is a matter of feeling, and we may not all feel the same about one problem. By scientific truth, with limited objective, we hope to bring people who can use their minds and who can be influenced by intellectual considerations to agreement

in certain areas of practice. In poetry, something true
crystallizes out; to plan our lives we need science. But
science boggles at the problem of human nature, and tends
to lose sight of the whole human being. [pp. 172–173]

In this passage, Winnicott not only reaffirms his empiricist belief that people "can be influenced by intellectual
considerations to agreement in certain areas of practice" but
also reveals the strong romantic tendencies in his thinking.
Romanticism, as it developed in the eighteenth and nine-
teenth centuries, emphasized many of the themes that were
to become central to Winnicott's thinking: the importance
of the subjective, spontaneous, individual who expresses a
psychosomatic authenticity; a preference for the creative
above the compliant, the "natural" inner life above the
"artificial" life imposed from without; a deepened appreciation of nature's beauty and the emotions as sources of
knowledge; a turning in upon the self and a heightened
examination of human personality; a view of the artist as a
supremely individual creator, whose creative spirit is more
important than strict adherence to formal rules; an emphasis
on imagination.

Perhaps Romanticism was particularly appealing to
Winnicott because it arose, in the words of Richard Holmes
(1991), "in a period when science and art were still talking
intelligently to each other" (p. 51). In the same way that
Winnicott saw the value of both poetic truth and scientific
truth, the leading figures of the Romantic era lived their
intellectual lives in both worlds: Sir Humphry Davy, the
greatest British experimental chemist of his day, published a
collection of his own poetry; Coleridge attended Davy's
lectures to "renew his stock of metaphors"; Wordsworth,
Coleridge, and Shelley all owned microscopes; Keats attended and made notes on the lectures of both Sir Astley
Cooper, chief surgeon at Guy's Hospital, and Cooper's
leading critic, William Hazlitt. For nearly two generations,
there was this ongoing and fruitful dialogue between scien-

tists and imaginative writers. As Holmes says, "There was no social gap between the Two Cultures" (p. 51).

Winnicott's relationship with Romanticism can probably best be understood as one of aesthetic affinity. It is not so much that Winnicott was directly "influenced" by the Romantic movement in any clear linear sense as it is that the "truths" explored by the Romantics resonated with Winnicott's own sensibilities. The cultured world of Winnicott's youth was, after all, permeated with the high Romantic evaluation of imaginative activity. In a sense, one could say that Winnicott created out of his own sensibility that which was already there to be found in his romantic predecessors. This is consistent with Fred Pine's (1990) notion of "appeal." Specific inner experiences, Pine says, "act like magnets, pulling in and incorporating those confirming and elaborating offerings from the surround that then add to and enrich the inner phenomena of particular moments of experience. Here, too, new meanings are added on" (p. 109).

The Romantics appealed to Winnicott; he "discovered" like-minded spirits and was consequently "influenced" by them. That is why he frequently acknowledged that many of his own insights were not entirely original—they were, after all, synonymous with what poets and artists described in terms of imagination. Although Winnicott was a great empirical observer, his ideas were not necessarily solely the result of empirical study. They were at least as much the product of his already formed personal aesthetic, which included a strong romantic bent. Winnicott's scientific inquiry was animated by the poetic spirit.

Romanticism in English literature began in the 1790s with the publication of the lyrical ballads of William Wordsworth. His description of poetry as "the spontaneous overflow of powerful feelings" became the manifesto of the English Romantic movement in poetry. Just as Winnicott had valued the "two roads to truth," Wordsworth (1974) was to declare in the preface to the Ballads: "Poetry is the breath and finer spirit of all knowledge; it is the impassioned expression which is in the countenance of all Science" (vol. 1, p. 141).

Although Winnicott does not display the same extravagance of expression, he does display what Madeline Davis (1981) referred to as "Wordsworthian overtones" (p. 6), as when he describes, for example, the "native honesty which so curiously starts in full bloom in the infant and then unripens to a bud" (Winnicott 1964a, p. 146). Winnicott quotes Wordsworth numerous times in his writings. A particular favorite of his was Wordsworth's "Ode on the Intimations of Immortality" (Winnicott 1962d). Winnicott felt that in this poem Wordsworth demonstrated a keen intuitive grasp of a child's transition from an unawareness of dependence to a recognition of the relative enclosures provided by mother, family, and social institutions.

At times, Winnicott alludes to Wordsworth without acknowledging that he is doing so. In his paper "Psychoses and Child Care" (1952), for example, Winnicott writes: "For the paediatrician there is a continuity of development of the individual; this development starts with conception, goes on throughout infancy and early childhood, and leads to the adult state, the child being father to the man" (p. 220).

Wordsworth uses the phrase "The child is father of the man" in two places: a short poem entitled "My Heart Leaps Up" and as a preface to his longer "Immortality Ode." Stephen Prickett (1970), in his book *Coleridge and Wordsworth: The Poetry of Growth*, argues that when Wordsworth employs this paradox he is, logically, "only playing." Prickett's rendering of Wordsworth, however, is that this seeming paradox can, and should, be resolved. He argues that Wordsworth is "using the shock-effect of the paradox to say something that is not really a paradox at all" (p. 129). Prickett points to other classical philosophical paradoxes, such as the Cretan who says that all Cretans lie or the blackboard with only one statement written on it that runs: "The only statement on the blackboard is untrue." Prickett says these paradoxes can be tackled by Bertrand

Russell's doctrine of types. According to Russell, there is a question as to whether a definer of a class may be legitimately included within that class. Similarly, Wordsworth's child as father to man is resolved once we recognize that he is writing this as an adult and so cannot be included in the class of children who see and understand truths that are beyond the reach of any adult. The resolution of the seeming paradox, therefore, is to be found in the faculty of memory. "Memory," writes Prickett, "permits Wordsworth to place side by side the vision that has been lost, and the present vision . . . " (p. 129).

Yet such an interpretation misses precisely that element in the poetry that was most alluring to Winnicott—the introduction of a logical impossibility that adds complexity and depth by facilitating intercourse between the articulate and the inarticulate, the known and the unknowable. It was the paradoxical quality of Wordsworth's intuition that resonated with Winnicott's aesthetic sensibility. For both Winnicott and Wordsworth, the child *is* father of the man, a paradox to be appreciated, not eliminated through logic. As Winnicott (1971c) says: "By flight to split-off intellectual functioning it is possible to resolve the paradox, but the price of this is the loss of the value of the paradox itself" (p. xii). Or, in Wordsworth's (1940–1949) words, there are times "we murder to dissect" (vol 4, p. 57).

Rosalie Colie (1966), in her book *Paradoxia Epidemica*, argues that paradoxes operate at the limits of discourse, directing our attention to the limited structures of our own thought. Paradox, in her view, "plays back and forth across terminal and categorical boundaries—that is, they play with human understanding, the most serious of all human activities" (p. 7).

That is precisely what both Wordsworth and Winnicott do. Both lived in a world in which the categories that John Turner (1988) has called "truths-to-be-believed or falsehoods-to-be-disbelieved" were never clearly demarcated (p. 482). This is a world where adults could transgress the categories of time and space by accepting the co-presence of the child's vision active within themselves. As Wordsworth (1940–1949) writes in his "Immortality Ode":

> Hence in a season of calm weather
> Though inland far we be,
> Our Souls have sight of that immortal sea
> Which brought us hither,
> Can in a moment travel thither,
> And see the Children sport upon the shore,
> And hear the mighty waters rolling evermore.
> [vol. 4, p. 162]

Or, as he says elsewhere, "Heaven lies about us in our infancy," an idea Winnicott (1962d) was to express thus: "The idea of eternity comes from the memory traces in each one of us of our infancy before time started" (p. 34).

Winnicott also discovered in Wordsworth a deep appreciation of the centrality of the caregiver's role in the psychological origins of the imagination. For both Wordsworth and Winnicott, imagination signified the human being's deep creative and symbolic activities—that which made life feel real and worth living. And Wordsworth, like Winnicott, intuited that the imagination is somehow causally associated with the "mirror relationship" between the infant and its mother. In his poem "The Prelude," Wordsworth (1987) anticipates Winnicott when he writes:

> Blest the Babe,
> Nursed in his mother's arms, who sinks to sleep
> Rocked on his Mother's breast: who when his soul
> Drinks in the feelings of his Mother's eye!
> For him, in one dear Presence, there exists
> A virtue which irradiates and exalts
> Objects through widest intercourse of sense.
> No outcast he, bewildered and depressed;
> Along his infant veins are interfused
> The gravitation and the filial bond
> Of nature that connect him with the world.
> [pp. 1469–1470]

It is precisely by drinking "in the feelings of his Mother's eye" that the infant is able to develop a creative habit of mind. The poetic spirit is imparted to the infant by the mother's gaze. Wordsworth, like Winnicott, believed that the living relational warmth of the first relationship becomes an integral part of the individual's power to be "creator and receiver both, working in alliance with the works which it beholds":

> Is there a flower, to which he points with hand
> Too weak to gather it, already love
> Drawn from love's purest earthly fount for him
> Hath beautified that flower; already shades
> Of pity cast from inward tenderness
> Do fall around him upon aught that bears
> Unsightly marks of violence or harm.
> Emphatically such a Being lives,
> Frail creature as he is, helpless as frail,
> An inmate of this active universe.
> For feeling has to him imparted power
> That through the growing faculties of sense
> Doth like an agent of the one great Mind
> Create, creator and receiver both,
> Working but in alliance with the works
> Which it beholds. Such, verily, is the first
> Poetic spirit of our human life. . . .
> [Wordsworth 1987, p. 1470]

Winnicott discovered an additional reservoir for his notions of creativity and creative living in his reading of a second Romantic poet—John Keats. While Winnicott and Wordsworth shared a vision as to the origins of the imagination, it was with Keats that Winnicott displayed an affinity when it came to the conditions or state of mind that make creativity possible. It is no coincidence that Winnicott quoted periodically from Keats's writing (Winnicott 1963b,h). They both were deeply concerned with the processes of enrichment of the imagination, although, strangely enough, the word "imagination" is hardly used by Winnicott at all.

The overlap between these two thinkers is found in Keats's notion of Negative Capability and Winnicott's parallel ideas about creative play. Keats's (1958) concept of Negative Capability took shape in a series of private letters he wrote during the winter and spring of 1817–1818 in which he explored the nature of poetic genius and imagination. It was at Christmas time, in 1817, that Keats described a "disquisition" he had with a friend on the way back from a Christmas pantomime. At that time, "several things dovetailed" in his mind and "at once it struck me what quality went to form a Man of Achievement . . . I mean Negative Capability." Negative Capability was, in Keats's words, that quality possessed especially by individuals of genius

> when a man is capable of being in uncertainties, Mysteries, doubts, without any irritable reaching after fact & reason—Coleridge, for instance, would let go by a fine isolated verisimilitude caught from the Penetralium of mystery, from being incapable of remaining content with half knowledge. This pursued through Volumes would perhaps take us no further than this, that with a great poet the sense of Beauty overcomes every other consideration, or rather obliterates all consideration. [p. 193–194]

As Brooke Hopkins (1984) points out, Keats's notion of Negative Capability was actually both a resolution and a new beginning for him. For several months, Keats had been engaged in speculations about the nature of poetic genius, and this new idea both resolved his own uncertainty and issued in a new way of thinking for him. Keats's use of the word "negative" is not meant to be in the judgmental sense, but rather in the sense of "absence" or "being devoid of, or lacking in" particular attributes. The term Negative Capability, therefore, embodies the kind of paradox Winnicott would have found attractive: being capable of lacking something.

For Winnicott, this is the same attribute the child manifests in creative "play": the ability to be open, in the presence of mother, to whatever spontaneous gestures may arise, without the need to flee into compliance. This allows the child to "feel real" and have a "truly personal experience." Or, as Keats (1958) writes in his comparison of the state with a "Bee hive":

> However it seems to me that we should rather be the flower than the Bee . . . let us open our leaves like a flower and be passive and receptive—budding patiently under the eye of Apollo and taking hints from every noble insect that favors us with a visit—sap will be given us for Meat and dew for drink. [p. 232]

Keats contends that it is precisely this receptivity to "uncertainties, Mysteries, doubts"—a receptivity uncontaminated by the need to flee "irritably" into intellectual or philosophic systems—that is the hallmark of creative genius. Like Winnicott, Keats is not necessarily opposed to "fact & reason"; he simply objects to the way they may be used at the expense of one's own true being. For both Winnicott and Keats, what is crucial is not the particular activities of the individual, but their way of being. That is the meaning of Keats's emphasizing "*being* in uncertainties" and Winnicott's (1971b) famous dictum: "After being—doing and being done to. But first, being" (p. 99).

What each of these thinkers is suggesting is a vision of creative play predicated on the capacity to, in Keats's words, "remain content with half knowledge." For Keats, this means, as Albert Hutter (1982) has pointed out,

> achieving identity by an absolute projection, to tolerate a loss of self and a loss of rationality by trusting in the capacity to recreate oneself in another character or in the environment: "That I might drink, and leave the world unseen,/And with thee fade away into the forest dim." [p. 305]

This loss, however, is not a negation of self but rather an affirmation of self through what Hutter calls "an exaggerated notion of object relating" (p. 305). From Winnicott's perspective, this entails a provisional return to an "unintegrated" state. As he (1971a) described the origins of his own notion of "transitional phenomena": "For a long time my mind remained in a state of not-knowing, this state crystallizing into my formulation of the transitional phenomena" (p. 113). "It is only in this unintegrated state of the personality," wrote Winnicott (1971d), "that that which we describe as creative can appear" (p. 75). The unintegrated state is one in which the individual is able to flounder, to be without orientation, to exist without needing to either act or react (Winnicott 1958a).

Winnicott attempted to create in therapy a specialized atmosphere that would allow two people to be together without having to "irritably reach after facts" or meaning. "The person we are trying to help," he writes,

> needs a new experience in a specialized setting. The experience is one of a non-purposive state, as one might say a sort of ticking over of the unintegrated personality. I referred to this as formlessness. . . . In the relaxation that belongs to trust and to acceptance of the professional reliability of the therapeutic setting . . . there is room, for the idea of unrelated thought sequences which the analyst will do well to accept as such, not assuming the existence of a significant thread. [1971d, pp. 64–65]

Perhaps what Winnicott shared most of all with Keats and other Romantic predecessors was an appreciation of the rhythm of life that cannot necessarily be put into words. Many poets claim that their poems often first appear in the form of an awareness of rhythm, not words. As Victoria Hamilton (1987) has noted:

> Working with the help of rhythm as well as words, poets can evoke the infant's experience of his original state of

nakedness and sense of exposure. The infant may feel that
he is as one cast out from the womb into a cold and
jangling world, or he may live and breathe and "have his
being" in the light of his mother's eye. Poetic language
conveys the underlying physicality or sensuous matrix, of
thought. [p. 45]

Out of his sensitivity to the rhythm of preverbal life,
Winnicott fashioned a somewhat idiosyncratic terminology
that appears, at times, poetic, but that is difficult to coordinate with the conceptual language of traditional theory.
Through his attunement to the "underlying physicality or
sensuous matrix," Winnicott (1967c) came to believe that
the answers to problems concerning early baby–mother
relationships are provided by patients once they are able to
reach back to early phenomena "without insulting the deli-
cacy of what is preverbal, unverbalized, and unverbalizable
except perhaps in poetry" (p. 131). No wonder he was
attracted to Wordsworth (1940–1949), who wrote in his
"Ode on Intimations of Immortality":

But for those first affections,
Those shadowy recollections,
Which, be they what they may,
Are yet the fountain-light of all our day,
Are yet a master-light of all our seeing.
[Vol. IV, p. 283]

The crucial difference, of course, between Keats and
Winnicott is the developmental perspective adopted by the
latter. Whereas Keats describes the creative attitude necessary for poetic genius, Winnicott poetically describes the
developmental conditions essential for the creative attitude.
Keats tells us nothing about the origins of Negative Capability. Winnicott, on the other hand, traces the "capacity to
be" back to the infant's earliest "identity" with its mother's
breast. Keats offers no theory as to the environmental

conditions that facilitate being able to tolerate "uncertainties, Mysteries, and doubts." Winnicott, on the other hand, shows how creativity, emerging from the infant's unintegrated state, needs to be reflected back by the mother if it is to become part of the organized individual personality.

It is precisely for this reason that it would be a mistake to dismiss the novelty of some of Winnicott's conceptualizations solely on the basis of the similarities one can find between Winnicott and various Romantic poets. Despite the clear aesthetic affinity between them, Winnicott added depth to their "truths" by laying out the developmental roots of the object relational aspects of the capacity to play, symbolize, and form illusion. Although his inquiry was animated by the poetic spirit, his genre and medium of investigation were clinical and scientific. As he said in his paper "Fear of Breakdown" (1963b):

> Naturally, if what I say has truth in it, this will already have been dealt with by the world's poets, but the flashes of insight that come in poetry cannot absolve us from our painful task of getting step by step away from ignorance towards our goal. [p. 87]

Winnicott, unlike the Romantic poets, took upon himself that painful scientific task. In fact, he was troubled by tendencies within the psychoanalytic movement to see analysis as an art form. When Ella Sharpe, for example, asserted in a letter she read before the British Psycho-Analytic Society in 1946 that psychoanalysis was an art, Winnicott quickly dispatched a private letter to her in which he voiced his discomfort. "From my point of view," he wrote,

> I enjoy true psycho-analytic work more than the other kinds, and the reason is to some extent bound up with the fact that in psycho-analysis the art is less and the technique based on scientific considerations more. Therefore when I hear you speak about psycho-analysis as an art I find

myself in difficulties; not wishing to completely disagree with you, but fearing lest this comment that you make should be given too much consideration. [quoted in Rodman 1987, p. 10]

Winnicott clearly appreciated the imaginative elements of psychoanalysis, but for him, these were secondary. As he said in his paper "Metapsychological and Clinical Aspects of Regression" (1954b), "The idea of psycho-analysis as an art must gradually give way to a study of environmental adaptation. . . . An analyst may be a good artist, but (as I have frequently asked): what patient wants to be someone else's poem or picture?" (p. 291).

THE DARWINIAN LEGACY

When Winnicott was at Cambridge, he spent many hours in the secondhand bookstalls in the local market. Letters that he wrote home at the time pleaded for birthday money to "buy some of those wonderful books I pass every day" (C. Winnicott 1983, p. 6). He spent the money collecting the works of Charles Darwin. In a lecture given at Saint Paul's School in 1945, Winnicott described the excitement he felt as a schoolboy when he came across Darwin's *Origin of Species*. "I could not leave off reading it," he said:

At the time I did not know why it was so important to me, but I see now that the main thing was that it showed that living things could be examined scientifically with the corollary that gaps in knowledge and understanding need not scare me. For me this idea meant a great lessening of tension and consequently a release of energy for work and play. [quoted in Davis and Wallbridge 1981, p. 8]

Twenty years later, he reiterated this idea when he told a group of senior British analysts that the moment he read

Darwin he "knew Darwin was my cup of tea . . . I felt this tremendously . . . " (Winnicott 1967b, p. 574). Winnicott's encounter with Darwin was even partly responsible for his decision to take a degree in biology at Cambridge as a preliminary to his study of medicine. What was it about Darwin that spoke so directly to Winnicott?

Fundamentally, it was the same thing that was later to attract him to Freud: the thrill of discovering an objective way of looking at things. According to Clare Winnicott (1983), the discovery of Darwin was a "revelation to him. . . . It changed his whole life" (p. 6). Winnicott was to see first in biology, and later in psychoanalysis, a method of inquiry that enables the individual to approach something without preconceived notions. This, in his mind, is the essence of science (Winnicott 1967b). Needing to know, and profoundly aware of feeling that he does not know enough—science was to be a vehicle for his native curiosity, a means of quelling the anxiety born of the gaps in his understanding, and a potential space for his imagination. As he said in a talk before the Oxford University Scientific Society:

> About scientists I would say this: that when a gap in knowledge turns up, the scientist does not flee to a supernatural explanation. This would imply panic, fear of the unknown. . . . For the scientist every gap in understanding provides an exciting challenge. Ignorance is held, and a research programme is devised. The stimulus for the work done is the existence of the gap. [1961a, p. 14]

Just as Darwin labored to fill the gaps in the historical evidence regarding the origins of species, Winnicott focused on the gaps in the historical evidence regarding the earliest relationship between mother and infant. Winnicott, like Darwin, believed in the truth value of his scientific endeavors. Theirs was a search for true causes. While Darwin concerned himself with the true origins of the anatomy of species, Winnicott concerned himself with the true origins of what feels real to individuals.

Darwin offered Winnicott a grand lesson in the way detailed observation could lead to creative theories. Darwin was a master observer, a collector of specimens and facts. He took meticulous notes on his five-year journey to survey the wildlife of the west coast of South America and the Pacific islands and displayed an avid curiosity about all natural phenomena. He keenly observed both the relics of demised species and the gestures of living organisms. In a characteristic passage, Darwin, in Winnicott-like fashion, focuses on patterns of breathing in a variety of human emotions. Beginning with a discussion of crying, wailing, and the shedding of tears, he goes on to say:

> But why the sounds which man utters when he is pleased have the peculiar reiterated character of laughter we do not know. Nevertheless we can see that they would naturally be as different as possible from the screams or cries of distress; and as in the production of the latter, the expirations are prolonged and continuous, with the inspirations short and interrupted, so it might perhaps have been expected with the sounds uttered from joy, that the expirations would have been short and broken with the inspirations prolonged; and this is the case. [Darwin 1965, p. 205]

And, like Winnicott, Darwin even applied his skill of observations to the study of infants. Writing about his own infant son he tells, for example:

> Before the present one was four and a half months old I had been accustomed to make close to him many strange and loud noises, which were all taken as excellent jokes. But at this period I one day made a loud snoring noise which I had never done before; he instantly looked grave and then burst out crying. . . . About the same time (viz on the 137th day) I approached him with my back towards

him and then stood motionless: he looked very grave and
much surprised, and would soon have cried had I not
turned round; then his face instantly relaxed with a smile.
[quoted in Murray 1989, p. 340]

Darwin's account is quite reminiscent of the detailed observations Winnicott made when he employed, for example,
his spatula technique for diagnosing children. Even more
striking, however, is the way in which Darwin, like Winnicott, focuses sensitively on the impact disruptions have on
the infant. Winnicott's notion of "impingements" makes
clear that it is precisely when things do not go well that the
infant becomes aware of the results of the failure of maternal
care. Darwin, too, focuses, not on the harmonious interactions but on the perturbations.

The meticulousness of Darwin's naturalistic observations were only part of what was appealing about him to
Winnicott. The actual theory of natural selection, which
Winnicott studied in great detail while at Cambridge, centered on the notion that the developmental history of a
species can be detected in that species' current form. It
placed particular emphasis on the way organic change led to
increasing adaptation between organisms and their own
environments. Winnicott was to be consistently preoccupied with the dialectics of adaptation between infants and
their environments. He envisioned the infant as a re-
sourceful organism making use of the environment. He
traced the way the mother adequately or inadequately
adapted at various stages. He formulated a theory of character based on the way the infant responded to its mother's
adaptations.

Adam Phillips (1988) argues that Winnicott actually
reversed the Darwinian equation by suggesting that development was frequently a struggle against compliance with
the environment. This line of thinking is a good example of
how Winnicott's own way of being in the world can sometimes be confounded with his theory. Winnicott frequently

spoke about his own need to struggle against compliance, but he did not represent the struggle against compliance as a driving force in development. The need to comply, according to Winnicott, arises only where the environment has failed to adapt adequately to the individual. The driving force behind development is what Winnicott (1954b) calls the "biological drive behind progress" or the "evolutionary progress of the psyche" (pp. 280–281). This is a Rousseau-like vision in which the individual naturally evolves. It is not a struggle "against"; it is an urge to become. As he said in a broadcast talk to parents in 1949:

> In each baby is a vital spark, and this urge towards life and growth and development is a part of the baby, something the child is born with and which is carried forward in a way that we do not have to understand. For instance, if you have just put a bulb in the window-box you know perfectly well that you do not have to make the bulb grow into a daffodil. You supply the right kind of earth or fibre and you keep the bulb watered just the right amount, and the rest comes naturally, because the bulb has life in it. [quoted in Davis 1987, p. 493]

What was relevant to Winnicott about Darwin's theory, therefore, was that evolution—more accurately referred to as "descent with modification"—depends as much on individuation as it does on reproduction. Although Winnicott (1970d) disliked the term "individuation," the idea was inherent in what he called the "maturational process."

Winnicott's notion of a "biological drive behind progress" may, however, be an indication that part of his view is rooted in what is a common misunderstanding of Darwin. Like many evolutionists, Winnicott uses the word "progress" in the sense of moving from lower to higher, or from simpler to more complex, forms. This carries with it the implication that the latter are an improvement over the former. For Darwin, however, evolution was in no way associated with progress. It was a measure of change, not of assumed improvement. As Stephen Gould (1977) points out, Darwin was frequently reminding himself never to say "higher" or "lower" in describing the structure of organisms. That is why he even disliked the term "evolution." His "descent with modification" was a description of the way organic change led only to increasing adaptation between organisms and their environments, not to an abstract ideal of progress defined by structural complexity.

Even Darwin's criterion of fitness—"improved design"—referred not to something "better" in the sense of an advance over what had come previously, but as in "better designed for an immediate, local environment." Since, in Darwin's (1965) view, local environments were changing constantly, evolution by natural selection was "no more than a tracking of these changing environments by differential preservation of organisms better designed to live in them" (p. 45). Although Winnicott may not have shared Darwin's adamant refusal to attach the connotation of progress to the idea of evolution, he certainly was inspired by him to track the differential preservation of infants and the changing environments in which they lived.

THE AREA OF FAITH

In the same talk Winnicott (1961a) gave to the Oxford University Scientific Society in which he articulated his views about how every gap in knowledge provides an exciting challenge, he added a characteristically paradoxical twist to his positivist assertions when he said:

The stimulus for the work done is the existence of the gap. The scientist can afford to wait and to be ignorant. This means he has some sort of faith—not a faith in this or in that, but a faith, or a capacity for faith. . . . [p. 14]

Winnicott believes that it is this capacity for faith that
enables the scientist to tolerate doubt, to "shudder" at the
thought of complete knowledge. For the scientist, the formulation of questions is everything; answers, when found,
lead to new questions. Winnicott contrasts this attitude with
the "certainty that belongs to religion." Religion, he says,
replaces doubt with certainty.

Winnicott's remarks highlight the complexity of his
relationship to religious faith. On the one hand, Winnicott
was to see organized religion as a form of escape into the
security of supernatural explanations. He rejected all notions
of miracles and afterlife. He detested the suffocation of spirit
and inhibition of individual creativeness suffered by children at the hands of moral educators. It was not religion
generally that he opposed, but religion as a closed dogmatic
system, thwarting individual creativity and demanding obe-
dient worshipers. The innate capacity for concern of the
child was, according to Winnicott (1963e), often "stolen"
by organized religion and then "injected" back into the
child in the name of moral education.

According to Clare Winnicott (1983), it was Winnicott's
exposure to Darwin that changed his attitude toward religion and prompted his allegiance to "a scientific way of
working" (p. 6). His understanding of the psychological
origins of religion, however, were decisively psychoanalytic. He saw religion as a form of projection rooted in the
dangerous and tenuous attainment of individuality. God's
name, after all, means "I AM THAT I AM." "Does not this
name given to God," writes Winnicott (1968b),

> reflect the danger that the individual feels he or she is in on
> reaching the state of individual being? If I am, then I have
> gathered together this and that and have claimed it as me,
> and I have repudiated everything else; in repudiating the
> not-me I have, so to speak, insulted the world, and I must
> expect to be attacked. So when people first came to the
> concept of individuality, they quickly put it up in the sky
> and gave it a voice that only a Moses could hear. [p. 57]

Despite the obvious implication that belief in God is a defense against the anxiety felt in attaining a sense of self, Winnicott continued to hold what can be characterized as a lingering religiosity. As Clare Winnicott (1983) insisted, he "was never anti-religion" and "was only too thankful if anybody could believe in anything" (p. 4). Sometimes, however, he even went beyond upholding the capacity for "belief in" as a sign of health and actually saw value in a particular belief. In his essay "Some Thoughts on the Meaning of the Word 'Democracy'" (1950), for example, he declares: "It is certainly helpful when the reigning monarch quite easily and sincerely . . . proclaims a belief in God" (p. 255).

Winnicott (1968d) believed that religiosity arises naturally out of benign human nature, not that a savage human nature needs to be rescued by organized religion. Nowhere does he display the kind of hostility toward religion that characterized most psychoanalytic thinkers, beginning with Freud. As he wrote in a private letter to Michael Fordham:

> One must be able to look at religious beliefs and their place in psychology without being considered to be antagonistic to anyone's personal religion. I found others who thought I was anti-religious in some of my writings but it has always turned out that what they were annoyed about was that I was not myself religious in their own particular way. [quoted in Rodman 1987, p. 74]

Winnicott does not share the Freudian conviction that there are two wholly incompatible styles of thinking in the world—the scientific, on the one hand, and the theological and metaphysical, on the other—the former to be cultivated and the latter to be banished (Gay 1987, p. 32). He also differed fundamentally with Freud's view of illusion as a distortion or contradiction of reality in the service of wish fulfillment. For Freud (1930), religion was fundamentally an attempt to "procure a certainty of happiness and a protection against suffering through a delusional remoulding of reality" (p. 81). Organized religion, therefore, was an example of mass delusion. Winnicott, on the other hand, emphasizes the positive creative aspects of religious experience. His dream was not that psychoanalysis would one day eliminate, through enlightenment, the hold the church held on its believers. Instead, he hoped that psychoanalysis could "save religious practice from losing its place in the civilization process" (Winnicott 1963e, p. 95). "It is not possible for me to throw away religion," he wrote to Wilfred Bion in 1967, "just because the people who organize religions of the world insist on belief in miracles" (Rodman 1987, p. 170). He saw a place for religion in the setting of high ethical standards.

Winnicott was raised as a Wesleyan Methodist, his home a ten-minute walk from the church. Religion was the core of the family's cultural life. As he (1989) said once: "I did not meet the cultural life (except in the form of an evangelical religion) until I was at public school" (p. 508). The whole family went to church every Sunday morning. They were thought of as "leading lights in the church" (C. Winnicott 1983), his father acting as treasurer and singing in the choir.

The ideology of British Protestantism in general, and the Methodists in particular, drew its inspiration from the idea of the individual's personal, direct, moral contract with God. This vision superseded the authority of both priests and Pope. In his autobiographical notebook, Winnicott (C. Winnicott 1989) gives us a glimpse of his religious upbringing when he writes:

> My father had a simple [religious] faith and once when I asked him a question that could have involved us in a long argument he just said: read the Bible and what you find there will be the true answer for you. So I was left, thank God, to get on with it myself. [p. 8]

Or, as he said in a talk given to the Christian Teamwork Institute of Education (1968d): "Brought up as a Wesleyan Methodist, I suppose I just grew up out of church religious practice, and I am always glad that my religious upbringing was of a kind that allowed for growing up out of" (pp. 142–143).

Notice that Winnicott is speaking of growing up out of religious *practice*; he is not referring to abandoning everything that can be associated with a religious outlook. He remained a religious person in the sense that he maintained a capacity for wonder and reverence for the objects of wonder. One can observe, describe, appreciate, and acknowledge the objects of wonder but not invade, conquer, or appropriate them.

What Winnicott apparently learned from his father was that the essence of religiosity is always personal. As Clare Winnicott (1983) said, the entire family was "profoundly religious, but it's not obvious" (p. 3). Theirs was a nonconformist and questioning religion, rather than a strict, oppressive, and doctrinaire one. It was based on the simple notion of helping people through love.

Winnicott attended the Methodist church regularly at Cambridge. Later, when he married, he joined the Anglican church to which his first wife belonged. Sometime around the age of 27, he was even confirmed. This conversion was not uncommon at the time; many young aspiring people abandoned the somewhat working-class and simplistic Methodist church for the more polished and intellectually sophisticated Anglican church. In light of what has been made of Winnicott's so-called maternal identification, it is noteworthy that his mother was originally from the Anglican church but had settled in the Methodist church when she married Sir Frederick. Although Winnicott's actual church attendance gradually dropped off in his adult years, he remained, throughout his life, what Peter Rudnytsky (1989) has called a "believing skeptic" (p. 332).

Methodism began in the eighteenth century as a religious society that aimed to reform the Church of England from within; by force of circumstance it eventually became separate from its parent body and took on the characteristics of an autonomous church.

It is striking how some of the fundamental doctrines of Methodism were given secular expression by Winnicott. These include insistence that the heart of religion lies in personal relationship with God; simplicity of worship; the partnership of ordained ministers and laity in the worship and administration of the church; concern for the underprivileged and the betterment of social conditions; tolerance for differences of conviction regarding various theological disputes; worship that is partly liturgical, but partly spontaneous, including extemporaneous prayer (Semmel 1973). Having grown up within the atmospheric conditions of this church, it is easy to see how Winnicott would be predisposed to a sensibility that emphasized the personal and spontaneous in human nature, a nondogmatic attitude toward theory, and mutuality in the therapeutic alliance.

John Wesley, the founder of the Methodist church, strove to make his work accessible to the common man without trying to forcibly convert him. As he said in one of his sermons:

> I design plain truth for plain people: therefore, of set purpose, I abstain from all nice and philosophical speculations; from all perplexed and intricate reasonings; and, as far as possible, from even the show of learning, unless in sometimes citing the original Scripture. I labour to avoid all words which are not easy to be understood, all which are not used in common life; and, in particular, those kinds of technical terms that so frequently occur in Bodies of Divinity. [quoted in Phillips 1988, p. 24]

An echo of Wesley's belief that the fundamentals of doctrine can be communicated in simple language devoid of all technical jargon and yet without diminishment of content can be found in every one of Winnicott's lectures before lay audiences. Or, as he wrote to his sister Violet when, in 1919, he wished to introduce her to Freud's "cleverly devised" cure:

> I am putting this all extremely simply. If there is anything which is not completely simple for anyone to understand I want you to tell me because I am now practising so that one day I shall be able to help introduce the subject to English people so that who runs may read. [Rodman 1987, p. 2]

Winnicott commented once that it is a paradox that children must be reared by parents that were not of their choosing. The same applies to the child's religious upbringing. But just as the child can fantasize substitute parents, so can identifications be made with alternative religious figures. In 1969, less than two years before his death, Winnicott began to take an avid interest in John Wycliffe and the nonconformist Lollard sect. He had heard about three BBC broadcasts about the Lollards and discovered that the author was Ian Rodger. Hoping to obtain a copy of the material, he wrote a letter to Rodger in which he characterized himself as "a natural Lollard [who] would have had a bad time in the 14th and 15th centuries" (Winnicott Correspondence, D. W. W. to Ian Roger, May 28, 1969). Four days later, Roger responded. He clarified for Winnicott that his material was in play form (Winnicott had mistakenly believed they were talks given by the author). He linked the dissident view of the Lollards with some of the innovative and controversial work being done by progressive educators in the Pre-School Playgroup Association who "at first diffidently and then with confidence assault the various rule books and bureaucratic entanglements which seek to bring their work to nothing." The playgroup world, with its "constant battle with Health and Education departments, provides a small

parallel with the situation of the Lollards." Roger went on to
place this within the larger context of historical change.
"Europe," he averred, "has been created by its heresies"
(Winnicott Correspondence, Ian Roger to D. W. W., June 1,
1969).

Winnicott had discovered an enriching source. Two
days later, he wrote back to Roger and confessed that he was
"very much drawn to the Pre-School Playgroup Association's work." What is more, it appeared to him that "but for
the early Lollards and Wycliffe all these people who come to
England to be accepted and to find refuge would not have
had anywhere to go." It was persecuted religious heretics
who, in Winnicott's mind, had the tolerance and sensitivity
to "lay the basis for liberal thinking in England and Europe."
He hoped to meet with Roger and "discuss with you the
book that gives me the source of what I feel I know about
these matters." Without elaborating, he explained that he
was "even interested in the word Lollard but it would be
very complex to describe to you in one letter how this comes
in in connection with my work" (Winnicott Correspondence, D. W. W., to Ian Roger, June 3, 1969).

Adam Phillips (1988) speculates that Winnicott's interest in the word "Lollard" derived from its origin from
"lollen," meaning "to mew, bawl, or mutter." Phillips
connects this with Winnicott's special interest in the development of infants who "mew, bawl and eventually begin to
mutter" (p. 38).

A more likely interpretation is that Winnicott was
referring to the actual derivation of the name of the religious
group, which is the Dutch "lollaert" meaning "mumbler"—
a term applied to certain European groups suspected of
combining pious pretensions with heretical belief. It is
obvious from Winnicott's letters that he identified with both
the ideas and the plight of the Lollards. Wycliffe's followers,
some of whom were burned at the stake for heresy, were
radical anticonformists. Long before the rise of Protestantism, they denied the doctrine of transubstantiation and the

authority of the Pope. They abhorred how many church practices had led to hypocrisy, idolatry, and denial. Clerical celibacy, for example, occasioned unnatural lust; the "feigned miracle" of transubstantiation led men into idolatry; vows of chastity by nuns led to the horrors of abortion and child murder. The Lollards condemned special prayers for the dead, pilgrimages, and offerings to images. They declared confession to a priest unnecessary for salvation. They believed that all men should have free access to the Scriptures in their own language and were responsible for a translation of the Bible into English.

Why did Winnicott, late in his life, see himself as a "natural Lollard"? Did he see himself as a "heretic" or "nonconformist" within his own movement? Was it because of his contempt for certain trends within psychoanalysis that, in his mind, smacked of subservience to authority and secular idolatry? Was he fearful that psychoanalysis might degenerate into an ossified belief system, built upon a stagnant cannon inaccessible to the common man? One wonders if there isn't, perhaps, a disguised allusion here to his own struggles against both the dogmatic Kleinians and the Freudian canonizers. Is it not likely that Winnicott saw a connection between the demands for compliance imposed upon the early heretics and his notions of True Self and False Self?

Or did Winnicott's interest in the Lollards have more to do with his relationship to the church than to psychoanalysis? The letter quoted above was written not long after he fell seriously ill in New York, in 1968. As Clare Winnicott (1989) indicated in her biographical sketch of him, he spent his final years trying to negotiate his own impending death. One wonders if Winnicott's interest in the Lollards at that time might not be connected to a desire on his part to come to terms with the church. Winnicott sensed that the oppressive, suffocating order within the organized church would lead to either unproductive rebellion or a similarly sterile and defeated submission on the part of its members. He wished for neither, but wanted to maintain a connection. This was possible for him only if the institution was based on spontaneous order, contained within boundaries, yet facilitative of experiment and growth. Such an approach is consistent with his belief that what is needed for the healthy development of the individual is "a well-graduated series of defiant iconoclastic actions, each of the series being compatible with the retention of an unconscious bond with the central figures or figure, the parents or the mother" (Winnicott 1960d, p. 92). Perhaps Winnicott saw in the Lollards a way of expressing his own iconoclastic defiance of and unconscious bond to his religious upbringing. Was this Winnicott's way, toward the end of his life, of "making peace with his maker"—his parents and his God?

Winnicott's lingering religiosity, however, is not to be found solely in the interest he displayed in a particular religious sect. It permeates his writing, both in form and content. In a talk he (1970) gave before the Progressive League, for example, while discussing the importance of the experience of omnipotence in infant development, he composes what he calls a "humanist hymn":

> O! to be a cog
> O! to stand collectively
> O! to work harmoniously with others
> O! to be married without losing the
>   *idea* of being the creator of the world. [p. 50]

It was Winnicott's view that the individual who did not start off life with the experience of being godlike would be forever destined to remain alienated from his fellow human beings. That individual would not be emotionally prepared to relinquish the desire to be the whole wheel or be capable of experiencing satisfaction as merely a cog. Instead, he would have to "go on pushing round omnipotence and creativeness and control, like trying to sell unwanted shares in a bogus company" (p. 50).

Winnicott's lingering religiosity is probably most evident in how akin so many of his ideas are to religious categories. His descriptions of mother's containment of her infant by means of boundary making and at the same time space-affording holding, for example, is reminiscent of the religious concept of "everlasting arms." The security of being held by these arms enables the individual to tolerate a world that is equally merciful and malign, supportive and indifferent, beautiful and horrific. Winnicott's concept of personalization, whereby the mother facilitates the entry of the infant into a full experience of his psyche-soma, is suggestive of the religious notion of incarnation in which a spirit comes to be embodied in flesh and blood and time and space. Another of Winnicott's notions—the capacity to be alone in the felt presence of the mother—parallels the traditional idea of the Presence of God as being both intimate and ultimate.

Winnicott's notion of True Self and False Self is equally akin to the distinction drawn by the Catholic philosopher Baron von Hugel between "Isness" and "Oughtness" (Lambert 1987, pp. 53–55). Both Winnicott and von Hügel are contrasting two distinct sorts of order. The False Self and "Oughtness" are forms of order imposed by outside authority upon people who are not necessarily ready for it or who haven't organically grown into it out of themselves. The True Self and "Isness" are descriptions of the sort of order that emerges spontaneously from within when there is both sufficient containment and space, as well as an absence of impingements from without. Religion, in von Hugel's view, had more to do with "Isness" than "Oughtness"; real living, according to Winnicott, is rooted in the True Self rather than the False.

An argument can be made that all these examples—holding, personalization, the capacity to be alone, the True Self—rather than demonstrating Winnicott's affinity for religious thought indicate how he was explicating the developmental origins of religious ideas. Although there is some

truth to this contention, it would be a mistake to draw a
simple reductionist conclusion. It is of great significance that
Winnicott, despite his fundamentally scientific and psycho-
analytic point of view, always cautiously hedges the religious issue in a way that both expresses respect and averts
reductionism. An example of this can be found in his 1935
paper "The Manic Defence." In looking for a word to
describe the total of defenses against the depressive position,
Winnicott chooses the religiously laden word "ascensive."
This naturally leads him to a discussion of the significance
of the Ascension in the Christian religion. If, Winnicott
acknowledges, he were to explain the Crucifixion and Resurrection to a Christian as a symbolic castration with subsequent erection, he would undoubtedly encounter indignation that "would have been justified by my having left out
the depressive-ascensive significance of the myth. . . . The
Ascension marks recovery from depression." He concludes
his discussion with the observation:

> Many find sadness near enough at hand without the help of
> religion and can even tolerate being sad without the
> support that shared experience affords, but it has some-
> times struck me, when I have heard people in analysis
> jeering at religion, that they are showing a manic defence
> in so far as they fail to recognize sadness, guilt, and
> worthlessness and the value of reaching to this which
> belongs to personal inner or psychic reality. [p. 135]

Rather than reduce the religious impulse to defensive com-
pensations or disguised substitutes, Winnicott turns the
Freudian legacy on its head and points out how intolerance
of religion might serve those functions.

    Winnicott's fundamental respect for religious experi-
ence stemmed quite naturally from his ideas regarding illusion and transitional phenomenon. From Winnicott's perspective, illusion is an important positive aspect of human
involvement in the world of experience, which is at one and

the same time objective and subjective (Meissner 1992). It is an area of experiencing that exists as a "resting place for the individual engaged in the perpetual human task of keeping inner and outer reality separate yet interrelated" (Winnicott 1971c, p. 3). Developmentally, its origins lie in the intermediate state between a baby's inability and his growing ability to recognize and accept reality. In this transitional area, the baby uses various objects as steps toward the symbolic function. The eventual successful use of symbols indicates the child has obtained the capacity to distinguish fantasy from fact, internal from external.

The capacity for illusory experience develops and evolves from the earliest transitional phenomena through the older child's play to the creative and cultural experiences of the adult. As Gilbert Rose (1978) has argued, psychological development can be understood as a lifelong "transitional process" in which a dynamic equilibrium is sought between a more or less "fluid" self and the shifting, changing patterns of external reality. Adaptation, in other words, requires an element of creative imagination. Religion and art are mature expressions of transitional experiences. As such, they are valuable means of establishing and maintaining a sense of self. As V. P. Gay (1983) has noted, they help keep the human personality from slipping into schizoid isolation and despair. Religion, in other words, like all transitional phenomena, is an essential illusory experience indispensable to selfhood. Furthermore, writes Winnicott (1971c), "we can share a respect for illusory experience, and if we wish we may collect together and form a group on the basis of the similarity of our illusory experiences. This is a natural root of grouping among human beings" (p. 3).

Although Winnicott recognized that individuals bond on the basis of shared illusions, his primary concern is not with the organizational aspects of religion. Religion, for him, needs to be respected because it is one more example of the kinds of illusory cultural experiences that make life feel real and without which there is an impoverishment of being.

These experiences are essential because they are simultaneously both objective and subjective and at the same time neither.

Symbols permeate all religions. As Meissner (1992) has pointed out, religious symbolic objects—the crucifix, the Torah, the bread and wine—become "vehicles for the expression of meanings and values that transcend their physical characteristics" (p. 187). These objects obtain their significance precisely because they are perceived neither as exclusively external and objective nor as simply produced by the imagination. In Meissner's words, "they evolve from the amalgamation of what is real, material, and objective as it is experienced, penetrated, and creatively reshaped by the patterns of meaning attributed to the object by the believer" (p. 187). Again, what is crucial for Winnicott is not that an individual hold a particular belief, but that he or she achieve the capacity to "believe in" something. These symbols help articulate and maintain the human experience of believing.

That is why, for example, Winnicott frequently drew a comparison between his ideas about transitional phenomena and the Christian doctrines about the eucharist. How can it be, he asks, that the host is considered both ordinary bread and the body of Christ at one and the same time? The controversies of transubstantiation that tore the Church apart arose, he concluded, because of attempts to resolve a paradox that should not be resolved (Fuller 1987).

Winnicott's subtle exposition of the psychology of religious experience has led Michael Eigen (1981a) to describe what he terms "the area of faith." Faith is a fundamental dimension for Winnicott, distinguishable, according to Eigen, from operations that emphasize ego mastery or introjection–internalization processes. It refers to a way of experiencing with one's whole being, with "all one's heart, with all one's soul, and with all one's might." Eigen traces how the capacity for faith evolves in Winnicott's developmental scheme, from transitional experiencing through object usage, and he demonstrates how Winnicott believes that the primary object of creative experiencing is not mother or father, but "the unknowable ground of creativeness as such" (p. 431).

Although Eigen is correct that for Winnicott the capacity for faith cannot be reduced to mother as an object, it is still central to his thinking that mother's active human reliability is an essential foundation of all beliefs. By allowing the baby to go easily to and fro between states of integration and relaxed unintegration, the mother silently facilitates the infant's belief in its own inner processes. The accumulated experiences become a pattern and form a basis for what baby expects. Eventually, as development proceeds and the infant acquires a clearer inside and outside, "environmental reliability becomes a belief," what Winnicott (1968e) calls "an introject based on the experience of reliability" (p. 97).

It is precisely for this reason that, from Winnicott's point of view, the "worst kind of mothering" is the kind that "tantalizes" at the very earliest stages (Rodman 1987, p. 145). To tantalize means to be so unpredictable that "she cannot even be relied on to fail to adapt to a need." Winnicott doubts whether a baby can ever really recover from such an experience, for it entails a disturbance in the basis of belief or the capacity for "belief in."

From Winnicott's perspective, it is precisely the capacity for faith, the ability to have a whole enough sense of self so as to be able to believe in something, that is the hallmark of mental health. In fact, without it, the individual can hardly go about with the activities of daily living. As he said at a conference of the Christian Teamwork Institute of Education:

> We are believing people. Here we are in this large hall and no one has been worried about the ceiling falling down. We have a belief in the architect. We are believing people because we are started off well by somebody. We received a silent communication over a period of time that we were

loved in the sense that we could rely on the environmental provision and so get on with our growth and development. [p. 147]

It is the True Self, in Winnicott's view, that is characterized by the feeling of genuine and authentic wholeness. This sense of wholeness is perpetually threatened by countertendencies toward disruption or perversion. The central battle within the soul, according to Winnicott, is over one's own sense of realness. In religious terms, this is the struggle to live one's life faithfully. It requires not intelligence or knowledge, but purity of purpose. For both theologians and Winnicott, this is the road to true wisdom (Winnicott 1968b).

Winnicott's emphasis on the wholling tendencies of the self led him to adopt a holistic approach toward treatment as well, what he referred to once as a "kind of religion of external relationship" (Winnicott 1970a, p. 112). The older he got, the greater his faith grew in what he called "natural processes." He criticized overly interpretive methods that communicated doubt about the patient's natural tendency toward self-cure. At one point, he even stopped prescribing medications. He demonstrated what Rodman (1987) has referred to as a "pattern of restraint, which amounted to an exquisite form of respect" (p. xviii). In a talk given to doctors and nurses in 1970, Winnicott (1970a) explained how the word "cure" points to a "common denominator in religious and medical practice" (p. 112). Although he acknowledged that the field of medical practice had become so vast that specialization is inevitable, he still claimed that "as thinkers we are not exonerated from the attempt on a holistic approach." The foundation of the holistic approach is reliability meeting dependence. It was Winnicott's belief (for he offers no empirical evidence) that the trust born of such reliability can even affect bodily tissues. As he said to his medical audience:

[I]f a doctor appears at the time arranged, he experiences a tremendous strengthening of the patient's trust in him (or

her) and this is not only important for the avoidance of
patient agony, but also it enhances the somatic processes
tending towards healing, even of tissues, certainly of
functions. [p. 117]

One can see how, despite having "grown up out of the
concept of miracles" (Winnicott 1966a, p. 134), Winnicott's
lingering religiosity affords him faith in his capacity to heal.

5

Making
Freud Real

And thus a store of ideas is created, born from man's need to make his helplessness tolerable. [Sigmund Freud]

Last season's fruit is eaten
And the fullfed beast shall kick the empty pail.
For last year's words belong to last year's language
And next year's words await another voice.
["Little Gidding," T. S. Eliot, *Four Quartets*]

No advance in psycho-analytic theory is made without nightmares. The question is: who is to have the nightmare? The further question—why does he need to have nightmares?—is not relevant and can be ignored. In our Society here, although we serve science, we need to make an effort every time we attempt to re-open matters which seem to have been settled. It is not only the inertia which belongs to the fear of doubt; it is also that we have loyalties. [D. W. Winnicott, *Psycho-Analytic Explorations*, 1989, p. 458]

In 1967, four years before his death, Winnicott was asked by a group of senior British analysts to speak on the subject of the relationship of his theory to other formulations of early development. The task was not an easy one for Winnicott, given both his personal and idiosyncratic style, as well as his inability to engage in systematic theory building. The thoughts Winnicott eventually shared with his British colleagues constitute the only recorded incident where he consciously tried to link his ideas with those whose work he felt had influenced him at various stages. Surviving only in the form of a poor recording, the talk illustrates how Winnicott was, at times, painfully aware of the price he paid for being unable to systematically link his thinking with the ideas of others. "I've realized more and more as time went on," he (1967b) began:

> what a tremendous lot I've lost from not properly corre-
> lating my work with the work of others. It's not only
> annoying to other people but it's also rude and it has meant
> that what I've said has been isolated and people have to do
> a lot of work to get at it. It happens to be my temperament,
> and it's a big fault. [p. 573]

It was really only thanks to Masud Khan that Winnicott's first writings were edited and appeared with a detailed conceptual index. Today, that same work is being carried out by the Winnicott Trust. In his acknowledgments for *The Maturational Processes and the Facilitating Environment* (1979), Winnicott commented revealingly that it was actually Khan who not only was the driving force behind the preparation of the book for publication but that "he is responsible for my gradually coming to see the relationship of my work to that of other analysts, past and present" (p. 11).

By temperament, Winnicott was always more an innovator than a curator. He needed to seemingly destroy certain facets of psychoanalytic theory so as to re-create them in his own image. Only then could theory feel real for him. As he (1960d) said once in a discussion about emotional maturity: "Mature adults bring vitality to that which is ancient, old and orthodox by re-creating it after destroying it" (p. 94).

Whether or not in the process the theory itself was altered in some way was of no real consequence to him. Nor did it matter that by maintaining a distinctly personal style he often set himself apart. What was important was that the vitality of the theory be sustained by genuinely personal statements. As he (1989) proclaimed: "Something new and valuable always turns up when old things are stated in a new way" (p. 427).

Winnicott's original contributions to psychoanalytic theory are best understood, therefore, as efforts to re-create for himself, in a personal way, aspects of theory that he had imaginatively destroyed. As such, they are always part of the ongoing dialogue he engaged in with his surroundings. As he acknowledged on a different occasion, referring to the debt he felt he owed his psychoanalytic colleagues:

> I have grown up as a member of this group, and after so many years of inter-relating it is now impossible for me to know what I have learned and what I have contributed. The writings of any one of us must be to some extent plagiaristic. Nevertheless I think we do not copy; we work and observe and think and discover, even if it can be shown that what we discover has been discovered before. [Winnicott 1979, p. 11]

What Winnicott is describing is his own vision of the essence of creativity. What began, according to Winnicott, as the infant's experience of finding exactly that which it created, has here evolved into a complex interrelationship where the boundaries between what one learns and what one contributes remain in dialectical tension. It is no coincidence that Winnicott focuses on this dynamic; it is part of what for him was, perhaps, the central theme of human

development: the continuously perilous struggle of the self
for an authentic individuated existence that did not preclude
intimate association with others. The dialectic between
originality and tradition is an expression of the way in which
an individual is both alone and together in respect to shared
reality. Winnicott recognized this dimension when he wrote
in *Playing and Reality* (1971a): "The interplay between
originality and the acceptance of tradition as the basis for
inventiveness seems to me to be just one more example, and
a very exciting one, of the interplay between separateness
and union" (p. 117).

Nowhere is the issue of the interplay between Winnicott's own theoretical "separateness" and "union" more
apparant than in his complex relationship with Sigmund
Freud. Freud was the theoretical luminary around whom
Winnicott orbited; he was sustained in his clinical endeavors
by remaining within Freud's gravitational field. At the same
time, however, Freud was the founding father against whom
Winnicott struggled to differentiate himself. Repeatedly,
Winnicott acknowledged his debt and gratitude for Freud's
discoveries while inveighing against any signs of blind allegiance to him.

Some authors have come to see Winnicott's stance
toward Freud as evidence of a willfully disingenuous attitude. Greenberg and Mitchell (1983), for example, in their
book *Object Relations in Psychoanalytic Theory*, argue that
Winnicott purposely misrepresents his positions as consistent with Freud when, in fact, he knew they were not.
According to them, Winnicott employed a "systematic strat-
egy" to represent his contributions as direct extensions of,
rather than departures from, Freud. Through "misreading"
and a "combination of assimilation, distortion and strategic
avoidance," Winnicott engages in an effort at "forced continuity." His interpretation of Freudian concepts is "so
idiosyncratic and so unrepresentative of their original formulation and intent as to make them unrecognizable."

Where areas of difference do obviously appear, he "side-steps" rather than directly challenges (pp. 189–222).

The polemical tone of Greenberg and Mitchell probably reveals more about the theoretical struggles in which the authors themselves are engaged than about Winnicott's true intentions. It is more emblematic of contemporary ideological cleavages than representative of Winnicott's way of thinking. The essential thesis of the Greenberg and Mitchell book is that there are two competing theoretical paradigms vying for primacy within psychoanalysis: Freud's drive/structural model, and the relational/structural model initiated in the work of Fairbairn and Sullivan. From Greenberg and Mitchell's perspective, these are mutually exclusive, alternative models for conceptualizing human development, experience, and the clinical enterprise.

Borrowing from the philosopher of science, Thomas Kuhn (1962), they argue that since truth is unknowable, the concern of science is actually problem solving and the history of scientific ideas consists of discontinuous evolving models, paradigms, or "ways of seeing the world" that are more or less heuristic tools. The reigning paradigm at any particular time determines what is accepted as scientific "data" and what methods are considered "valid." Because these paradigms are models of reality taken for the "truth," they inspire enduring groups of adherents and intense loyalties. At some point, however, "retooling" is inevitable: old paradigms fade and are replaced with new ones based on a new set of "cognitive" or "metaphysical" commitments.

Greenberg and Mitchell (1983) believe that Kuhn's approach to the evolution of scientific ideas and his notion of models or paradigms as metaphysical commitments are "highly applicable to the history of psychoanalytic thought and constitute a useful way to approach the different strategies of theory-construction" (p. 19). Although Greenberg and Mitchell's application of Kuhn's work to a comparison of efforts at psychoanalytic theory construction yields a

great many valuable insights and highlights important
shifting thrusts in orientation, it also artificially dichoto-
mizes in a way that would have been anathema to Winnicott.
Between Freud and Winnicott lies a very large area of
overlap and much smaller areas of divergence, although the
divergences can be highly significant. By assuming that there
is an inevitable incongruity between the drive/structural
model, on the one hand, and the relational/structural model,
on the other, Greenberg and Mitchell are compelled to see
Winnicott's attempts to make sense of clinical data using
both drive and relational hypotheses as necessarily disingenuous.

The problem with Greenberg and Mitchell's stance is
twofold. First, it fails to appreciate the relational elements of
Freud's metapsychology. Second, it dilutes the true significance of the instinctual elements in Winnicott's organic
conception of human development. Winnicott's ideas,
rather than being an effort at "forced continuity," are an
honest attempt to understand clinical and developmental
phenomena from a truly object relational point of view that
takes into account essential drive components. This is not to
say that on every theoretical point there is agreement between the two. There are, as mentioned before, some areas
of difference that are quite significant. But to remove the
instinctual elements from Winnicott, or to represent them as
mere "lip service" that he paid to Freud, is to dilute the
significance of many of his truly original ideas.

Contemporary critiques of Freud's "metapsychology"
and controversies between so-called object relations and
classical perspectives tend to cloud and distort precisely
those elements in Freud's thinking that appealed most to
Winnicott. Winnicott genuinely believed that Freud understood his own metapsychological assertions were nothing
more than speculations. He also never doubted the extent to
which "relational" or "interpersonal" considerations fig-
ured into Freud's motivational hypotheses. That is why
Winnicott could assert with conviction, as he did in a private

letter to Harry Guntrip, "Any theories that I may have which are original are only valuable as a growth of ordinary Freudian psycho-analytic theory" (Rodman 1987, p. 75).

But is it not possible that Winnicott's view of his own work as a continuation of Freud's is based on distortion? After all, a thinker is not necessarily the best judge of the significance of his own work or its relation to the work of others. And what, exactly, does Winnicott mean by a "growth" of Freudian theory? What was Winnicott's fundamental relationship to Freudian theory?

Guntrip suggested that Winnicott had two relationships with Freud: one public and one private. Publicly, he emphasized his continuity; privately, he acknowledged his departure from Freud's drive-based approach to psychopathology. "We disagree with Freud," Guntrip reports Winnicott as having told him. "He was for curing symptoms. We are concerned with whole living and loving persons" (quoted in Mendez and Fine 1976, p. 361). This open modification of Freud was not evident in his public pronouncements because, according to Guntrip, Winnicott was "clinically revolutionary and not really interested enough in pure theory to bother to think it out." Guntrip's view of Winnicott as a disguised modifier, unwilling or unable to acknowledge his theoretical departure from Freud, is certainly consistent with Greenberg and Mitchell's reading of Winnicott. Winnicott, they say, rather than remain loyal to Freud's "original vision," perpetuates a "distorted icon" of Freud for his own "political positioning of himself in continuity with Freud" (Greenberg and Mitchell 1983, p. 209).

The problem with this rendering of Winnicott is twofold. First, although Guntrip is correct in asserting that Winnicott was not particularly interested in "pure theory," it is a misjudgment of his character to imply a hypocritical or opportunistic motive. Winnicott had no difficulty staking out consistently individual positions for himself, nor did he recoil from openly disagreeing with Freud where he felt a need to do so. In fact, in a sometimes irritating way, he could

not do otherwise. "I have never been able to follow anyone
else," Winnicott (1962c) declared, "not even Freud" (p.
177). A central issue in his life was his absolute insistence on
being himself. For years, he preferred to be an outsider in the
British Psycho-Analytic Society rather than take comfort in
false allegiances or group loyalties. He was denied teaching
positions because of his refusal to clearly align himself with
existing camps. Temperamentally, he was allergic to icons.
What Greenberg and Mitchell perceive as "political postur-
ing" can be better understood as ambivalence: Winnicott
was enormously devoted to Freud but needed to defend his
own sensitive imagination. He was engaged in a personal
balancing act that paralleled what he described theoretically:
between ruthless assertion of his unique individuality and
rigorous opposition to schisms. If Winnicott avoided polemical breaks, it was not because he was disingenuous; in his
typically British way, Winnicott always looked for the
common meeting ground, rather than the battlefield.

Furthermore, Winnicott was not constrained by the
kind of unresolved transference toward Freud that characterized many of his psychoanalytic colleagues. He had no
compelling need to engage in intractable idealizations of
Freud or to represent Freud's assertions or speculations as
veridical evidence. Unlike many other psychoanalytic thinkers, Winnicott frequently dared to criticize, analyze, and
assess Freud from a subjective point of view. He appears
relatively free of any anxiety or fear that by diverging from
Freud he may destroy or sabotage his own faith in the
psychoanalytic method.

Winnicott's relatively conflict-free relationship with
Freud was rooted, at least in part, in the fact that there was
no actual personal contact between the two men. His relationship was not complicated by having to contend with
Freud personally. It is well known that many of Freud's
followers found intellectual autonomy difficult in his presence. Whether this be due to a tyrannical streak in Freud or
an artifact of his intellectual brilliance, it is a fact that the

people in his movement who meant most to him—Fliess, Rank, Jung—were compelled to sunder their relationships with him. Ferenczi's (1988) private diary speaks of Freud's "fear of allowing any one of his sons to become independent" (p. 185). The final entry describes how he felt "trampled under foot . . . as soon as I go my own way and not his" (p. 212). Soon after, Ferenczi died of pernicious anemia. Freud's propensity for authoritarian closure, both on a personal and therapeutic level, would most certainly have clashed with Winnicott's preference for dialectical openness. Winnicott was under Freud's intellectual shadow, but he was spared having to feel he was under his thumb.

The second problem with seeing Winnicott as a disguised modifier is the assumption that Freud's life work is reducible to a single, correct, "original vision." Freud's pioneering, subtle, and oft-changing formulations, based on accumulating clinical experience and a willingness to readily discard earlier propositions, is misrepresented as an easily identifiable schema. The *spirit* of Freud's work is extinguished, as elements of *content* are canonized. The truth of the matter is that Freud's legacy is so rich that each analyst can have in mind a different Freud that reflects crucial aspects of his own personal struggles.

The issue, therefore, is what is truly *essential* about Freud and what is not. Is Winnicott's rendering of Freud congruous with what is essential? Is Winnicott's representation of Freud sufficiently consistent with what Freud actually believed? The question is not whether Winnicott "distorts" or "misreads" Freud, but whether or not his individual way of understanding Freud is plausible. Which Freud did Winnicott have in mind? How did he internalize him and make his theory feel real to himself?

Taken from this perspective, Winnicott was justified in his subjective sense that he was extending rather than altering Freudian theory. Just as he believed that pediatrics, with the advent of antibiotics, could now afford to turn its attention from purely physical concerns to the emotional development of children, psychoanalysis, with the advances made in understanding the internal world of unconscious processes, could extend its inquiry into the full importance of external conditions affecting early psychological development. What Freud had done to reconstruct the childhood roots of adult mental life, Winnicott would attempt for the infantile roots. Since Freud's theory of neurosis convincingly explained how whole people can be in conflict within themselves, it was possible to now extend investigations to include the psychological difficulties of more severely disturbed individuals who could not experience themselves as whole. Because Freud's theory provided a powerful way of exploring what makes an individual's life unbearable, it could now be extended to examine what it is that makes life feel real and worth living. Winnicott's image of himself was certainly that he was standing on the shoulder of a giant reaching upward.

Both Freud and Winnicott grappled with the same fundamental issue: how the quality of human experience can be accounted for given the interworkings of endogenous and exogenous stimulation, developing mental life, desire, fantasy, veridical memory, meaning, relationship, and representation. At different points, and in different ways, each of these authors focused on various aspects of the complex interplay of these forces. But both were consistently sophisticated in their thinking to recognize that human experience encompassed real and imagined happenings emanating from within and without.

A METHOD OF INVESTIGATION

What resonated most profoundly for Winnicott, when he first encountered Freud in his early twenties, was that the latter had developed a method of investigation that allowed for the complexity of both mind and body. He was particularly impressed that it was out of dissatisfaction with his own results that Freud, as a distinguished neurologist and pioneer in neuropharmacology, abandoned prior avenues of investigation and fashioned his own method of inquiry. A similar experience of dissatisfaction led Winnicott, as a young medical student, to abandon "cold" physiology and seek emotional explanations for somatic processes. As he (1957d) later recalled:

> The physiology I learned was cold. . . . Every effort was made to eliminate variables such as emotions, and the animals as well as human beings seemed to me to be treated as if they were always in a neutral condition in regard to instinctual life. One can see the civilizing process which brings a dog into a constant state of frustration. Consider the strain that we impose on a dog that *does not even secrete urine into the bladder* until some indication is given that there will be opportunity for bladder discharge. How much more important it must be that we shall allow physiology to become complicated by emotion and emotional conflict when we study the way the human body works. [p. 35–36]

There was something about medicine, as he was trained to practice it in England, that was inherently unsatisfactory to him. Too many questions were left unasked. As early as 1931, Winnicott (1931) wrote in *Clinical Notes on Disorders of Childhood:*

> If enuresis is explained as a disturbance of the pituitary or thyroid gland, the question remains, how is it that these glands are so very commonly affected in this way? If cyclical vomiting is explained along biochemical lines the question must be asked: Why is the biochemical balance so easily upset, when everything points to the stability of the animal tissues? The same applies to the toxaemic theory of tiredness, the glycopoenic theory of nervousness and the theory that stuttering is due to lack of breath control. All these theories lead to blind alleys. [p. 5]

Identifying with Freud's pioneering spirit and his search for a personal and creative response to his own dissatisfaction, Winnicott was impressed that psychoanalysis offered a method in which new questions about the mind and body could be asked. He also tended to identify with the personal price inevitably paid by Freud as a creative individual. Winnicott understood that a creative innovator is invariably in a fragile state and suffers isolation. Drawing on his own experience, but echoing Freud's, Winnicott wrote in one of his letters to Melanie Klein: "The initial statement is usually made at great cost and for some time afterwards the man or woman who has done this work is in a sensitive state as he is personally involved" (Rodman 1987, p. 36).

Eventually, Winnicott came to accept, without reservation, certain of Freud's central tenets. These were to include infantile sexuality and instinctual life as developmental phenomena, the notion of unconscious conflict, and the recognition of psychic reality, which, from Winnicott's point of view, meant what is real to the individual apart from what is actual. Winnicott (1988) believed that Freud had "done unpleasant things for us" by getting to the pain, anguish, and conflict that "invariably lie at the root of symptom formations" and by putting forward "arrogantly if necessary" the importance of instincts and childhood sexuality. "Any theory that denies or bypasses these matters," Winnicott told a group of students, "is unhelpful" (p. 36).

But Winnicott's true loyalty was to the method of clinical work, rather than to any one of the oft-changing and ever-evolving formulations put forth by Freud at various times. This was a method that Freud had evolved prior to World War I when he was most deeply engaged in actual clinical work. As Steve Ellman (1991) has noted, the bulk of Freud's groundbreaking clinical work was prior to the war. After that, his attention turned primarily to consolidating his movement and to elaborating theoretical questions. His practice became increasingly limited to conducting training analyses for people interested in psychoanalysis, rather than individuals in need of therapeutic analyses. It was the heuristic spirit of the clinical method devised in this early period that resonated most profoundly for Winnicott. The system of thought that tended toward institutional rigidity was of little import to him. As he said to his colleagues in 1967:

> I suppose that if there's anything I do that *isn't* Freudian, this is what I want to know. I don't mind if it isn't, but I just feel that Freud gave us this method which we can use, and it doesn't matter what it leads us to. The point is, it *does* lead us to things; it's an objective way of looking at things and it's for people who can go to something without preconceived notions, which, in a sense, is science. [p. 574]

Winnicott believed that Freud was a genius who, in a scientific manner, gleaned from the clinical setting provisional hypotheses about the human mind. It did not matter to him that, by employing the same method, one was led to alternative formulations. Freud was easy to criticize, Winnicott (1962c) once averred, "because he was always critical of himself" (p. 177). To blindly accept all of Freud's propositions would have been, from Winnicott's perspective, "absurd" and a betrayal of Freud's legacy. As he wrote in his paper "Growth and Development in Immaturity" (1950a):

> The reader should know that I am a product of the Freudian or psychoanalytic school. This does not mean that I take for granted everything Freud said or wrote, and in any case that would be absurd since Freud was developing, that is to say changing his views (in an orderly manner, like any other scientific worker) all along the line right up to his death in 1939. As a matter of fact, there are some things that Freud came to believe which seem to me and to many other analysts to be actually wrong, but it simply does not matter. The point is that Freud started off a scientific approach to the problem of human development . . . he gave us a method for use and for development

which we could learn, and whereby we could check the observations of others and contribute our own. [p. 21]

Freud's achievement was so great, as far as his method and provisional hypotheses were concerned, that no defect, extension, alteration, or divergence could, in Winnicott's mind, detract from it.

THE "WITCH" METAPSYCHOLOGY

"There is nothing for it but to 'summon help from the Witch'—the Witch Metapsychology," wrote Freud (1937) two years before his death. "Without metapsychological speculations and theorizing—I had almost said 'fantasy'—we shall not get a step further" (p. 326). The crux of Freud's dilemma was simply this: he placed a very high premium on metapsychological formulations but was never consistent as to what he considered to be the essence of psychoanalytic metapsychology (Holt 1982). He saw it as the "consummation of psycho-analytic research" (Freud 1915, p. 114) and as "crude" or "nebulous, scarcely imaginable" (Freud 1914, p. 77). In the absence of hard data on the relationship between brain functioning and mental happenings, he employed a concept of physical energy as a metaphor for psychical energy. Freud put it quite clearly in Chapter 7 of *The Interpretation of Dreams* (1900) when discussing the metaphorical quality of the idea of "psychical locality":

Analogies of this kind are only intended to assist us in our attempt to make the complications of mental functioning intelligible . . . And since at our first approach to something unknown all that we need is the assistance of provisional ideas, I shall give preference in the first instance to hypotheses of the crudest and most concrete description. [p. 536]

Or, as he wrote in 1926: "In psychology, we can only describe things by the help of analogies . . . we have constantly to keep changing these analogies, for none of them lasts us long enough" (p. 195).

Winnicott identified with a Freud who recognized his own metapsychological constructions as "metaphors" (1900, p. 610), "fictions" (1911b, p. 220n), and "scientific phantasies" (1916–1917). This was the Freud (1933) who wrote to Albert Einstein: "It may perhaps seem to you as though our theories are a kind of mythology. . . . But does not every science come in the end to a kind of mythology like this? Cannot the same be said today of your own Physics?" (p. 211).

Reflecting similarly on his own theoretical beliefs, Winnicott (1971b) remarked:

> There is little doubt that the general attitude of our society and the philosophic atmosphere of the age in which we happen to live contribute to this view, the view that we hold here and that we hold at the present time. We might not have held this view elsewhere and in another age. [p. 76]

Winnicott was probably particularly attuned to this quality of Freud's thinking because, by nature, he did not think in terms of absolute truths. As F. Robert Rodman (1987) has noted:

> One has a sense that Winnicott did not set his sights on Truth with a capital T, but on truths that would not stay still, the truth that is contained in the continuous interplay of people. He did not seem to require what Nietzsche has called "metaphysical solace," of the sort one may get, for example, from a convincing philosophical system. [p. xxvii]

Of course, as J. P. M. Tizard (1981) pointed out, Winnicott's way of thinking constitutes a kind of philosophy of its own. It was a philosophy which, as he wrote in a letter to Anna Freud, made him deeply suspicious whenever metapsychological formulations were presented in a way that created the illusion of understanding when no such understanding really existed (Rodman 1987). To some extent, it was also a philosophy rooted in his own liabilities. "It is quite one thing," he wrote to Charles Rycroft, "to come at a problem through clinical work and to formulate something in one's own language, and another thing to take ideas and interrelate them, thus contributing to the building of theory" (Rodman 1987, p. 87).

For years, Winnicott felt himself "absolutely unable" to take part in metapsychological discussions of any kind. He confessed to Ernest Jones that he suffered from "inhibitions in regard to the reading of Freud" (Rodman 1987, p. 33). Privately, he confided to Michael Balint that he felt that if he lived long enough, he might, one day, be able to "join in from time to time." As time passed, he gained confidence and began "to see a glimmer of light" (pp. 127–128). Eventually, he joined in, in his own way.

Winnicott was able to join in by having in his mind a version of Freud that resonated with crucial aspects of himself. This was a Freud who, as a scientist inbued with the freedom to speculate, never really constricted himself by loyalty to particular metapsychological formulations. For Winnicott, therefore, there was never a question in his mind about being "loyal" or "disloyal" to Freud. What Winnicott (1989) wrote about Freud's Death Instinct is emblematic of the way he made Freud feel real to himself:

> There is no trouble if we feel something is wrong with Freud's Death Instinct formulation because he himself seems to have had doubts, doubts proper to a scientist who knows that no truth is absolute or final, and that it is the thinking and the feeling and the freedom to speculate that counts. [p. 460]

Winnicott admired tremendously Freud's ability to change his mind; and it was always more important for him to "play" with Freud's ideas than to adhere to them.

INSTINCTS, RELATIONS, AND THE SELF

The Freud internalized by Winnicott was one who postulated both endogenous and exogenous sources of stimulation operating upon the psyche. Current disputes between so-called drive and relational theories often cloud the extent to which Freud flexibly attempted to account for clinical findings using both drive *and* environmental hypotheses (Steve Ellman, personal communication, May 15, 1992). The failure to appreciate the relational elements of Freud's metapsychology derives primarily from the historical tradition of equating Freud's instinct theory with a simple drive-discharge model. It is an interesting historical question, beyond the scope of this book, why this came to be. Suffice it to say that the systematization of Freud's thought by such people as Abraham, Fenichel, Hartmann, and Rapaport tended to omit from Freud's metapsychology those elements that Freud consistently depicted as rooted in environmental or relational experience (Reisner 1989). To appreciate how Winnicott understood Freud, however, it is quite relevant that those who reduce Freud's theorizing to a simple drive-discharge model underestimate the extent to which Freud himself was cognizant that any description of mental functioning had to take into account both internal and external as well as biological and psychological sources of motivation. Winnicott believed his own theorizing was wholly consistent with Freud because he was convinced that Freud continuously strove to go beyond the limitations imposed by purely neurological or experiential explanations. Winnicott internalized a Freud who never lost sight that human beings had two realities with which they had to contend.

Freud's efforts at incorporating both sources of motivation began with his "Project for Scientific Psychology" and continued when he turned his attention to the origins of neuroses. In fact, what Steven Reisner (1989) has referred to as Freud's "dual motivation theory of the psyche" runs as a constant thread—despite changes in the content of the hypotheses—throughout Freud's lifetime. Even after he purportedly discarded his own seduction hypothesis, Freud did not really abandon the notion of environmental or relational stimulation. What he did do, however, is transform trauma into a broadened sensual stimulation, placing increased emphasis on the ideation and fantasies derived from the experience. Freud expanded the role of ideation and fantasy; he didn't abandon the notion that relationships and environment play a role. He focused on how the individual reacted to environmental stimulation; he didn't claim that environmental stimulation was irrelevant.

Freud pursued the view that psychic disturbance was invariably engendered by a combination of both endogenous and exogenous forces even after he introduced the concept of drive into his metapsychology. In his *Three Essays on the Theory of Sexuality*, Freud distinguished between drives such as hunger, which were derived from endogenous buildup up of tension, and sexual drives, which consisted of "germs of sexual impulses" combined with interpersonal stimulation of erotogenic zones (Laplanche 1976). Freud (1905) made it clear that sexuality was evoked by the external stimulation of an "erotogenic zone":

> We can distinguish in the [sexual drives] . . . an instinct not in itself sexual which has its source in motor impulses, and a contribution from an organ capable of receiving stimuli (e.g., the skin, a mucous membrane or a sense organ). An organ of this kind will be described in this connection as an

"erotogenic zone"—as being the organ whose excitation lends the instinct a sexual character. [p. 168n]

It was, in Freud's new theory as outlined in *Three Essays* (1905), the presence and subsequent removal of a gratifying other that created a sexual drive from an endogenous "germ of an impulse." From this, Freud was able to conclude that mother's breast is the prototype of every relation of love. Or, as he put it, "The finding of an object is in fact a refinding of it" (p. 222).

Martin Bergmann (1987) believes that this statement of Freud's is his "most profound contribution" to understanding human love (p.159). In essence, Freud's contention is that love is the restoration of a happiness with an external object that was lost; intrapsychically, the parents who were the original love objects remain important. Once Freud realized that the root of sexuality goes back to infancy, he recognized that love, too, has its origins in the earliest years. Desire and love constitute, in Freud's thinking, two separate currents. "Should these currents fail to converge," wrote Freud (1905), "the focusing of all desire upon a single object will be unobtainable" (p. 200). For Freud, the crucial developmental task of adolescence is the remingling of the two currents, the bringing together of love and lust. The child who has been overstimulated sexually is at high risk of reaching premature genitality and therefore is more likely to remain fixated on the original parental figures.

At the same time that Freud was distinguishing between love and desire, he was also contrasting the sexual instincts with what he called "needs" or "functions of vital importance." In *Three Essays* he claims that the sexual instincts come into existence by first attaching themselves to these functions. Referring to this as anaclisis, Freud believed that bodily functions furnish sexuality with its source or erotogenic zone. In the oral activity of the infant at the breast, for example, the pleasure obtained from sucking is a sort of "bonus pleasure" attached to the need for taking nourishment. Later, the need for repeating this sexual satisfaction will become detached from the need for taking nourishment.

While maintaining the fundamental notions that external stimulation contributes to both infantile sexuality and love and that a distinction must be made between vital ego needs and sexual instincts, Freud began to hypothesize about the numerous developmental steps along the path to final object choice. Because he adopted a developmental point of view, he postulated that the aim and the object of libido are not intimately connected, but rather change over time. This developmental hypothesis is often mistakenly understood to mean that Freud believed the sexual drive itself was paramount, while the object of satisfaction was secondary or inconsequential.

That Freud represented the object of sexuality as mobile rather than fixed, however, doesn't necessarily imply that the drive is solely endogenous or necessarily independent of object. All it means is that sexual satisfactions can be derived from various sources and that these sources change developmentally. And, as the sources of sexual satisfaction shift, so does the current of love. Ultimately, however, the object of love remained, in Freud's mind, determined by the pleasure experienced in the earliest object relationship. "There is thus good reason," Freud (1905) wrote, "why the sucking of a child at his mother's breast has become a prototype of every relation of love" (p. 222).

As a "prototype" of future love, mother's role is not only as a passive recipient of drive discharge, but as an active facilitator of the infant's learning to experience its own vitality in a constructive way. As Freud wrote in *Three Essays*:

> A mother would probably be horrified if she were made aware that all her marks of affection were rousing her child's sexual [drive] and preparing for its later intensity . . . [But] if the mother understood more of the importance

of the part played by the drives in mental life as a whole
. . . she would spare herself any reproaches. . . . She is
fulfilling her task in teaching the child to love. After all, he
is meant to grow up into a strong and capable person with
vigorous sexual needs and to accomplish during his life all
the things that human beings are urged to do by their
instincts. [p. 223]

It was precisely Freud's view of the mother as "fulfilling
her task in teaching the child to love" that became the
cornerstone of Winnicott's unique contribution to psychoanalysis. What Freud implies, Winnicott amplifies; what
Freud mentions in passing, Winnicott elaborates. Although
his writings span a wide range of topics—from delinquincy
to the moon landing—Winnicott's main contribution remains the study of the earliest relationships. "Teaching the
child to love" meant, for Winnicott, facilitating ego development such that the child's own drive experiences and
spontaneous inner promptings could be incorporated into a
tenuously emerging sense of self capable of relating to
others. For this reason, instincts and relations cannot be
separated in Winnicott's theory. His emphasis was on how
the developing personality eventually comes to terms with
itself—meaning it's relationship to what is both inside and
outside. Like Freud, Winnicott grappled with the relative
significance of the contending influences emanating from
within and without.

But how did Winnicott understand instincts? And how
did he see them in terms of external relationships? Was his
use of the term equivalent to Freud's? Winnicott was consistent in his belief that instincts were a central part of
human experience; he uses the term, however, in ways that
sometimes correspond to Freud, but at other times take on a
slightly altered meaning.

"Instinct is the term given to the powerful biological
drives which come and go in the life of the infant or child
and which demand action," Winnicott (1988) once told a
group of students. He continued:

The stirring of instinct cause the child, like any other
animal, to make preparations for satisfaction of the full-
blown instinct when it eventually reaches a climax of
demand. If satisfaction can be provided at the climax of
demand, then there is a reward of pleasure and also a
temporary relief from instinct. Incomplete or ill-timed
satisfaction results in incomplete relief, discomfort, and an
absence of a much-needed resting period between waves
of demand. [p. 39]

Here, Winnicott is offering a view of instincts that corresponds to Freud's instinct discharge model. Like Freud,
Winnicott (1931) tended to see instincts as a vestige of man's
animal nature but was reluctant to enter into a discussion
about classification of instincts, or even to decide exactly
how many there were. And he agreed with Freud that what
distinguished man from other animals was the "much more
complicated attempt on the part of the former to make the
instincts serve instead of govern." This is the root of all the
illnesses that are "common in man and practically absent in
animals" (p. 5). Winnicott also accepted Freud's central
hypothesis that when considering instinctual excitement it is
necessary to take into account the body function most
powerfully involved. He expanded, however, the description of the body functions that might be dominant at a
particular time. For Winnicott (1988), it could mean "the
mouth, the anus, the urinary tract, the skin, one or other part
of the male or female genitals, the nasal mucous membrane,
the breathing apparatus, or the musculature generally, or the
ticklish groins or armpits" (p. 40).

By expanding the potentially dominant areas, Winnicott was indicating that he took a slightly different view of
instincts than the one generally held by Freud. First, Winnicott's emphasis is always on the instinctual *experience* rather
than the instinct as impersonal force. It is the developing
person's relationship to the instinct rather than the development of the instinct within the person that most concerns
Winnicott. Second, Winnicott tended to emphasize the

more sensual aspects of experience in addition to the rapacious quality of the drive. Although Freud (1905) indicated that he appreciated the distinction when he spoke in *Three Essays* of an instinct "not in itself sexual" that is affected by "an organ capable of receiving stimuli" (p. 168n), his emphasis was primarily on the sexual. The voracious sexual impulse that Freud focused on as central was recast by Winnicott to include sensual sensory experience. In Winnicott's (1988) words, "skin eroticism" was "spread out from the oral and the anal and the urethral" experiences (p. 42).

Nevertheless, Winnicott shared Freud's belief that the individual must contend with dominant patterns of excitement that progress and develop over time. And, most significantly, Winnicott, like Freud, recognized that instinctual experiences could arise either endogenously or as the result of external stimulation. Whatever the source, the aim was climax. Freud's work clearly reverberates when Winnicott (1969a) asserts:

> From time to time the person becomes excited: that is to say, in some way or other instincts are aroused. It does not matter what is the nature of the instinct; once the instincts have been aroused either through the rhythm that comes from within or in reaction to stimuli from outside (whether real or imagined), then the body has started along a path which in terms of pure physiology ought to lead to a climax: hunger leading to a meal; a certain type of sensation that leads naturally to an excretory activity; or sexual excitement that can end in genital orgasm; or an accumulation of aggressive impulses that can lead to a fight. [pp. 561–562]

Here we have Winnicott echoing the issues Freud grappled with as he "abandoned" his seduction theory and attempted to formulate a theory of neuroses that emphasized internal fantasy without discarding the subtle impact of external happenings.

In Winnicott's view, regardless of whether they originate from within or without, some physiological awakenings are more easily satiated than others. But the principle remains the same: once aroused, the person has to manage either to bring the impulse to climax or else to live through a phase in which the body has to tolerate and absorb the changes brought by the excitement without there being any climax. What is more, Winnicott believed that "life is quite a lot concerned with the management of these failed climaxes" and that people frequently "organise themselves as far as possible to be distracted so that over long periods of time excitements do not arise." "Everyone could write a book," Winnicott (1969a) said, "called 'The Technique for Living,' which would be a description of the ways he or she has learned to adapt in order to avoid the beginnings of excitements, and alternatively to arrange for excitements to reach a climax" (p. 562).

Like Freud before him, Winnicott linked the management of excitements to questions of pathology. In some of his writings on psychosomatic illnesses, for example, Winnicott echoes Freud's earliest formulations regarding the actual neuroses. Freud had referred to anxiety neurosis and neurasthenia as actual because the origins of the disturbance were to be found in the subject's contemporary, rather than childhood, life. "Actual" also refers to the fact that the symptoms remain somatic, as opposed to being transformed symbolically. Winnicott retained these notions when he discussed, for example, how bodily excitement, which is a precondition for instinctual experience, can be mismanaged and lead to coronary thrombosis. The delay, accumulation, or displacement of excitements could also be linked, according to Winnicott (1957d), to "mental states that we call abnormal" such as hysteria, depression, depersonalization, and a sense of unreality or general tension (p. 37). The difference, nevertheless, between Freud and Winnicott's conceptualizations is that whereas the former emphasized the singular role of the sexual instinct in the etiology of the actual neuroses, the latter was vaguer about the nature of the emotional experience involved.

Winnicott also follows Freud's lead in connecting psychological illness to the precocious overwhelming of a child by stimuli. Freud's seduction theory was restated by Winnicott in terms of "impingements." Like Freud, he emphasizes both the external component and the infant's reaction. Just as Freud, after 1897, focused on the role of ideation and fantasy in the origins of trauma, Winnicott (1962b) believed that "whatever the external factors, it is the individual's view (fantasy) of the external factor that counts" (p. 61). "Trauma," Winnicott (1967d) asserts, "is an impingement from the environment and from the individual's reaction to the impingement that occurs prior to the individual's development of the mechanisms that make the unpredictable predictable" (p. 198).

But again, whereas Freud (even after he presumably "abandoned" his seduction theory) exclusively emphasized sexual overstimulation of children, Winnicott focused on more diverse contingencies of inappropriate parental handling of infants. Unlike Freud, Winnicott emphasized that a child can be overwhelmed not only by what a parent does, but by what a parent fails to do. His concern was not with the libidinal economy, but with the integrity of the self. Winnicott—and here his pediatric training can be discerned—was a more subtle interpreter of the actual parental role than was Freud. Impingements could be the result of a parent intruding when the infant needed to be alone, or being absent when his or her presence was called for. They may take the form of repeated changes in techniques of care, loud unexpected noises, misattunements to the infant's natural rhythms, insufficient physical support, or abandonment for a time period beyond which the infant can cope. Erratic or "tantalizing" care constituted a particularly toxic form of impingement because it undermined the infant's fundamental need for stability and reliability—to make the "unpredictable predictable." An accumulation of traumatic impingements puts the infant at risk for future mental instability. Recurring impingements, writes Winnicott (1962b), "set[s] going a pattern of fragmentation of being. The infant whose pattern is one of fragmentation of the line of continuity of being has a developmental task that is, almost from the beginning, loaded in the direction of psychopathology" (pp. 60–61).

The most important thing about impingements is that they compel the infant to react. All failures in good-enough parental ego coverage bring about a reaction of the infant, and "this reaction cuts across the going-on-being" (p. 60). Winnicott suggests a dichotomy between being and reacting. In extreme cases, a whole life may be built on the pattern of reacting to stimuli. "In order to be and so have the feeling that one *is*," writes Winnicott (1970e), "one must have a predominance of impulse-doing over reactive doing" (p. 39). But is this dichotomy tenable? Are these really two discrete and separable psychical phenomena? And if so, does the former necessarily point in the direction of health and the latter toward pathology?

The dichotomy between being and reacting can be seen as an interesting amplification, in terms of the self, of Freud's ideas about primary and secondary processes. In primary process, psychical energy flows spontaneously, without obstacles, from one idea to another, tending to attach itself to those satisfying experiences that are at the root of unconscious wishes. In secondary process, the energy is bound and flows in a controlled manner; satisfaction is postponed allowing for mental experiments that test out the viability and safety of various paths leading to satisfaction. At first, the infant attempts to discharge instinctual tension immediately, by means of hallucination. When this primary process activity of trying to establish "perceptual identity" by the shortest possible route fails, secondary process activity takes over. It is the nonoccurrence of the expected satisfaction, the disappointment experienced by the infant, that leads to the abandonment of attempts at satisfaction based solely on primary process. Secondary process, in other words, can be understood as a form of reaction to the failure of primary process to achieve satisfaction. Waking thought, attention, judgment, reasoning, and controlled action all begin to exercise a regulatory function. As necessary as they may be for survival, however, they are at the expense of what is the more primary and spontaneously generated part of the psyche.

Winnicott's dichotomy between being and reacting is an attempt to retain the idea of a primary and spontaneously generated core of the self. But Winnicott goes beyond Freud's theory in that he postulates a state of being that is prior to instinct and the source of experiences that feel real. What is more, unlike Freud, who frequently emphasized the dangers to the individual under the sway of solipsistic and unrealistic primary processes, Winnicott elevated that which is authentic and spontaneously generated to nearly sacred status. Without it, life was virtually without meaning; it could not feel real. The so-called True Self—which is Winnicott's attempt to give structural form to his ideas—was essential to "living" as contrasted with mere "existing."

The theory of the True Self as an inherited personality potential is in some ways equivalent to Freud's hypothetical notion of the primary repressed unconscious (Bollas 1991). As Freud (1915b) wrote in *The Unconscious*: "The content of the unconscious may be compared with an aboriginal population in the mind. If inherited mental formations exist in the human being—something analogous to instinct in animals—these constitute the nucleus of the unconscious" (p. 195).

Freud postulated the idea of primary repression because of his prior notion that an idea cannot be repressed unless there is an attraction exerted on it by contents that are already unconscious. But this raised the immediate dilemma of how to account for an aboriginal nucleus in the unconscious that could attract repressed content. Freud resolved this problem by adopting a Lamarckian theory of mental

preformation. His primal fantasies were essentially unconscious schemata transcending individual lived experience
and supposedly transmitted through heredity.

But whereas Freud's primal fantasies underscored the
fundamental universality of psychological life, Winnicott's
True Self celebrated the unique individuality of each person.
Winnicott's emphasis is on the idiosyncratic or temperamental way in which individuals interpret the world. Furthermore, the True Self need not be construed as a Lamarckian transmission of acquired characteristics; it refers
to an intrinsic personality potential that may or may not be
in part genetically sponsored. It can be understood as a form
of dispositional knowledge about *processes* of self-
experiencing rather than as a storehouse of preformed
mental *contents*.

Still, as Adam Phillips (1988) points out, Winnicott
posits what is basically an essentialist theory, but with an
essence barely describable. Minimalist definitions allowed
him maximal variety of description. The True Self is a
"theoretical position" and "does no more," writes Winnicott (1960f), "than collect together the details of the experience of aliveness" (p. 148). Living from the True Self
enables an individual to "feel real," which means to "exist
as oneself" (Winnicott 1967c, p. 138). It was this unique
individuality, or innate authenticity, that was threatened by
impingements that compelled the person to react.

It was Winnicott's implicit belief that the "experience
of aliveness" could not be taken for granted; a sensitive
facilitating environment in earliest infancy was an absolute
prerequisite. The True Self only begins to have a life of its
own "through the strength given to the weak ego by the
mother's implementation of the infant's omnipotent expressions" (Winnicott 1960f, p. 145). Mother must naturally take
baby's innate predispositions into account. A mother who
does too much or responds too little to what the infant needs
at a particular time interrupts the baby's continuity of being;
reactive defenses are, therefore, needed. Mother's task was

doubly delicate, however, because she not only had to facilitate True Self expression but she had to allow for and protect the fundamental isolation of the core of the personality. It was axiomatic for Winnicott (1960h) that the concept of the isolation of this central self is an aspect of health. Any threat to this isolation constitutes a "major anxiety," and defenses of earliest infancy appear "in relation to failures on the part of the mother . . . to ward off impingements which might disturb this isolation" (p. 46).

How toxic the impingements were to the infant's emotional well-being was determined, to a large extent, by the stage in development in which they occurred. Winnicott unambiguously adopted Freud's genetic view of pathology; but, rather than emphasize the libidinal fixation points of the neurotic, he focused on the environmental failures that were at the root of psychosis. The etiology of psychoses could be found, according to Winnicott, in the failure of environmental adaptation at the earliest stage of absolute dependence. Psychoses were "environmental deficiency diseases" organized as defenses that distorted the individual's relationship with external reality and created a sense of unreality.

Winnicott describes two categories of psychotic illness. The first involves distortions of the ego organization that lay down the basis for schizoid characteristics. It includes infantile schizophrenia, autism, latent schizophrenia, and schizoid personality. What these have in common is a defense organization that makes the individual invulnerable to experiencing once again some unthinkable anxiety or primitive agony. This unthinkable anxiety was experienced initially in a "moment of failure of the environmental provision when the immature personality was at the stage of absolute dependence" (Winnicott 1967d, p. 198). Unthinkable anxieties could be experiences of going to pieces, falling forever, having no relation to the body, having no orientation, or complete isolation because of there being no means of communication. Each of these engendered a terrifying fear of annihilation. Baby had been horrifically let down by the environment. The result: a distortion in ego development.

Winnicott's (1960f) second category of illness arising from early environmental failure is "the development of a caretaker self and the organization of a self that is false." The "True Self" is protected, while the "False Self" copes with reacting. "True" and "False" selves are really just two different aspects of one individual's sense of self. There are, in Winnicott's view, degrees of false self organization. At the healthy end of the spectrum is "that which can develop in the child into a social manner, something which is adaptable." This social manner represents a workable compromise which "ceases to become allowable when the issues become crucial." When matters of vital significance are involved, the "True Self is able to override the compliant self" (p. 150).

At the pathological extreme, however, the "truly split-off compliant False Self" is "taken for the whole child." Because the true self has no relationship to external reality under these circumstances, life becomes futile. As a result of a certain degree of failure of adaptation, or a chaotic adaptation at the earliest stages of development, the individual develops two types of relationships split off from each other (Winnicott 1988). One type is a "silent secret relationship to an essentially personal and private inner world of subjective phenomenon." It is, according to Winnicott, only this relationship that "contains the spontaneity and the richness which seems real." The impulses and the spontaneity and the feelings that seem most real, in other words, are bound up in a relationship that to an extreme degree is incommunicable. At the same time, however, the infant develops "a relationship from a false self to a dimly perceived external environment." This second relationship is based on compliance, is "plain for all the world to see, and is easy to manage." The compliant relationship to external reality creates an experience of unreality for the individual, yet it is frequently maintained as a way of "gaining time" until perhaps the first relationship "may some day come into its own" (p. 109). In the most extreme cases, the child has no reason to live at all. In less severe cases, there is a sense of futility in regard to false living, and a "constant search for the life that feels real, even if it leads to death" (p. 108).

"Instead of cultural pursuits," writes Winnicott (1960f), "one observes in such people extreme restlessness, an inability to concentrate, and a need to collect impingements from external reality so that the living time of the individual can be filled by reactions to these impingements" (p. 150). The False Self, in this schema, is a self-protective defense against "that which is unthinkable, the exploitation of the True Self, which would result in annihilation" (p. 147). In severe cases of environmental failure, the child's mind feverishly compensates for parental deficits by precocious self-sufficiency. A pathological split-off part of the mind usurps responsibility from an environment that has failed; it frantically memorizes and catalogs every reaction disturbing the continuity of being. Mind becomes dissociated from body. In the absence of firm grounding in the body, mental functioning, or what Freud calls secondary process thought, becomes an "encumbrance . . . to the individual being's continuity of being which constitutes the self" (Winnicott 1949a, p. 248).

It is crucial, from Winnicott's (1960h) perspective, that even instinctual satisfactions and object relationships can, under certain conditions, become impingements. The fact that an infant is feeding at the breast and obtaining nourishment and oral gratification does not reveal the true quality of the experience. It does not indicate

> whether he is having an ego-syntonic id-experience or, on the contrary, is suffering the trauma of a seduction, a threat to personal ego continuity, a threat by an id-experience which is not ego-syntonic, and with which the ego is not equipped to deal. [p. 47]

Winnicott's fundamental view of the infant at the earliest stage of development, therefore, is not as a person who gets hungry and whose instinctual drives are either met or frustrated. Rather, he tends to see the baby as an immature being living a precarious existence on the brink of unthinkable anxieties. One moment there is the uninterrupted bliss of going-on-being, and the next there is the potential for annihilation. When all goes well—and it usually does—the unthinkable anxiety is kept away by mother's capacity to "put herself in baby's place and to know what the baby needs in the general management of the body, and therefore of the person" (Winnicott 1962b, pp.57–58). Mother's good-enough empathic care is the sacred guardian of baby's experience of life as real and meaningful.

Through both the management and the natural ebb and flow of excitements, the individual invariably experiences both excited and quiet states. Excited states imply, for Winnicott, the operation of instinct. Winnicott (1988) adopts Freud's notion that there is a developmental progression of instinct dominance according to the function and fantasy involved—pregenital, phallic, genital. Central are the notions that the dominant zone changes over time and that bodily functions always include what Winnicott calls "imaginative elaboration." The individual not only experiences physiological sensations but develops ideas or fantasies that invariably accompany those sensations. At times he intimates, although he is far from certain about this point, that the closer the experience is to concrete physiological sensation, the farther the fantasy is from consciousness.

Essentially, Winnicott was concerned with elaborating the implications of Freud's (1923) famous assertion that the ego is first and foremost a body ego, deriving from bodily sensations. The difficult questions, of course, are where does body end and mind begin and how does mind come to dwell within the body. Winnicott accepted Freud's assumption that thought begins with fantasy and that thinking in pictures is but an incomplete form of becoming conscious.

But before fantasy can even become visual, Winnicott implied that it took the form of being experienced *in* the body, yet not yet associated *with* the body. The initially immature psyche, although based on bodily functioning, has crude unvisualized fantasies that are not closely bound to the body. Only later are these followed by fantasies *about* the body that perhaps represent the first mental images of the separate self. Winnicott employed the term "personalization" to try to capture the process whereby the psyche gradually comes to be more or less firmly placed within the body and the whole body becomes the dwelling place of the self.

As the process of personalization proceeds, particular zones predominate. At first, it is the mouth and the whole intake mechanisms, including the grasping of hands, that form the basis for fantasy. Later, a genital type of excitement comes to dominate the life of the child. Development, in other words, includes the natural progression of these various types of excited sensations and ideas. The richness of the personality is built up, according to Winnicott, through satisfactory and unsatisfactory experiences of excitement.

Still—and this is crucial for Winnicott—these instinctual moments do not cover *all* of human experience. They are a *part* of experience that must be dealt with and that can be either potentially satisfying or severely complicating. It was not to Winnicott's liking that Freudian theory focused too narrowly at times on the instinctual elements of relationships. A developmental theory that ignores instincts is misguided; but one based *solely* on the notion of instinctual conflict is inaccurate and leaves too much out. It is inaccurate because a mother who is sensitive to her infant's inner prompting can substantially reduce inner conflict. Furthermore, instinctual conflict covers only a narrow range of experience. As Winnicott wrote regarding the significance of instincts:

> No claim is being made that these matters cover the entire range of human experience. It would seem that only

comparatively recently have analysts begun to feel the
need for a hypothesis that would allow for areas of infancy
experience and of ego-development that are not basically
associated with instinctual conflict. [Quoted in Phillips
1988, p. 102]

What Winnicott is implying—and here he explores an
area insufficiently captured by Freud's ideas about sublimation—is that in the course of development instincts come to
serve the self; they don't constitute it. Instinctual life needs
to be freed as much as tamed. Well-being, in other words,
entails not only the attainment, either direct or indirect, of
instinctual satisfactions, but the existence of a sense of self
that can remain uncomplicated by the demands of desire.
The basic drive, for Winnicott, is for total development, not
pleasure. Instincts, therefore, become subsumed under this
greater process. In Winnicott's mind, psychoanalysis had
correctly identified the importance of instinctual experience
and of reactions to frustration in the origins of neurotic
illness, but it had failed to explore with comparable conviction the tremendous significance of nonclimactic experiences. "We now see," he (1971a) wrote in "The Location of
Cultural Experience,"

> that it is not instinctual satisfaction that makes a baby begin
> to be, to feel that life is real, to find life worth living. In
> fact, instinctual gratifications start off as part-functions
> and they become seductions unless based on a well-
> established capacity in the individual person for total
> experience. . . . [p. 116]

Feeling real, or the meaningfulness of experience, sup-
plements physical gratification as the primary criterion for
satisfaction. Creativity, play, work, and cultural pursuits are
not mere transformations of instinctual energy; instinctual
energy can easily disrupt the individual's capacity to enjoy
life. "Id-relationship," writes Winnicott (1958a), "is a recur-

ring complication in what might be called ego life" (pp. 30–31). Drawing on his extensive observations of children, he notes that the healthy child can feel satisfied playing a game "without feeling threatened by a physical orgasm of local excitement." By contrast, a deprived child might be "unable to enjoy play because the body becomes physically involved" (p. 35). Bodily excitement in erotogenic zones "constantly threatens playing, and therefore threatens the child's sense of existing as a person" (Winnicott 1971e, p. 60). Since instinct arousal beyond a certain point must lead to either direct climax, discomfort and confusion due to lack of climax, or a search for alternative forms of climax, the pleasure derived from play "carries with it the implication that the instinctual arousal is not excessive" (p. 61). "In my opinion," writes Winnicott (1958a),

> if we compare the happy play of a child or the experience of an adult at a concert with a sexual experience, the difference is so great that we should do no harm in allowing a different term for the description of the two experiences. Whatever the unconscious symbolism, the quantity of actual physical excitement is minimal in the one type of experience and maximal in the other. [p. 35]

Meaningful ego experiences, in other words, require freedom from bodily excitement. Eventually, Winnicott was to label this experience, perhaps inappropriately, an "ego orgasm." He chose such a term so as to capture the quality of climax or deep satisfaction afforded by experiences of music or friendship, which differ qualitatively from so-called id experiences. Play and all its derivatives have, for Winnicott, an inherent excitement that derives not from the arousal of drives but from the precarious tension between one's subjectivity and that which is objectively perceived.

Toward the end of his life, Winnicott (1966b) speculatively linked some of these ideas to varieties of object relating and to what he called "pure male" and "pure female" elements of the personality. He attempted to distinguish not between men and women per se, but between the masculine and feminine elements in people. Object relations, backed by instinct drive, he thought, "belongs to the male element in the personality uncontaminated by the female element" (p. 180). Classical object relations, notions about finding, using, oral sadism, and so on, "arise out of the life of the pure male element" (p. 180). The study of the "pure distilled uncontaminated female element," on the other hand, leads to what Winnicott called BEING. BEING "forms the only basis for self-discovery and a sense of existing" (p. 180); it enables the individual to develop an inside, to be a container, and to have a capacity to use the mechanisms of projection and introjection. What Winnicott is implying by such a distinction is that object relations, although definitely tied to instinctual drive through the "male element," cannot be explained solely on the basis of instinctual life. A "female" element, by necessity, had to precede it.

Winnicott's speculative ideas about "male" and "female" elements are consistent with his fundamental notion that in earliest infancy the ego must obtain a certain level of development *before* instinct experiences can be real. Whatever instinctual life there is apart from ego functioning is essentially irrelevant, according to Winnicott, until such time as there is an entity, or ego, capable of experiences. "There is thus no sense in making use of the word 'id,'" writes Winnicott (1962b), "for phenomena that are not covered and catalogued and experienced and eventually interpreted by ego-functioning" (p. 56). Where Freud frequently pictured the ego as emerging from an undifferentiated id–ego matrix, Winnicott reverses the order and asserts that id experiences depend on prior ego development. In the absence of a self with sufficient discriminatory abilities to distinguish inside and outside, id satisfactions have no meaning. If the instincts are not yet clearly defined as internal to the infant, then they "can be as much external as can a clap of thunder or a hit'' (Winnicott 1960f, p. 141). Once the ego has built up strength, the id satisfactions become important enhancers of self-experience. But before such a point, the ego is not yet able to include instinctual experiences nor contain the risks and frustrations involved in managing them.

Having formulated this developmental sequence—from an ego incapable of meaningful impulse experience to an ego capable of such experience—Winnicott introduces an essential distinction between needs and wish fulfillment. Needs arise earlier and are more fundamental than wish fulfillment. According to Winnicott, they start with body needs and gradually turn into ego needs inasmuch as a psychology emerges out of the imaginative elaboration of physical experience. Needs are not satisfied or frustrated; they are met or not met. The effect of their being either met or not met is quite different from the effect of instinctual gratification or frustration. As an example, Winnicott refers to the ''lulling'' type of rhythmic pleasures that the infant enjoys. It would be inappropriate, he argues, to say that the infant who is not lulled reacts with anger as to a frustration. Instead, the inadequately held and rocked infant suffers a distortion in ego development. It is not ''frustrated,'' it is ''maimed.''

To some extent, Winnicott's distinction between needs and wishes can be seen as an elaboration of Freud's ideas about anaclisis. Freud's idea that the sexual instincts originally borrow their source and object from the ego instincts suggests that he fully recognized a basic difference in kind between two sorts of phenomena. The vital distinction is evident from Freud's own repeated use of the words ''function'' and ''need'' in describing the ego instincts (Laplanche and Pontalis 1973). Winnicott preferred, however, both to remove the label ''instinct'' from these primary needs and to extend and elaborate their content.

Psychoanalytic theory was severely hampered, Winnicott thought, by a failure to distinguish clearly between earliest ego needs and later instinctual gratifications. Before the mid-1940s he was constantly frustrated because scientific meetings of the British Psycho-Analytic Society dealt exclusively with "wishes." As a pediatrician acutely aware of infantile dependence, he found it "exasperating that the only dependence my colleagues could envisage was dependence on the kind of provision that leads to id satisfactions." The clinical implications were clear to him:

> Progress in the study of what a psycho-analyst can do in reference to borderline and schizoid personalities depends more than anything else on the recognition of dependence as something that refers to need. For instance, in anorexia nervosa . . . oral satisfaction has become a dissociated phenomenon, a kind of seduction. What is more important to the child is *not eating*, which at any rate leaves the child unseduced and existing as an individual (even if dying). [Winnicott Correspondence, D. W. W. to Lili Peller, April 15, 1966]

Increasingly, the psychotic and the infant became mirror images for Winnicott. The emotional life of the latter could be reliably inferred from the former. This is not to say that a normal infant was psychotic. Rather, what apparently needed to go right to ensure the healthy development of the infant was implicit in what had obviously gone wrong in the psychotic. Thus schizophrenia was an "environmental deficiency disease" traceable to the first year of life (Winnicott 1959–1964, pp. 135–136). Winnicott's conviction about the developmental origins of psychotic disturbance led him to quite specific genetic interpretations about presumed infantile traumas that are, at times, questionable.

Carrying his research deeper into the realms of borderline and psychotic phenomena, Winnicott became increasingly convinced that psychotic-type anxieties "cluster round the word need" and "have nothing to do with instincts" (Winnicott Correspondence, D. W. W. to Lili Peller, April 15, 1966). He drew a clear distinction between regression to dependence and regression in terms of instinct stages. "Regression to dependence," Winnicott wrote to Enid Balint,

> seems to me not to be specifically linked to the oral phase, and indeed I want to cut it loose from the phases and from the instinctual development and allow it therefore to relate to ego relatedness which precedes instinctual experience that is accepted as such. [Rodman 1987, p. 98]

Winnicott's position on regression to dependence left him open to frequent accusations that he was minimizing both the importance of drives and of interpretive work. He was placing the therapeutic value of the patient–analyst relationship—so the charge goes—above the interpretive process. This reading of Winnicott, however, trivializes his complex position on these issues. Winnicott felt there was simply no need to emphasize instincts and interpretions because they could be taken for granted as part and parcel of the psychoanalyst's work. What was worth stressing, especially in public papers, were his own personal and innovative contributions that had meaning precisely because they were founded on and grounded in shared theory. As he wrote in a letter to Hanna Ries:

> I find myself that when I talk about regression and very early infantile problems people very easily think that I am unable to do an ordinary piece of analysis involving instincts and the ordinary work in the transference situation, which as a matter of fact I am all the time taking for granted, knowing that there is no point at all in going on to discover new things if one forgets the old things. [Rodman 1987, p. 55]

Winnicott's "new discovery" was that crucial ego relatedness was absolutely dependent upon good-enough maternal care. It was his unshakable conviction that, without a facilitating mother, the individual was doomed: a vital sense of self would fail to thrive, leaving the person prone to unthinkable anxieties and a life plagued by futility and unreality. The maturational process inherent in the individual from birth is inextricably linked to the facilitating environment of maternal care.

It was Winnicott's understanding of Freud that the latter simply took for granted that there was good-enough maternal care at the outset. He neglected to elaborate on its significance because he dealt with neurotic patients for whom good-enough care could be assumed. Built in to the analytic setting, Winnicott believed, was Freud's implicit, perhaps unconscious, recognition of the maternal function. "In reading Freud's own work," Winnicott (1960b) commented, "although Freud uses the mind and the intellectual processes and the verbalised part of feeling, he never lets us forget that he is talking about phenomena that have their roots in non-verbal material" (p. 468).

Nonverbal material, of course, assumes the active presence of a mothering figure capable of meeting unspoken needs; otherwise, the infant could not survive. One did not have to accept Winnicott's extreme statement—"There is no such thing as an infant"—to concede that, at least to some extent, mother and baby constitute a single unit. Freud articulated this idea most clearly in a footnote in his "Formulations on the Two Principles of Mental Functioning" (1911b):

> It will rightly be objected that an organization which was a slave to the pleasure-principle and neglected the reality of the external world could not maintain itself alive for the shortest time, so that it could not have come into existence at all. The employment of a fiction like this is, however, justified when one considers that the infant—*provided one includes with it the care it receives from its mother*—does almost realize a psychical system of this kind. [p. 215]

What Freud put in a footnote, Winnicott made his life work to explicate.

PATHS TO OBJECT LOVE

Winnicott was acutely aware that Freud never gave a final, definitive account as to the particular way stations the individual needed to reach en route to true object love. Instead, he offered changing hypotheses derived from growing clinical experience. But he was always consistent in his belief that true object love was a developmental achievement of a loving self. As such, every effort to delineate the paths toward object love invariably brought him to consider, in addition to instinctual trends, various aspects of self or narcissistic experience (Steve Ellman, personal communication May 15, 1992). As he said quite explicitly in "Instincts and Their Vicissitudes" (1915a): "Love and hate cannot be made use of for the relations of instincts to their objects, but are reserved for the relations of the *total ego* to objects" (p. 137). Winnicott sensed, however, that the two sides of the coin had not been equally explored: Freud's primary emphasis was on the achievement of true object love; his own contribution would be to give greater specificity to the idea of a developing self.

Freud's views on the development of object choice shifted over time, and so too did his understanding of the nature of the self and its relation to others and to drives. He obviously wrestled with the phenomena of narcissism, without ever coming to a definitive formulation.

Between 1910 and 1939, Freud proposed different, in some ways mutually exclusive, models of the developmental line to object love (Smith 1985). The first of these models appears in such works as the Schreber analysis (Freud 1911a), "The Disposition to Obsessional Neuroses" (1913b), and "Totem and Taboo" (1913a). In these papers, Freud describes a sequence of maturational stages beginning with a stage of autoeroticism, extending through stages of narcissism, and culminating in heterosexual object choice.

Autoeroticism, in this model, had four cardinal attributes: primary unintegration of the sexual drive, object-lessness, seeking of satisfaction in the subject's own body, and absence of an ego. Freud is hypothesizing an initial primordial state in which, for the infant, there is a complete absence of representations. From the autoerotic infant's point of view, there is no recognition of outside sources of frustration and gratification. Consequently, there is no internal representation of a self distinguishable from objects.

The developing infant moves from autoeroticism to narcissism, when there is a unification of the component drives, the formation of the ego, and the finding of the first object. The first object of the unified sexual current is the "ego" or self-representation. One possible reading of Freud is that it is the formation of the self-representation that is the cause of the unification of the sexual components.

The term "narcissism" appears in Freud's work for the first time in a footnote added in 1910 to *Three Essays* (1905). Freud discusses the way in which homosexuals in the earliest years of their childhoods "pass through a *phase*" of very intense fixation to a woman and, "after leaving this behind" identify with the woman and "take themselves as their sexual object. That is to say, they proceed from a narcissistic basis and look for a young man who resembles themselves and whom they may love as their mother loved them" (p. 145).

The narcissistic choice Freud outlines here is secondary narcissism and is a form of object choice; the narcissistic object choice follows upon a disappointment in the primary love object. A year later, in the Schreber case, Freud posits the existence of narcissism as a normal stage in sexual development. In 1914, in his classic paper "On Narcissism" (1914), Freud emphasizes the structural and economic characteristics of narcissism: the "original libidinal cathexis of the ego" can be "put forth" upon objects and "drawn back" again. Assuming a principle of conservation of libidinal energy, Freud postulates a constant reciprocity between the libidinal energy invested in the ego and the libidinal energy invested in the object: "The more the one is employed," he writes, "the more the other becomes depleted" (p. 76).

But what is the relationship between this form of narcissism—the "original libidinal cathexis of the ego"—and autoeroticism? In "On Narcissism," Freud maintains a clear distinction between the two. "It is impossible to suppose," he writes,

> that a unity comparable to the ego can exist in the individual from the very start; the ego has to develop. But the autoerotic instincts are primordial; so there must be something added to autoeroticism—some new operation in the mind—in order that narcissism may come into being. [p. 77]

In this version, the period of infantile narcissism ensues with the formative moments of the ego. The ego as a "unity" must develop before it can become the object of libidinal investment. But how does it become such a unity? How does the ego become a distinct psychical unit? What are its constituent parts and what makes it whole such that libido begins to "flow" toward it?

Although Freud fails in "On Narcissism" to answer these central questions, implicit in his writing is a particular vision of primitive emotional life that Winnicott amplifies with greater specificity. Logically consistent with Freud's formulation is the argument that, psychologically speaking, an individual does not exist at the outset of extrauterine life. There is not yet an "I" on the scene. At best, there is what Lear (1990) has called a "proto-I," or archaic precursor from which an "I" will later emerge. There are, for this "proto-I," no clear boundaries between inside and outside or between self and other. Given this primitive mental state in which there is no established sense of self, or "unified ego," a person cannot libidinally invest either an object or itself. The "I" must have psychological reality for itself before it can do so. And the "I" begins to achieve psychological reality for itself only gradually, as it achieves some distinction between inner and outer and between subject and object. Until this is the case, there is no person for whom there can be psychological meaning. Even drives, insofar as they are conceptualized psychologically as internal sources of pressure, can have no meaning or reality, and therefore, from the infant's perspective, do not yet exist.

Winnicott creatively elaborates these themes. At the very outset, Winnicott (1968e) suggests, the infant is in a condition of "primary unintegration." Integration appears only gradually. For long periods the infant is but an "armful of anatomy and physiology" (p. 89) with unconnected feeling states, disparate impressions, and disjointed motility phases; emotionally, baby does not mind "whether he is in many bits or one whole being, or whether he lives in his mother's face or in his own body," provided that "from time to time he comes together and feels something" (Winnicott 1945a, p. 150). The infant is not aware that the particular sensations felt while lying peacefully in a crib belong to the same hungry self screaming for milk a moment later. There is no integration between the child awake and the child asleep. Visual images and tactile bodily experiences are not yet brought together: the breast that is seen is not connected to the warm softness felt in the mouth and the smooth surface that meets the fingers (Wright 1991).

Periodically, however, and with ever growing frequency, the infant has unifying experiences. Visual-tactile schemata are built up gradually. Various psychic and somatic components come together to create "I AM" moments. These are described by Winnicott (1955) as "raw" because the assertion of a distinct self invariably brings with it an expectation of persecution from the "not-me," which is momentarily felt as separate and rejected.

Still, for Winnicott, this is a momentous developmental achievement. As he (1966a) said at a conference of nursery school workers:

The most aggressive and therefore the most dangerous words in the languages of the world are to be found in the assertion "I am." It has to be admitted, however, that only those who have reached a stage at which they can make this assertion are really qualified as adult members of society. [p. 141]

Integration, being such a hazardous risk on which so much hinges, leaves the infant "infinitely exposed." "Only if someone has her arms round the infant at this time," writes Winnicott (1955), "can the I AM moment be endured, or rather, perhaps, risked" (p. 148). A breakdown in the mother's sensitive adaptation can lead, in other words, to a continuing expectation of persecution.

The natural, though perilous, tendency to integrate is helped, according to Winnicott (1945a), by two sets of experience: the technique of infant care whereby the baby is "kept warm, handled and bathed and rocked and named" and also the "acute instinctual experiences which tend to gather the personality together from within" (p. 150). These two orders of events, repeated again and again over time, gradually gather together the disparate "bits" of the infant to create a dawning sense of self as a specific person rooted in a particular body experiencing a continuity in time. Motor and sensory and functional experiences are linked together and a limiting membrane, which to some extent is equated with the surface of the skin, gradually distinguishes "me" from "not-me." In Winnicott's words, "It is instinctual experience and the repeated quiet experiences of body care that gradually build up what may be called satisfactory personalization" (p. 151).

It is characteristically paradoxical of Winnicott that instinctual experiences are a real factor contributing to integration and become real only once integration has occurred. An argument could be made that in one way or another the whole of Winnicott's work relates to the examination of the conditions in infancy that sponsor integration in the infant. He sees integration as both a capacity present in the mother, which she makes available to the infant through her reliable maternal care, and as a growing capacity in the infant that is brought together intrapsychically through a complex interplay of the maturational development and of the body ego, ego functions, and the experience of the environment as such.

Paradoxically, however, insofar as mother's ego support is reliable enough to facilitate integration, it enables the infant to return, periodically, to unintegrated experiences without a threat to personal continuity. Unintegration is the precursor of the adult capacity to relax; it implies that the individual feels no compelling need to integrate. In a fragmentary transcript of an unpublished lecture, Winnicott (1948a) describes it thus:

> In the quiet moments let us say that there is no line but just lots of things they separate out, sky seen through trees, something to do with mother's eyes all going in and out, wandering round. Some lack of need for any integration. That is an extremely valuable thing to be able to retain. Miss something without it. Something to do with being calm, restful, relaxed and feeling one with people and things when no excitement is around.

A decade later, Winnicott's ideas crystallized into his essay "The Capacity to Be Alone" (1958a). The sophisticated capacity to be alone, to enjoy solitude, can come about only when the mother's active life presence at the beginning makes possible periodic returns to unintegrated states. If she fails to allow such experiences, if she compels the infant to integrate too frequently or too precociously, a reactive False Self will emerge. The capacity to be unintegrated without loss of personal going-on-being depends on the mother's unobtrusive presence and is absolutely vital for "a life that has reality instead of futility." "It is only when alone (that is to say, in the presence of someone)," writes Winnicott, that the infant can discover his own personal life. . . . When alone in the sense that I am using the term, and only when alone, the infant is able to do the equivalent of what in an adult would be called relaxing. The infant is able to become unintegrated, to flounder, to be in a state in which there is no orientation, to be able to exist for a time without being either a reactor to an external impingement or an active person with a direction of interest or movement. The stage is set for an id experience. In the course of time there arrives a sensation or an impulse. In this setting the sensation or impulse will feel real and be a truly personal experience. [p. 34]

The mother's crucial function, therefore, is to be with the infant in a way that enables the infant to be alone. Baby can experience moments of satisfying self-communion without needing to be too preoccupied with mother's presence or absence. The infant then has the opportunity for a large number of experiences in which spontaneously arising impulses are graciously received by her. The infant is alone enough to feel that what is endogenous is really coming from within, and mother is present enough to be a recipient or participant according to baby's need. The endogenously arising impulse is then "fruitfully" linked to an external object. Instincts, in this way, become gradually tied to object relations.

Winnicott's ideas about integration and personalization can be linked to some of Freud's inconsistent notions about primary narcissism. Winnicott (1962b) assumed that integration emerges out of the "stuff of primary narcissism" (p. 60). In Freud's work, primary narcissism refers in a general way to the child taking itself as its love-object before choosing external objects. But he is inconsistent as to when, exactly, this occurs. At times he uses the term to mean a first state of life, prior to ego formation, epitomized by life in the womb. At other times, however, Freud makes "primary narcissism" contemporaneous with the emergence of a unified subject (Laplanche and Pontalis 1973, pp. 337–338). Winnicott and

Freud, it seems, were grappling with the same issue: how and when does an infant come to have an experience of itself as an "I AM." Freud, working from the vantage point of libidinal cathexes, called this obscure process "primary narcissism"; Winnicott, approaching the issue more experientially, spoke of "integration."

What they share is the assumption that there is an early phase of emotional development in which, as Winnicott (1960g) put it, "nothing has yet been separated out as not-me, so there is *not yet* a ME" (p. 17). No object external to the self is known. The mother's actions, heartbeat, warmth, and breath cannot be distinguished from the baby's own. What Winnicott added to the description, however, which Freud merely implied, is that the ongoing presence and reliability of the mother's ego support is a crucial component of this state. She holds and handles the baby, making the weak ego into a strong one, reinforcing everything like "power-assisted steering on a bus" (Winnicott 1962a, p. 70). Paradoxically, the "objectless" state of "primary narcissism" necessarily presumes an intersubjective element.

This intersubjective element, however, should not be confused with object relating or object seeking. As long as the baby was unaware of the early environmental provision, Winnicott felt that it was inappropriate to call it a relationship. He rejected Balint's use of the term "primary love" to describe early infancy because "the infant has not yet established the capacity to make relationships and in fact is not there to be related except in an unintegrated way" (Rodman 1987, p. 128). In a similar vein, Winnicott strenuously objected to Fairbairn's idea that libido, from the outset, seeks objects. For Winnicott, until there is sufficient integration to differentiate self from mother, the notion of seeking an object is meaningless. "Now if the object is not differentiated," he (1989) wrote:

> it cannot operate as an object. What Fairbairn is referring to then is an infant with needs, but with no "mechanism"

by which to implement them, an infant with needs not
"seeking" an object, but seeking de-tension, libido seeking
satisfaction, instinct tension seeking a return to a state of
rest or unexcitement; which brings us back to Freud.
[p. 419]

What Winnicott adds to Freud, however, is precisely that
part of the total experience that is beyond the infant's own
mental activities: maternal provision. Mother provides baby
with a way out of its own instinctual episode. If all goes well,
the infant may develop a capacity to relate the object to its
own desire. Then, and only then, will baby begin to seek an
object.

In 1915, with the publication of "Instincts and Their
Vicissitudes" (1915a), Freud was to offer a different way of
understanding primitive mental life. This paper is considered one of Freud's most difficult. As Paul Federn has noted,
however, Freud is hardest to understand when he is struggling against himself (Bergmann 1987). Although entitled
"Instincts and Their Vicissitudes," the essay is no less concerned with love and its vicissitudes. Among other things,
Freud is concerned with how loving admits of not merely
one, but of three antitheses: loving/being loved, loving/
hating, and loving-hating/indifference.

Characteristically, Freud does not explicitly repudiate
his former developmental model, nor does he offer clear
reasons why he has chosen to do so. He simply takes it for
granted that formulations shift as theory is calibrated with
accumulating clinical observation. Winnicott deeply identified with the way Freud derived theory by learning from
patients. In Freud's new version, autoeroticism as a separate
developmental stage no longer appears. It is plausible that
Freud introduced this change to correspond with alterations
in his views on the origins of the ego. In the 1915 paper, he
clearly postulates an ego present from the beginning of
psychological life. No longer does the ego emerge between
autoeroticism and narcissism. Freud also adds two new
substages to the narcissistic phase: a stage of the "original

reality ego" and a stage of a "purified pleasure ego." In both these formulations, it is evident that Freud conceives of the infant as primarily concerned with sources of pleasure and unpleasure (Bergman and Ellman 1985).

During the period of the "original reality ego," the "ego-subject" coincides with what is pleasurable; the external world with what is indifferent. Under the sway of the pleasure principle, however, a new development takes place. The original "reality ego" changes into what Freud calls a "purified pleasure ego." Objects, insofar as they are pleasurable, are "absorbed" or "introjected" into the ego, while sources of pain are "projected" upon the external world. For the "purified pleasure ego," the outside world is divided between that which is pleasurable and incorporated into itself and a "remainder that is alien to it." The ego has separated off a part of itself, projected it into the outside world, then related to it as hostile.

What accounts for the infant's transition from the stage of "reality ego" to the stage of "purified pleasure ego"? And how do these forms of narcissistic love become transformed into object love? Freud does not tackle these questions head on, but he suggests a way of thinking about them that Winnicott devotes his life to elaborating.

In an important footnote added to "Instincts and Their Vicissitudes," Freud (1915a) describes the infant's initial state in this way:

> [T]he primal narcissistic condition would not have been able to attain such a development were it not that every individual goes through a period of helplessness and dependence on fostering care, during which his urgent needs are satisfied by agencies outside himself and thereby withheld from developing along their own line. [p. 135]

Freud then proposes three classes of instincts operating within the narcissistic matrix of helplessness: sexual instincts capable of autoerotic satisfaction, sexual instincts that from the outset require an object; and ego, or self-preservative instincts, which are never capable of autoerotic satisfaction. It is the latter two that, according to Freud, "interfere" with the narcissistic condition and "prepare the way for progress." The need for object relations, in other words, propels development forward.

A logically consistent implication of Freud's suggestive explanation is that the transition from narcissistic to object love is linked with the care given to the infant by caretakers (Steve Ellman, personal communication May 15, 1992). In the beginning, Freud implies, the baby can be entirely preoccupied with its own physical sensations of pleasure because the caretaker's provision is so quick, automatic, unobtrusive, and appropriate to vital needs that the infant takes the source of gratification for granted. The infant has no reason to be aware that there is an outside. That is why the infant's own body can be perceived subjectively as the source of its own pleasure. Narcissism, in other words, is based on the illusion of self-generated pleasure, dependent, in actuality, on the caretaker's ministrations (Smith 1985).

As the child matures, the caretaker gradually responds less and less automatically to the infant's needs. The infant is awake for longer and longer periods of time, and there are increasing delays between need arousal and satisfaction. Wholly compatible with Freud's model is the assumption that as the child needs to "work" harder to obtain gratification, the illusion of self-sufficiency is punctured; there is an increase in frustration. The recognition of dependency causes pain that is dealt with through the introjective and projective processes of the purified pleasure ego. This is the infant's attempt to recapture paradise lost. Narcissism is gradually transformed into object love to the extent that the infant becomes capable of tolerating frustration and its dependence on others for experiences of gratification.

What Freud alludes to in a broad stroke, Winnicott enriches with fine detail. So great was Winnicott's interest in this area that he developed his own specialized and specific vocabulary to describe it. Whereas Freud's account focuses almost entirely on the internal psyche, Winnicott's is always a double narrative: the maturational process and the facilitating environment. In his mind, these were instrinsically inseparable.

What Freud described as "a period of helplessness and dependence on fostering care," Winnicott called the stage of absolute dependence. Mother, during this sensitive phase, is in a state for which he coined the term "primary maternal preoccupation." Her pronounced single-minded involvement with the newborn nearly resembles an illness, except that a woman must be healthy in order to enter and recover from this state. "This organized state," writes Winnicott (1956a),

> could be compared with a withdrawn state, or a dissociated state, or a fugue, or even a disturbance at a deeper level such as a schizoid episode in which some aspect of the personality takes over temporarily. . . . I do not believe that it is possible to understand the functioning of the mother at the very beginning of the infant's life without seeing that she must be able to reach this state of heightened sensitivity, almost an illness, and to recover from it. [p. 302]

Primary maternal preoccupation begins as body involvement during pregnancy but becomes specifically linked in fantasy with an "internal object," which, Winnicott (1960g, 1989) implies, is tied to the good-enough mother of the expectant mother's own early infancy. This internalized environment, or memory, of her own infancy constitutes an inner reserve upon which the mother can rely during the trying period of managing her infant. It enables her to drain interest from her own self on to the baby. One implication of Winnicott's theory is that if the mother's internalized early environment is poor, she will have difficulty sustaining a whole live child in fantasy, which will lead to difficulties in her actual relationship with her newborn. As Winnicott (1966d) said in a talk to the Nursery School Association of Great Britain entitled "The Ordinary Devoted Mother":

> There is nothing mystical about this. After all, she was a baby once, and she has in her the memories of being a baby; she also has memories of being cared for, and these memories can either help or hinder her in her in her own experiences as a mother. [p. 6]

The actual relationship to the newborn is a highly complex affair because it involves sensitive adaptation to the infant's idiosyncratic rhythms and maturational processes. This places tremendous demands on the caretaker. The parents, after all, "do not produce a baby as an artist produces a picture or a potter a pot." They have only

> started up a developmental process which results in there being a lodger in the mother's body and then in her arms and then in the home provided by the parents, and what this lodger will turn out to be like is outside anyone's control. The parents are dependent on the infant's inherited tendencies. [Winnicott 1963f, p. 85]

Winnicott, more so than Freud, was acutely sensitive to how babies vary inherently. He observed and gave weight to their temperamental differences as expressed through such states as alert wakefulness, fidgetiness, arousal, quiescence, hesitation, and irritability. From the outset, Winnicott emphasized both the inexorable individuality of the newborn and its nonexistence in isolation from the mother. The infant must survive its absolute dependence on maternal care, as the mother must survive the infant's innate drive to preserve its personal integrity.

In most cases, mother and baby traverse this potentially treacherous path: Mother does not let her infant down, and baby is thereby able to proceed according to an internal developmental blueprint. During the stage of absolute dependence, mother meets the infant's needs so automatically and unobtrusively that baby lacks awareness of either need or maternal care. Internal promptings are met so quickly that they need not become desires. Again, in Winnicott's view, there is not yet an "I" on the scene to actually experience desire. There is also no need for symbols, even of the most primitive type, since symbols are required only when there is desire. Mother, for a brief period, makes the absence of desire possible. Ogden (1990) refers to this as "the illusion of invisible oneness" (p. 173). Mother and baby are within a homogeneous psychological field, without vantage points or perspective.

Mother makes this possible, but cannot humanly do so in an absolutely perfect fashion. As Winnicott (1966c) said: "Perfection has no *meaning*" (p. 108). Winnicott understood that inevitably there must be relative failures of adaptation. These relative failures, however, have a positive value in that they communicate to the infant mother's overall reliability. They introduce perspective into the infant's psychic field allowing it to feel loved. As Winnicott (1968e) described it:

> Human beings fail and fail; and in the course of ordinary care a mother is all the time mending her failures. These relative failures with immediate remedy undoubtedly add up eventually to a communication, so that the baby comes to know about success. . . . It is the innumerable failures followed by the sort of care that mends that build up into a communication of love, of the fact that there is a human being there who cares. [p. 98]

Gradually, the integrated "I" begins to emerge from the "matrix of the infant–mother relationship" (Winnicott 1962b, p. 57). Baby is entering a stage Winnicott refers to as one of relative dependence. By meeting baby's needs in a good-enough manner, mother affords the tenuously inte-

grated "I" experiences of actual omnipotence in which
fantasy and reality correspond. Freud had suggested a similar idea when he introduced his notion of hallucinatory
wish fulfillment. As he wrote in "Formulations Regarding
the Two Principles of Mental Functioning" (1911), baby
"hallucinates the fulfillment of its inner needs; it betrays its
pain due to increase of stimulation and delay of satisfaction
by the motor discharge of crying and struggling, and then
experiences the hallucinated satisfaction" (p. 220).

Winnicott adopted Freud's notion, but added two important reservations. First, from Winnicott's point of view,
the experience of omnipotence emerges only after there has
been an experience of absolute dependence. It is not there,
as Freud believed, from the outset. Second, Winnicott distinguishes between an actual experience of omnipotence
and one that serves a defensive function. Actual omnipotence was not a quality of feeling due to a denial of impo-
tence and helplessness in the face of external reality, as
Freud had presumed. Instead, after the gradual build up of
memories,

> the baby eventually gets the illusion that this real breast is
> exactly the thing that was created out of need, greed, and
> the first impulse of primitive loving. Sight, smell and taste
> register somewhere, and after a while the baby may be
> creating something like the very breast that mother has to
> offer. A thousand times before weaning the baby may be
> given just this particular introduction to external reality by
> one woman, the mother. A thousand times the feeling has
> existed that what was wanted was created, and found to be
> there. From this develops a belief that the world can
> contain what is wanted and needed, with the result that
> the baby has hope that there is a live relationshp between
> inner reality and external reality, between innate primary
> creativity and the world at large which is shared by all.
> [Winnicott 1964a, p. 90]

Primary creativity is one of Winnicott's most original
contributions to psychoanalysis. It was his way of going

beyond both the pleasure principle and the idea of projection, notions he found insufficient to describe the human spirit. The human being is capable of more than just projection of that which has been previously introjected. There is an innate creative potential. Even at the theoretical first feed, the infant has a personal contribution to make. If mother adapts well enough, baby assumes that the nipple and the milk are the results of a gesture that arose out of need. Primary creativity, or absolute originality, is the psychological root that enables an individual of any age to have a sense of the reality of any experience or object. It implies that the infant is essentially active, probably more so than Freud ever believed. It is vitally important, Winnicott believed, that the infant be allowed to enjoy its true creative potential and bask in the naive belief that the world is personally created. Gradually, there will come an intellectual understanding of the fact of the world's existence prior to the individual's, but nothing is more important than the feeling that remains that the world is personally created.

Emotional development, for Winnicott (1988), is the joining up of the "innate primary creativity" of the infant with the actual details of the world at large. Emotional well-being requires that in the earliest months the actual details of the world be presented in such a manner that the child's capacity for primary creativity is not undermined. Mother's adaptation is the delicate art of "giving the infant the illusion that what is created out of need and by impulse has real existence" (p. 104).

Mother must present the world in accordance with the infant's growing capacity to tolerate new experiences. She must titrate her adaptations so that the baby is not precociously overwhelmed by reality. But she must also respond to the infant's increasing interest in and ability to tolerate that reality. If, during the phase of absolute dependence, a near-perfect adaptation to the infant's needs was required, now, as baby becomes increasingly separate, mother must sensitively "de-adapt." Whereas before, mother understood her infant's needs based on empathy, she now changes over to an "understanding based on something in the infant or small child that indicates need" (Winnicott 1960h, p. 51). She begins to read the infant's signals rather than rely on her intuitive understanding. Of course, this, too, is a complex task since "children vacillate between one state and the other; one minute they are merged with their mothers and require empathy, while the next they are separate from her, and then if she knows their needs in advance she is dangerous, a witch" (pp. 51–52).

Winnicott's ideas about adaptation leading to de-adaptation parallel Freud's notions of the gradual introduction of the reality principle and the ego's progressive differentiation of subject and object. But whereas Freud describes these primarily from the vantage of the infant, Winnicott includes the point of view of maternal care. He adds rich detail to Freud's implication that the transition from narcissistic to object love is fundamentally linked with the care given to the infant by caretakers. Both Winnicott and Freud are concerned with the process by which an original illusion of self-sufficiency is altered by an increasing awareness of external reality.

Unfortunately, the terminology Freud employs in his 1915 developmental model makes it difficult to understand his intention. He confusingly labels the initial stage in which there is not yet any clear psychological differentiation between subject and object an "original reality-ego." What he apparently means by this is that for the ego at this stage the external world is absolutely neutral (Laplanche and Pontalis 1973). Although the infant has perceptual powers that enable it to perceive external reality, it has no emotional need to relate to it. The subject commands a rudimentary grasp of external reality but can remain indifferent to it. As Freud (1915a) states, the ego "coincides with what is pleasurable and the external world with what is indifferent" (p. 135). The infant, therefore, is "objective"—it can receive pleasurable and unpleasurable stimuli without necessarily being concerned that they belong to the external world. In Freud's words, it "distinguishes internal and external by means of a sound objective criterion" (pp. 135–136). Pleasure, of course, is that criterion. This phase, however, does not last long. The boundaries of the ego—its inside and outside—are gradually laid down. The ego, or self, is beginning to emerge as a separate psychological agency. This is painful. As a result, both the subject and the external world are split into pleasurable and unpleasurable parts. The new "purified pleasure ego" identifies with the pleasurable as opposed to the unpleasurable: the portion of the objects in the external world that are sources of pleasure are introjected and the causes of unpleasure emanating from within are projected outward. All unpleasure is now located outside.

The stage of the purified pleasure ego is, in Freud's 1915 model, a defensive effort on the part of the infant to maintain the pleasurable illusion that separation does not exist. It is an attempt to deny the absolute dependence of the ego on pleasure coming from without. The gradual introduction of the reality principle, however, makes the solipsistic denial increasingly untenable. Eventually, the infant develops what Freud (1925) calls a "definitive reality-ego," which seeks to find an object in the outside world that is essentially equivalent to the image of the lost satisfying object (now recognized to be separate) of the more primitive period.

Winnicott, grappling with the same phenomena, suggested formulations that both overlap with and diverge from those of Freud. Both Freud and Winnicott conceived of earliest infancy as a period in which the infant is, initially at least, partially insulated from external reality. Freud employed the term "protective shield" to describe the means by which the human organism is guarded against excitations deriving from the outside world that threaten to destroy it by their intensity. The protective shield, or stimulus barrier, is part of Freud's larger energy model. Beginning with his

"Project for a Scientific Psychology" (1895), Freud adhered to an economic discharge theory in which the primal tendency of the system was to keep quantity of excitation at zero. In "Beyond the Pleasure Principle" (1920), Freud postulates that the protective barrier functions to protect against outside stimuli that are incomparably stronger than the internal energy. Trauma, from this point of view, is a breach in the protective shield introducing more external stimuli than can be handled.

Winnicott, too, believed that at the outset the infant cannot tolerate the full blast of external reality. However, the protective shield for Winnicott is not an internally generated one. Mother, in a state of primary maternal preoccupation, acts as a stimulus barrier. Winnicott shifts the epistemologic focus from the developing infant to the developing mother–infant relationship. Furthermore, mother's role is primarily one of assuring homeostatic balance, or optimal frustration, rather than energy discharge. Although instinctual pressures require climax and discharge, according to Winnicott, overall self-development requires a subtle and individual balance between appropriate arousal and quiescence. For Winnicott, as for Freud, the introduction of a separate reality and the reality of separation was a process with which the maturing infant had to contend. His notion of the tenuous "I AM," expectant of external persecution, parallels Freud's formulation of a purified pleasure ego except that in Winnicott's version the ego is still too unsophisticated to employ projection. In general, whereas Freud saw the gradual introduction of reality and separation as necessarily deeply painful and requiring defenses, Winnicott saw it as only a potential insult that could be at least partially mitigated by mother's ministrations and the child's innate capacity for creativity. For Freud, the baby's central task was to recognize and accept external reality; for Winnicott, it was to find healthy ways of creating reality. For Freud, reality was a frustrating blow from which people never truly recover; for Winnicott, reality afforded relief and satisfaction from the alarming effects of unbridled fantasy.

Nevertheless, for Winnicott (1961b), exposure to reality still constituted an insult because, in his words, "the reality principle is the fact of the existence of the world whether the baby creates it or not"; it is the "arch-enemy of spontaneity, creativity and the sense of Real" (p. 236). The "Real," for Winnicott (1945a), emanated primarily from inner reality, fantasy, being "more primary than reality" (p. 153). But Winnicott's aim was to describe how the infant copes with the insult of the reality principle—how the gap between fantasy and reality is bridged—without falling into absolute despair.

The key, in Winnicott's mind, is the capacity for illusion. Early development does not center on psychological functions by which the infant cares for itself in the face of anxiety but on the infant's capacity (assuming mother's supportive ego-functions) to relate to mother as a subjective object. A subjective object is not an internal object; it is truly external but, "subjectively perceived, that is to say it comes out of the creative impulses of the child and out of the child's mind" (Winnicott 1966a, p. 133). Objective perception, in Winnicott's view, is at work; the baby could "not have invented exactly what the mother's left ear looks like" (p. 133). And yet, baby reaches out and creates "that particular ear that happened to be there to be discovered" (p. 133). Baby has the illusion that internal and external reality are one and the same.

Nevertheless, echoing the idea implicit in Freud's "original reality ego," Winnicott still distinguishes between the infant's sensorial aliveness, or nascent perceptual capabilities, and its initial inability to distinguish between self and object. Because mother allows delayed recognition of separateness by meeting needs before they become desires, the infant can tolerate fleeting moments of recognition of external reality. Maternal provision makes exposure to reality potentially tolerable. "In this respect," writes Winnicott (1962f),

> the baby can meet the reality principle here and there, now and then, but not everywhere all at once; that is, the baby retains areas of subjective objects along with other areas in which there is some relating to objectively perceived objects, or "not-me" ("not-I") objects. [p. 57]

And yet—and this is typical of Winnicott's paradoxical thinking—it is not sufficient that mother merely shield baby from premature separateness. She must also allow the baby to experience the full force of its own internal zest. The integrity of baby's separateness must be respected by allowing for its natural instinctual rhythms. "It is too easily assumed," writes Winnicott (1954a),

> that a feed is followed by satisfaction and sleep. Often distress follows this fobbing off, especially if physical satisfaction too quickly robs the infant of zest. The infant is then left with: agression undischarged . . . or a sense of "flop"—since a source of zest for life has gone suddenly, and the infant does not know it will return. [p. 268]

Mother's task, in other words, is to enable the infant to enjoy simultaneously both invisible oneness and unfolding individuality. In a sense, Winnicott's entire developmental theory—and the diachronic developmental sequence it presumes—is an effort to chart the subtle shifts in the quality of the dialectic between invisible oneness and individuality.

As baby matures and mother de-adapts, inside and outside begin to become distinct. Desire emerges and frustration increases. During this stage of relative dependence, mother now provides the illusion that baby has the omnipotent power to create precisely what it desires. Baby uses mother in a new way as a subjective object. For Winnicott, creativity is primary; omnipotence is not just a defense against anxiety. Whereas Freud was more of a learning theorist in the sense that the infant changed in response to external stimuli, Winnicott consistently believed that the infant—provided good-enough mothering—brings reality under omnipotent control.

The movement is from mother–infant unity toward mother and infant as separate. Winnicott suggests that this can occur in a nontraumatic way if there is a potential space between mother and infant. The illusion that fills this potential space is that oneness and separateness coexist.

Winnicott's notion of potential space is one of his most original, yet enigmatic, ideas. Grounded in his own acute visual and spatial imagination, it is a general term he used to refer to an intermediate area of experiencing that lies between fantasy and reality. "Potential space," writes Winnicott (1971c),

> is the hypothetical area that exists (but cannot exist) between the baby and the object mother or part of mother) during the phase of the repudiation of the object as not-me, that is, at the end of being merged in with the object. [p. 126]

He mentions specific forms of potential space, such as the area of transitional phenomena, play space, the area of cultural experience, analytic space, and the area of creativity. What these have in common is that they all "have a place in which they occur." That place, potential space, is

> not inside by any use of the word. . . . Nor is it outside, that is to say, it is not part of the repudiated world, the not-me, that which the individual has decided to recognize (with whatever difficulty and even pain) as truly external, which is outside magical control. [p. 47]

The essential feature of this area of experiencing is

the paradox, and the acceptance of the paradox: the baby creates the object, but the object was there waiting to be created. . . . In the rules of the game we all know that we will never challenge the baby to elicit an answer to the question: did you create that or did you find it? [p. 104]

By offering this paradox, Winnicott rejects both phylogenetic and strictly empiricist views. Baby's subjective experience is neither the product of innate ideas nor the imprinting of external reality. Furthermore, the paradox is not only that the infant both discovers and creates the objects of desire but that the potential space both joins and separates the individual and the object. The insult of reality is tolerable because playing and creativity and symbols fill the space between mother and infant allowing them to remain united though separate. In Winnicott's words:

This is the paradox that I accept and do not attempt to resolve. The baby's separating-out of the world of objects from the self is achieved only through the absence of a space between [the infant and the mother], the *potential* space being filled . . . with creative playing, with symbols, and with all that eventually adds up to a cultural life. [pp. 126–128]

The "absence of space" or the creation of potential space, is a by-product of mother's reliability expressed during the stage of relative dependence. Gradually de-adapting, she no longer automatically meets dependency needs but affords the infant the opportunity to move from dependency toward autonomy. That is why Winnicott (1971c) says that potential space "depends for its existence on living experiences, not on inherited tendencies" (p. 127). Each baby has a unique experience with a particular mother; mother's trust and reliability directly impacts on the individual's capacity for autonomous self-realization. "One baby," writes Winnicott, is given sensitive management here where the mother is separating out from the baby so that the area for play is immense; and the next baby has so poor an experience at this phase of his or her development that there is but little opportunity for development except in terms of introversion or extroversion. The potential space, in the later case, has no significance, because there was never a built-up sense of trust matched with reliability, and therefore there was no relaxed self-realization. [p. 127]

Winnicott is more concerned with the process of separating than the effects of separation. The "built-up sense of trust matched with reliability" facilitates the infant's capacity to be alone, to enjoy relaxed solitude. The infant internalizes mother not as object, but as total environment. Mother is absent as an object but is still vitally present as a containing space for the child. As Ogden (1990) states, "The child must have the opportunity to play alone in the presence of the absent mother, and in the absence of the present mother" (p. 182). The gradual weaning of the infant from the maternal provision of the holding environment—the titrated disillusionment that mother provides—enables the infant to begin to generate its own potential space. This is the space in which baby will relax "formlessly," dream, play, and enjoy the use of symbols. It implies a feeling of confidence on the part of the baby, "confidence being the evidence of dependability that is becoming introjected" (p. 118).

Thus is born the area of life in which the individual feels free (Eigen 1991). One feels most alive and real and free when one is not boxed in by either inner or outer (what Winnicott refers to as introversion and extroversion). The only way to avoid being boxed in is to sustain an unending dialectic between inner and outer. Winnicott's image of the mind is like an hourglass—one bulb internal reality, one bulb external reality—that, paradoxically, stands on both ends at the same time. A life that feels real is experienced in the narrow area of convergence where the grains of sand flow continuously in both directions. Individuals are faced with the perpetual task—and potential strain—of keeping inner and outer reality separate but interrelated. A collapse of the dialectic in either direction—reality subsumed by fantasy, or fantasy subsumed by reality—leads to various forms of pathology (Ogden 1990). Sustaining the dialectic, on the other hand, enables one to profit handsomely from what is within and without. After all, according to Winnicott (1945a), "fantasy is only tolerable at full blast when objective reality is appreciated well" and "we are poor indeed if we are only sane" (p. 153).

The Survival
of the Real

The closer Winnicott came to the end of his life, the more he focused on the issue of survival. Life had sensitized him to how individuals endure: the loss of friends in World War I; the devastation of the bombings he witnessed in World War II; the suffering of the children he treated in the hostels during their evacuation from London; the grief of not having a son to unconsciously destroy him; the death of his parents; the breakup of his first marriage; the fight to be productive despite repeated heart ailments. The older he grew, the greater he appreciated the way people go on living, day by day, despite the stresses and strains imposed by all that is beyond control.

The idea of survival had always been inherent in his writings. As a young medical student, he was deeply influenced by Darwin's theories about adaptation and survival. When, in the early 1930s, he first began to formulate his own views on emotional disturbances in children, he adopted the position that symptoms are a form of commu-

197

nication that have survival value. Later, when he explored in subtle detail the mother–infant relationship, he concluded that baby's precarious sense of being was threatened by impingements. Without a good-enough holding environment, he argued, inherited potential and continuity of being were at risk of annihilation. Mother's task, in other words, was to facilitate the survival of baby's authentic individuality.

When Winnicott turned his attention to clinical matters, the issue of survival surfaced as well. The introduction of the notion of True and False Self in the early 1960s brought with it the assumption that the False Self can serve as a "caretaker," or protector, ensuring the survival of the True Self. As Winnicott (1960f) put it, this is "the clearest example of clinical illness as an organization with a positive aim, the preservation of the individual in spite of abnormal environmental conditions" (p. 143).

Winnicott's description of adolescent psychology also centered on the notion that adolescence was essentially a struggle for the survival of one's inner authenticity. His work in the evacuation scheme convinced him that the adolescents benefited from the resiliency of the hostels; the staff members were of value to the displaced youngsters when they successfully demonstrated that continuity of care was not disrupted, despite adolescent destructiveness. Even under normal conditions, Winnicott believed, the adolescent passes through a period of "doldrums" before learning to tolerate compromise without a feeling of "personal extinction." "They feel unreal," he (1963g) wrote, "except in so far as they are refusing the false solutions, and feeling unreal leads them to do certain things which are only too real from the point of view of society" (p. 152). Since the only solution for adolescence is the passage of time, the task of parents is to "hold and to contain, avoiding both the false solution and the moral indignation which stems from jealousy of youthfulness" (Winnicott 1964c, p. 157–158). Parents, in other words, should not attempt to cure adolescence; they need only survive it.

In January 1969 Winnicott wrote a letter to F. Robert Rodman in which the implicit theme of survival was made quite explicit:

> In the extreme of a borderline case everything boils down in the end to what I have tried to describe as the survival of the analyst, only it may take years for the patient to become sufficiently confident in the transference to be able to take the risk of a relationship in which the analyst is absolutely unprotected. [Rodman 1987, p. 181]

Winnicott's proposition regarding the survival of the analyst was an important theme in a controversial talk given two months earlier at the New York Psychoanalytic Society. The talk, entitled "The Use of an Object and Relating through Identifications" (Winnicott 1968c, pp. 218–227), was to be Winnicott's last. He was stricken with Asian influenza from which he developed pulmonary edema, bringing him close to death for some time. Never fully recovering, he died a little over a year later. In "The Use of an Object" paper, Winnicott's personal struggle to survive converged with his ideas about survival.

Winnicott's main contention in the paper has to do with what he calls the "positive value of destructiveness." Paradoxically linking object permanence with destructiveness, he argues that objects become real by virtue of their capacity to survive the subject's destructiveness. Otherness comes through mother's survival of baby's fantasied attacks. When frustration reaches a certain level, baby attacks the fantasied image of mother and destroys her. But then real mother gives real comfort and contradicts the imagined state of affairs. Repeated experiences of this kind gradually lead to a distinction between inner and outer, imaginary and real. Objects begin to exist "outside the area . . . set up by the

subject's projective mental mechanisms'' (p. 227). Only
then, Winnicott argues, can a world of shared reality be
created "which the subject can use and which can feed back
other-than-me substance into the subject" (p. 227). Object
use, in other words, constitutes a more advanced and sophisticated stage of development than does object relating.

Winnicott drew clear therapeutic implications from his
own line of reasoning: the analyst's interpretations have
little meaning if they cannot be "used" by the patient, and
they can only be used if the patient is able to "place the
analyst outside the area of subjective phenomena" (p. 219).
Winnicott is alluding to the delicate balance that is struck
between safety and assertion. The survival of the destroyed
analyst means that this same analyst can be safely hated,
repudiated, and rebelled against, all of which strengthens
his being loved and relied upon. Conversely, Winnicott
implies that unless one tolerates the ruthless side of one's
character, it is impossible to have the full experience of the
survival of the analyst. From the standpoint of technique,
Winnicott was arguing that the analyst must learn to "wait
and wait for the natural evolution of the transference arising
out of the patient's growing trust . . . and avoid breaking up
this natural process by making interpretations" (p. 219).
Trust, in other words, is the confidence gained by the
analyst's survival of the patient's destructiveness.

"The Use of an Object" is a dazzling piece of insight,
condensing many of the themes that were of concern to
Winnicott and demonstrating both the depth of his dialogue
with psychoanalytic theory and his profound need to make
a personal and creative statement. It amplified his view of
aggression as traceable to the prenatal mobility of the infant,
the aliveness of the tissues, the twisting and turnings of the
unborn baby, the impulses of the fetus that make for movement rather than stillness. Winnicott called this a life force.
"At origin," Winnicott (1950–1955) writes, "aggressiveness
is almost synonymous with activity" (p. 204). Instinctual
aggressiveness, he (1939) asserted elsewhere, is "originally

part of appetite, or some form of instinctual love. It is something that increases during excitement, and the exercise of it is highly pleasurable" (pp. 87–88).

This view of aggression is actually consistent with Freud's earliest formulations. Originally, Freud (1915a) was reluctant to postulate a specific instinct to account for aggressive tendencies because he saw them as an essential characteristic of instincts in general. "Every instinct," he wrote, anticipating Winnicott, "is a piece of activity" (p. 122). In 1920, however, Freud first postulated the idea of a death instinct, which, from Winnicott's perspective, was totally unacceptable. Winnicott (1971b) saw no evidence for it and felt it "could be described as a reassertion of the principle of Original Sin" (p. 82).

Winnicott also rejected the conventional wisdom that aggression was solely reactive to frustration. Characteristically, he turned the idea on its head and suggested that the aggressive impulse actually invites opposition; it seeks obstacles. "In the early stages," writes Winnicott (1950–1955), "when the Me and the Not-Me are being established, it is the aggressive component that more surely drives the individual to a need for a Not-Me or for an object that is felt to be external" (p. 215). The resistance of the external world establishes a boundary through which differentiation and self-definition come into being.

It is most striking how Winnicott's ideas about the positive value of aggression parallel, in an uncanny way, his personal process of differentiation and self-definition, especially in regard to Melanie Klein. Winnicott knocks up against Kleinian doctrine, strikes at it, tears it down, and, in the process, appreciates its resilience, yet establishes his own distinct identity. In "The Use of an Object" (1968c) this is specifically evident in respect to two themes: projection and morality.

In Winnicott's view, the Kleinian model failed to give a coherent account of the reality of the external world. It eliminated from its purview environmental factors, except insofar as the environment was understood in terms of projective mechanisms. Instead, Winnicott argues, the object, if it is to be used, "must necessarily be real in the sense of being part of shared reality, not a bundle of projections" (1968c, p. 221). From Winnicott's perspective, projective mechanisms "assist in the act of *noticing what is there*, but they are not *the reason why the object is there*" (p. 223). Again, the implications for treatment were evident: the analyst must "take into account the nature of the object, not as a projection, but as a thing in itself."

For decades, Winnicott had been trying to influence Klein to give greater consideration to the significance of environmental factors. As John Padel (1978) noted, nearly all Winnicott's papers had,

> as a counterpoint to their explicit themes, a ground-base of persuasion to her to let up a bit . . . to accept that mother and infant began as one and stayed as one until the infant began to develop a self with a boundary between the inside and the outside . . . to bethink her that the infant's psychopathology was the mother's own in the first instance. [pp. 28–29]

Winnicott's descriptions of mother–infant interactions, dependence, actual omnipotence, primary maternal preoccupation, transitional objects, holding, handling, object presenting, de-adaptation, and impingements were all ways of including the actual environmental conditions in the equation of psychic development.

"The Use of an Object" not only reinforces Winnicott's contention that real objects play a vital role by virtue of their resiliency, but offers a radical model as to how all of external reality—and not only objects—is constituted. "The baby's use of the non-human environment," Winnicott (1968e) wrote elsewhere, "depends upon the previous use of a human environment" (p. 93).

On the one hand, Winnicott (1968c) stakes a claim for

what he calls "primary creativity" in which there must necessarily be a subjective constructivist element in perception for it to feel real. Creative apperception is an essential element of perception. At the same time, however, implicit in his argument is that there is a continuous unconscious destructive process. The moment reality is objectively perceived, it is destroyed in unconscious fantasy. It is the indifference of the material world to the ruthless fantasies that allows the child to emerge from the cocoon of omnipotence. The child appreciates the survivability of the external world and "gains immeasurably" because now the external world can "contribute in to the subject according to its own properties" (p. 223). Perception itself, Winnicott implies, operates on a backdrop of reality being continuously destroyed and created so as to achieve and reachieve a status beyond the individual's omnipotent control.

It is difficult to appreciate Winnicott's views about the positive value of destructiveness in constituting external reality unless one includes in the account his fundamental suppositions regarding morality. After all, temperamentally, he was far from nihilism. "We need to abandon absolutely," he (1966c) wrote, "the theory that children can be born innately amoral" (p. 111). Winnicott believed—and he seemed to differ on this point from Klein—that individuals are born with an innate morality that expresses itself in a powerful urge to ensure the survival of personal integrity. As he (1963e) put it,

> The fiercest morality is that of early infancy, and this persists as a streak in human nature that can be discerned throughout an individual's life. Immorality for the infant is to *comply at the expense of a personal way of life*. For instance, a child of any age may feel that to eat is wrong, even to the extent of dying for the principle. [p. 102]

Together with this fierce and uncompromising preservation of integrity, however, comes a developing concern for others. This part of Winnicott's theory owed much to Melanie Klein, who linked guilt to the capacity to tolerate ambivalence and introduced the notion of reparation. The infant begins to experience anxiety, writes Winnicott (1963a), "because if he consumes the mother he will lose her" (p. 76). The newly integrated infant, in other words, is beginning to experience some sense of responsibility for its own destructive fantasies. What mitigates the anxiety is the "growing confidence that there will be an opportunity for contributing-in, for giving to the environment-mother, a confidence which makes the infant able to hold the anxiety" (p. 77).

A benign cycle is established: instinct drives lead to ruthless usage of objects, then to a sense of guilt that is allayed by opportunities to contribute to the environment-mother. When confidence in this process is established, the "infant is now becoming able to be concerned, to take responsibility for his own instinctual impulses and the functions that belong to them" (p. 77). What distinguishes Winnicott's formulation from that of Klein's is his emphasis on how it is the mother's reliable presence which is absolutely crucial for the benign cycle to be completed; she must be there to give opportunities for, and acknowledge the effort behind, reparative gestures.

Winnicott's vision of maturity is incomplete without taking into account the twin capacities for concern and use of objects. In each, the survival of the object plays a central role, and both result in the ability to tolerate ambivalence and personal aggression. The use of an object does not mean its ruthless exploitation; it refers to the joy inherent in being enriched by the particular qualities found outside one's omnipotent control. The beginnings of social responsibility and the ability to make use of other-than-me substances for personal growth are rooted in the survival of objects.

But—and this is typical of Winnicott—in fiercely but gently revising the Kleinian suppositions, he offers an idiosyncratic vocabulary that introduces some confusion and doubt. First, his use of the term "survival" is somewhat vague. At times, he seems to be referring to the mother or analyst's continuing availability or presence. At other times, survival implies that there is nonretaliation for aggressive acts. At still other times, survival appears to refer to the patient's verbal expression of destructive impulses, followed by the experience that these verbalized impulses don't destroy the actual object that leads to an abandonment of magical thinking.

Furthermore, Winnicott (1968c) suggests a previously unheard of distinction between object relating and object usage. Object relating he reserves for the experience of the subject as an isolate. In object relating the subject "allows certain alterations in the self to take place, of a kind that has caused us to invent the term 'cathexis' " (p. 220). The object, in other words, becomes meaningful to the subject. But because object relating is essentially based on projective mechanisms, the object is still inside the area of the subject's omnipotent control. Object usage, on the other hand, implies that the subject has developed the capacity to tolerate the recognition of the object as an entity in its own right, as beyond its power, and, therefore, real. The object must do something for this capacity to develop: it must survive.

Winnicott's use of the term "use" had a history of its own. His first known reference to it appeared in some notes he made in April 1965 while he rode home on a train after giving a talk about freedom and control in progressive schools (Winnicott 1989). Two years later, he (1968e) ended a public lecture by remarking how great a compliment it is to be both found and used. Surprised by his own usage, he next set out to explore what he, himself, had meant when he employed the term. What he discovered was that he was referring both to the use the patient may make of an analyst and to the prototype, "the use the baby makes of the mother in a healthy experience of the nursing couple" (Winnicott

1989, p. 233). He recognized that for a long time, during many analyses, patients were actually protecting him from being used by them.

The creative origins of the "Use of an Object" paper, however, ran far deeper than his idiosyncratic use of the term "use." Winnicott not only knew how to evolve a theory out of clinical moments, but he was also in incessant and fruitful dialogue with his own unconscious processes. In this particular case, the ideas articulated in the paper came to him first in the form of a dream he had in 1963 while reviewing Jung's autobiography (Winnicott 1989, pp. 228–230). The backdrop for the dream was his impression, while reading the autobiography, that Jung was not suffi- ciently in contact with his own primitive destructive im- pulses. The dream had particular significance to Winnicott because, as he wrote to a colleague,

> it cleared up the mystery of an element of my psychology that analysis could not reach, namely, the feeling that I would be all right if someone would split my head open (front to back) and take out something (tumor, abscess, sinus, suppuration) that exists and makes itself felt right in the centre behind the root of the nose. [p. 228]

The dream had three parts. In the first, there was absolute destruction and Winnicott was "part of the world, and of all people, and therefore I was being destroyed." In the second part, there was absolute destruction and Winni- cott was the destructive agent. In the final scene, Winnicott, in the dream, awakens, and, as he does, he is cognizant of each of the first two segments. "I was awake in the dream," writes Winnicott, "and I knew I had dreamed of being destroyed and of being the destroying agent." This had tremendous import for Winnicott in analyzing the dream, for it signified that there was no dissociation, that "the three I's [in the dream] were altogether in touch with each other" (p. 229).

The conclusions Winnicott drew from this dream anticipated the ideas he was to express five years later in "Use of an Object." As he wrote to a colleague:

> I had an acute awareness . . . that destructiveness belongs to relating to objects that are outside the subjective world or the area of omnipotence. In other words, first there is the creativeness that belongs to being alive, and the world is only a subjective world. Then there is the objectively perceived world and absolute destruction of it and all its details. . . . In health the infant is helped by being given (by ordinary devoted Mum) areas of experience of omnipotence while experimenting with excursions over the line into the wasteland of destroyed reality. The wasteland turns out to have features in its own right, or survival value, etc, and surprisingly the individual child finds total destruction does not mean total destruction. [pp. 229–230]

Winnicott's "Use of an Object" paper generated a lively response among the discussants at the New York Psychoanalytic Society. Edith Jacobson (1968) led off the discussion by questioning Winnicott's idiosyncratic distinction between object relating and object use. She sharply differed from his view, arguing that his portrayal of object relating was better described as narcissistic object relationships and identifications. Jacobson could also not understand Winnicott's meaning of "destructive attack" and "survival" or why he felt that there is necessarily a destruction of the object in fantasy between the stage of relating to and using an object. The case material that accompanied the paper was, in her opinion, unconvincing. Although she agreed that aggression has some positive value, she felt that Winnicott had "overlooked those psychotic persons who are extremely destructive and whose patient therapists survive the destructive impulse without the positive results such as he describes" (p. 4). All in all, Jacobson felt that Winnicott had "made a rather extreme statement."

Jacobson was followed by Samuel Ritvo (Milrod 1968), who also noted Winnicott's different usage of the term "object relating." Ritvo, like Jacobson, could not understand the statement that "acceptance of the object outside the subject's omnipotent control meant the destruction of the object" (p. 4). He believed that the developmental process by which objects are accepted as existing outside the self outlined by Winnicott could be better reformulated in terms of the "functional capacity of the ego to tolerate the qualities of delay and lack of gratification, and their accompanying anxiety reaction" (p. 4). Adopting an ego perspective, Ritvo suggested that object permanence is "based on the capacity to tolerate frustration, a capacity which depends on the neutralization of aggression" (p. 4). He accepted, however, that the ability to neutralize aggression can "depend heavily on the facilitating environment."

The third discussant, Bernard Fine (1968), was equally critical of Winnicott's formulations. As one of the editors of the American Psychoanalytic Association's *Glossary of Psychoanalytic Terms and Concepts* and chairman of the indexing committee, Fine found it particularly irksome that Winnicott was loose in the way he employed words. "Psychoanalytic literature and communication has," he argued, "often foundered or at least became confused when it took over widely used terms from the general language" (p. 8). The idiosyncratic use of the word "use" does "us and Dr. Winnicott a disservice, and can make for considerable ambiguity. . . . As a scientific label, it has many drawbacks" (p. 8). More importantly, it was Fine's view that Winnicott's sharp separation between object relating and object usage "does not seem to be born out by previous usage in the literature, nor does it seem to me to add any significant clarification or convenience to our theoretical or clinical language or concepts" (p. 8).

Fine's criticism was not restricted to semantics. He argued that it is neither clear nor proven that the subject destroys the object. He noted as well the absence of any reference to "the significance of libidinal components in helping toward the survival of the object" (p. 3). The libidinal tie, he argued, exists both before and after separation from the object, and so "it is involved in the feeling of 'basic trust' in the object" (p. 3). It is the positive libidinal tie to the analyst that makes it possible that the "affective storm of rage at 'destruction' of the analyst in conscious or unconscious fantasy is traversed safely" (p. 3). Fine also felt that Winnicott had paid insufficient attention to the contribution of ego development in developing a "preponderance of pleasure in separate functioning." Winnicott's idea of the destruction of the object upon separation was, in his mind, "a great modification" that "is not substantiated."

Jacobson, Ritvo, and Fine were obviously somewhat bewildered by Winnicott's formulations. They were put off by his personal use of language. They felt that many of his ideas were just another way of stating what could be better described using the vocabulary of narcissistic identifications, libidinal economy, and the functional capacities of the ego. Winnicott's central proposition regarding the destruction of the object in unconscious fantasy as a prelude to its use seemed to them perplexing, extreme, or unwarranted.

How did Winnicott respond to these criticisms? The question is important, particularly since a myth has emerged that Winnicott's ensuing illness was a result of the way he was treated by the New York Psychoanalytic Society. According to a summary of the proceedings prepared by David Milrod (1968), Winnicott responded to the discussants in a "charming and whimsical fashion," saying that his "concept was torn to pieces and that he would be happy to give it up" (p. 6). He felt that "he had been trying to say something but had not succeeded" (p. 6).

It is evident from Winnicott's remarks that what was of greatest importance to him—more so than the theoretical propositions—was what his clinical intuition led him to believe to be true: that "there are patients, not ordinary patients, for whom arriving at a point where they can use him as an analyst is more important than his interpretations to them" (p. 6). The crucial issue with these patients is that "they never take the risk of something and they protect the analyst from something" (p. 6). What is it, he wondered, that the analyst is protected from? "It is not merely anger," he thought, "but it is destructive" (pp. 6–7).

Winnicott undoubtedly felt that he had failed to communicate something that was vitally important to him. He was convinced that the primitive love impulse contains an irreducible core of aggressiveness, but he didn't know how to make this intuition, which felt so real to him, feel real to others. He had avidly wanted his colleagues to receive his gesture, but he left feeling he hadn't gotten through to them. This was reminiscent of similar experiences he had had with the Kleinian group in general, and with his second analyst, Riviere, in particular. Once again, he was "wanting something which I have no right to expect," something "in the nature of a therapeutic act" in which others move "towards the gesture that I make in this paper" (Rodman 1987, p. 34).

On the basis of the available evidence, however, the assertion that Winnicott's physical illness is linked to the way he was received by his colleagues at the Psychoanalytic Society remains problematic at best. On the one hand, the discourse was in many ways within the traditional parameters for that scientific community. A review of the transcripts alone points to a spirited intellectual exchange without signs of personal animosity or rancor. Still, some participants at the meeting clearly recall an atmosphere of profound intolerance towards Winnicott's originality (Annie Bergman, personal communication, June 16, 1992). In the aftermath of the formal presentation, one participant noticed Winnicott to be visibly shaken and overheard him commenting that he now understood better why America was in Vietnam (Steve Ellman, personal communication, May 15, 1992). Winnicott obviously felt he was the target of aggression. The least one could say is that there was an

absence of openness in respect to the ingenuity of Winnicott's formulations. Both Winnicott's exceptional need to
find a personal route from clinical experience to theory
building and his desire to make theory feel real to himself by
being splendidly original had apparently engendered suspi-
cion among the more doctrinaire and close-minded elements
within the New York Psychoanalytic Society.

What is more, Winnicott went into the proceedings
feeling ill. This might help explain why he may have felt
particularly vulnerable. In a private letter to Anna Freud
written while he was convalescing at home in January 1969,
he confided in her that he was already ill before the talk, but
that "I think this was not noticed." He also confessed having
gotten "considerable benefit from the reaction of the three
discussants, so that I am now in the process of rewriting it in
a quite different language." Still, he was obviously peeved
that the three discussants had monopolized all the available
time such that there "could be no response from the very
large audience which collected for some reason unspeci-
fied" (Rodman 1987, p. 185). Perhaps Winnicott was still
hoping for some sign that someone in New York—if not
Jacobson, Ritvo, and Fine—had received his gesture.

Winnicott developed pulmonary edema while he was
still in New York. He was taken to the cardiac care unit at
Lenox Hill Hospital, where he was treated by a Dr. Cramp-
ton. A few weeks later he was released and returned to
London, where he continued to rest. In late January 1969, he
wrote a letter to his treating physician:

> I recognise that I was in a rather peculiar state of mind
> during the illness and I am sure that you and your col-
> leagues found me at times rather trying as a patient. As you
> did say to my wife, and this was helpful, you knew that the
> dependence of a patient who is very ill is a difficult thing,
> especially for a doctor who has at any rate some knowl-
> edge of what is going on. [quoted in Rudnytsky 1991, p.
> 338]

Once again the theme of dependence, so central to Winnicott's view of infancy, reemerged in his private life. It was obviously difficult for Winnicott to acknowledge and accept his dependence on others. Fifty years earlier, after breaking his collarbone, he decided that becoming a physician was the "only way out" of the terrible situation whereby, "for the rest of my life I should have to depend on doctors if I damaged myself or became ill" (C. Winnicott 1989, p. 10). No wonder he was so extraordinarily sensitive to the primacy of dependence both in development and treatment.

Winnicott's capacity to play survived despite the enforced dependence he was compelled to endure. His final year was spent in revising and editing his papers, corresponding extensively with colleagues, well-wishers, students, and people seeking his help. He still played with his wife Clare. It is emblematic of his playful spirit that his final words, spoken to his wife after viewing a televised film about antique cars, were: "What a happy-making film." He died in his sleep.

"The Use of an Object" was Winnicott's last attempt to make public his obscure sense of what enables the individual to survive as both scientist and dreamer. One can only be a scientist if the external world is perceived as being real and distinct enough to be worthy of objective investigation. One can only be a dreamer if internal reality has become sufficiently real and distinct enough to respect. Winnicott—the scientist and dreamer that he was—plumbed the depths of both worlds, in search of what felt real.

References

Bergman, A., and Ellman, S. (1985). Margaret S. Mahler: symbiosis and separation-individuation. In *Beyond Freud: A Study of Modern Psychoanalytic Theorists*, ed. J. Reppen, pp. 231–256. Hillsdale, NJ: The Analytic Press.

Bergmann, M. S. (1987). *The Anatomy of Loving*. New York: Fawcett Columbine.

Bollas, C. (1991). *Forces of Destiny: Psychoanalysis and Human Idiom*. London: Free Association.

Brome, V. (1983). *Ernest Jones: Freud's Alter Ego*. New York: W. W. Norton.

Carroll, L. (1960). *The Annotated Alice: Alice's Adventures in Wonderland & Through the Looking Glass*. New York: Clarkson N. Potter.

Casement, P. (1985). *Learning From the Patient*. New York: Guilford.

Cavell, M. (1988). Interpretation, psychoanalysis, and the philosophy of mind. *Journal of the American Psychoanalytic Association* 36:859–880.

Clancier, A., and Kalmanovitch, J. (1987). *Winnicott and Paradox: From Birth to Creation*. London: Tavistock.

_____ (1990). A splash of paint in his style. In *Tactics and Techniques in Psychoanalytic Therapy*, ed. P. Giovacchini, pp. 41–59. Northvale, NJ: Jason Aronson.

Colie, R. L. (1966). *Paradoxia Epidemica: The Renaissance Tradition of Paradox*. Princeton, NJ: Princeton University Press.

Darwin, C. (1965). *The Expression of Emotions in Man and Animals*. Chicago: University of Chicago Press.

Davis, M. (1987). The writing of D. W. Winnicott. *International Review of Psycho-Analysis* 14:491–502.

Davis, M., and Wallbridge, D. (1981). *Boundary and Space: An Introduction to the Work of D. W. Winnicott*. New York: Brunner/Mazel.

Eigen, M. (1981a). The area of faith in Winnicott, Lacan and Bion. *International Journal of Psycho-Analysis* 62:413–433.

_____ (1981b). Guntrip's analysis with Winnicott: a critique of Glatzer and Evans. *Contemporary Psychoanalysis* 17:103–117.

_____ (1991). Winnicott's area of freedom: the uncompromisable. In *Liminality and Transitional Phenomena,* ed. N. Schwartz-Salant and M. Stein, pp. 67–88. Wilmette, IL: Chiron.

Ellman, S. (1991). *Freud's Technique Papers: A Contemporary Perspective*. Northvale, NJ: Jason Aronson.

Fenichel, O. (1945). *The Psychoanalytic Theory of Neurosis*. New York: W. W. Norton.

Ferenczi, S. (1988). *The Clinical Diary of Sandor Ferenczi*. Ed. J. Dupont. Trans. M. Balint and N. Z. Jackson. Cambridge, MA: Harvard University Press.

Fine, B. (1968). Discussion of Dr. D. W. Winnicott's paper, "The Use of an Object," November 12, 1968. Unpublished Manuscript. Courtesy of New York Psychoanalytic Society.

Freud, S. (1895). Project for a scientific psychology. *Standard Edition* 1:283–387.

_____ (1900). The interpretation of dreams. *Standard Edition* 4,5:xxiii–627.

_____ (1905). Three essays on the theory of sexuality. *Standard Edition* 7:125–245.

_____ (1911a). Psycho-analytic notes on an autobiographical account of a case of paranoia. *Standard Edition* 12:1–82.

_____ (1911b). Formulations on the two principles of mental functioning. *Standard Edition* 12:218–226.

_____ (1913a). Totem and taboo. *Standard Edition* 13:ix–161.

_____ (1913b). The disposition to obsessional neuroses. *Standard Edition* 12:311–326.

_____ (1914). On narcissism: an introduction. *Standard Edition* 14:67–102.

_____ (1915a). Instincts and their vicissitudes. *Standard Edition* 14:117–140.

_____ (1915b). The unconscious. *Standard Edition* 14:159–215.

_____ (1916–1917). *A General Introduction to Psychoanalysis*. Trans. J. Riviere. New York: Pocket Books.

_____ (1920). Beyond the pleasure principle. *Standard Edition* 18:3–64.

_____ (1923). The ego and the id. *Standard Eition* 19:1–66.

_____ (1925). On negation. *Standard Edition* 19:233–239.

_____ (1926). The question of lay analysis. *Standard Edition* 20:177–258.

_____ (1930). Civilization and its discontents. *Standard Edition* 21:59–145.

_____ (1933). Why war? *Standard Edition* 22:197–215.

_____ (1937). Analysis terminable and interminable. *Standard Edition* 23:209–253.

Fromm, M. G. (1989). Winnicott's work in relation to classical psychoanalysis and ego psychology. In *The Facilitating Environment: Clinical Applications of Winnicott's Theory*, ed. M. G. Fromm and B. L. Smith, pp. 3–26. Madison, CT: International Universities Press.

Fuller, P. (1987). Mother and child in Henry Moore and Winnicott. *Winnicott Studies: The Journal of the Squiggle Foundation* 2:72–86.

Gaddini, E. (1969). On imitation. *International Journal of Psycho-Analysis* 50:475–484.

Gay, P. (1987). *A Godless Jew: Freud, Atheism, and the Making of Psychoanalysis*. New Haven, CT: Yale University Press.

Gay, V. P. (1983). Winnicott's religious studies: the resurrection of the cultural hero. *Journal of the American Academy of Religion* 51:371–395.

Gillespie, W. H. (1971). A tribute read at Dr. Winnicott's funeral. *International Journal of Psycho-Analysis* 52:227.

Gould, S. J. (1977). *Ever Since Darwin: Reflections in Natural History*. New York: W. W. Norton.

Greenberg, J., and Mitchell, S. (1983). *Object Relations in Psychoanalytic Theory*. Cambridge, MA: Harvard University Press.

Grolnick, S. (1990). *The Work and Play of Winnicott*. Northvale, NJ: Jason Aronson.

Grolnick, S., and Barkin, L. (1978). *Between Reality and Fantasy: Winnicott's Concepts of Transitional Objects and Phenomena*. Northvale, NJ: Jason Aronson.

Grosskurth, P. (1986). *Melanie Klein: Her World and Her Work*. New York: Alfred A. Knopf.

Guntrip, H. (1975). My experience of analysis with Fairbairn and Winnicott. *International Review of Psycho-Analysis* 2:145–156.

Hamilton, V. (1987). Rhythm and interpretation in maternal care and psychoanalysis. *Winnicott Studies: The Journal of the Squiggle Foundation* 2:32–48.

Holmes, R. (1991). Review of *Romantic Medicine and John Keats* by Hermione de Almeida. *New York Review of Books*, June 27, 1991, pp. 51–52.

Holroyd, M. (1973). *Unreceived Opinions*. New York: Holt, Reinhart and Winston.

Holt, R. R. (1982). The Manifest and Latent Meanings of Metapsychology. *The Annual of Psychoanalysis* 10:233–255.

Hopkins, B. (1984). Keats' "Negative Capability" and Winnicott's creative play. *American Imago* 41:85–100.

Hughes, J. (1989). *Reshaping the Psychoanalytic Domain: The Work of Melanie Klein, W. R. D. Fairbairn, and D. W. Winnicott.* Berkeley, CA: University of California Press.

Hutter, A. (1982). Poetry in psychoanalysis: Hopkins, Rossetti, and Winnicott. *International Review of Psycho-Analysis,* 9:303–316.

Jacobson, E. (1968). Discussion of "The Use of an Object" by Dr. D. W. Winnicott, Nov. 12, 1968. Unpublished Manuscript. Courtesy of New York Psychoanalytic Society.

James, M. (1982). Review of *Boundary and Space: An Introduction to the Work of D. W. Winnicott. International Journal of Psycho-Analysis* 63:493–497.

_____ (1988). Review of human nature by D. W. Winnicott. *British Journal of Psychotherapy* 5:263–266.

Keats, J. (1958). *The Letters of John Keats 1814–1821.* Ed. H. E. Rollins. Cambridge, MA: Harvard University Press.

Khan, M. (1961). Private letter to Dr. Frankel, June 22, 1961. D. W. Winnicott Correspondence. Archives of Psychiatry, New York Hospital-Cornell Medical Center.

_____ (1975). Introduction to D. W. Winnicott. In *Through Pediatrics to Psychoanalysis,* pp.11–48. New York: Basic Books.

Klein, M., and Isaacs, S. (1952). *Developments in Psychoanalysis.* London: Hogarth.

Kohon, G., ed. (1986). *The British School of Psychoanalysis: The Independent Tradition.* London: Free Association.

Kuhn, T. (1962). *The Structure of Scientific Revolutions.* 2nd ed. Chicago: University of Chicago Press.

Lambert, K. (1987). Some religious implications of the work

of Freud, Jung and Winnicott. *Winnicott Studies: The Journal of the Squiggle Foundation* 2:49–70.

Laplanche, J. (1976). *Life and Death in Psychoanalysis*. Baltimore: Johns Hopkins University Press.

Laplanche, J., and Pontalis, J.-B. (1973). *The Language of Psychoanalysis*. New York: W. W. Norton.

Lear, J. (1990). *Love and its Place in Nature*. New York: Farrar, Straus & Giroux.

Limentani, A. (1989). *Between Freud and Klein*. London: Free Association.

Little, M. L. (1990). *Psychotic Anxieties and Containment: A Personal Record of an Analysis with Winnicott*. Northvale, NJ: Jason Aronson.

Meisel, P., and Kendrick, W., eds. (1985). *Bloomsbury/Freud: The Letters of James and Alix Strachey, 1924–1925*. New York: Basic Books.

Meissner, W. W. (1992). Religious thinking as transitional conceptualization. *The Psychoanalytic Review* 79:175–196.

Mendez, A., and Fine, R. (1976). A short history of the British School of Object Relations and Ego Psychology. *Bulletin of the Menninger Clinic* 40:357–382.

Miller, J. (1987). Neither fish nor fowl nor good red herring. In *Winnicott Studies: The Journal of the Squiggle Foundation* 2:4–18.

Milner, M. (1969). *Hands of the Living God: An Account of a Psychoanalytic Treatment*. London: Hogarth.

_____ (1972). For Dr. Winnicott Memorial Meeting, January 19, 1972. London, British Institute of Psychoanalysis.

_____ (1978). D. W. Winnicott and the two-way journey. In *Between Reality and Fantasy: Winnicott's Concepts of Transitional Objects and Phenomena*, ed. S. Grolnick and L. Barkin, pp. 37–42. Northvale, NJ: Jason Aronson.

Milrod, D. (1968). Summary of Discussion of "The Use of an Object" by D. W. Winnicott, November 12, 1968. Unpublished Manuscript. Courtesy of New York Psychoanalytic Society.

Modell, A. H. (1983). Review of *Boundary and Space: An Introduction to the Work of D. W. Winnicott*. *International Journal of Psycho-Analysis* 64:111–112.

Murray, L. (1989). Winnicott and the developmental psychology of infancy. *British Journal of Psychotherapy* 5:333–348.

Ogden, T. (1989). *The Primitive Edge of Experience*. Northvale, NJ: Jason Aronson.

——— (1990). *The Matrix of the Mind*. Northvale, NJ: Jason Aronson.

Padel, J. (1978). Positions, stages, attitudes, or modes of being? *Bulletin of the European Psycho-Analytic Federation* 12:26–31.

——— (1991). The psychoanalytic theories of Melanie Klein and D. W. Winnicott and their interaction in the British Society of Psychoanalysis. *The Psychoanalytic Review* 78:325–345.

Phillips, A. (1988). *Winnicott*. Cambridge, MA: Harvard University Press.

Pine, F. (1990). *Drive, Ego, Object, and Self*. New York: Basic Books.

Pribram, K. H., and Gill, M. M. (1976). *Freud's "Project" Reassessed*. New York: Basic Books.

Prickett, S. (1970). *Coleridge and Wordsworth: The Poetry of Growth*. Cambridge, MA: Cambridge University Press.

Rayner, E. (1991). *The Independent Mind in British Psychoanalysis*. Northvale, NJ: Jason Aronson.

Reisner, S. (1989). Reclaiming metapsychology: classical revisionism, seduction, and the self in Freudian psychoanalysis. Paper presented at the APA, Division 39, April, Boston, Mass.

Riviere, J. (1991). *The Inner World and Joan Riviere: Collected Papers, 1920–1958*. Ed. A. Hughes. London: Karnac.

Rodman, F. R., ed. (1987). *The Spontaneous Gesture, Selected Letters of D. W. Winnicott*. Cambridge, MA: Harvard University Press.

Rose, G. (1978). The creativity of everyday life. In *Between Reality and Fantasy: Winnicott's Concepts of Transitional Objects and Phenomena*, ed. S. Grolnick and L. Barkin, pp. 345–362. Northvale, NJ: Jason Aronson.

Rudnytsky, P. L. (1989). Winnicott and Freud. *Psychoanalytic Study of the Child* 44:331–350. New Haven, CT: Yale University Press.

_____ (1991). *The Psychoanalytic Vocation: Rank, Winnicott, and the Legacy of Freud*. New Haven, CT: Yale University Press.

Rycroft, C. (1985). *Psychoanalysis and Beyond*. Chicago: University of Chicago Press.

Semmel, B. (1973). *The Methodist Revolution*. New York: Basic Books.

Siegelman, E. (1990). *Metaphor and Meaning in Psychotherapy*. New York: Guilford.

Smith, D. (1985). Freud's developmental approach to narcissism: a concise review. *International Journal of Psycho-Analysis* 66:489–497.

Solomon, J. C. (1963). Alice and the red king: a psychoanalytic view of existence. *International Journal of Psycho-Analysis* 44:63–73.

Strachey, J. (1934). The Nature of the Therapeutic Action of Psycho-Analysis. *International Journal of Psycho-Analysis* 15:427–459.

Ticho, E. (1974). Donald W. Winnicott, Martin Buber, and the theory of personal relationships. *Psychiatry* 37:240–252.

Tizard, J. P. M. (1971). A tribute read at Dr. Winnicott's funeral. *International Journal of Psycho-Analysis* 52:226.

_____ (1981). Donald Winnicott: the President's view of a past president. *Journal of the Royal Society of Medicine* April, 1981.

Turner, J. (1988). Wordsworth and Winnicott in the area of play. *International Review of Psycho-Analysis* 15:481–497.

Winnicott, C. (1978). D. W. W.: a reflection. In *Between Reality and Fantasy: Winnicott's Concepts of Transitional Objects and Phenomena*, ed. S. G. Grolnick and L. Barkin, pp. 15–34. Northvale, NJ: Jason Aronson.

_____ (1983). Interview with Dr. Michael Neve, June, 1983. D. W. Winnicott Correspondence. Archives of Psychiatry, New York Hospital–Cornell Medical Center.

_____ (1989). D. W. W.: a reflection. In *Psycho-Analytic Explorations*, pp. 1–18. Cambridge, MA: Harvard University Press.

Winnicott Correspondence (1949–1970). Courtesy of Archives of Psychiatry, New York Hospital–Cornell Medical Center.

Winnicott, D. W. (undated). Introduction on the Occasion of the 8th Ernest Jones Lecture. Winnicott Correspondence. Courtesy of Archives of Psychiatry, New York Hospital–Cornell Medical Center.

_____ (1931). A note on normality and anxiety. In *Collected Papers: Through Paediatrics to Psycho-analysis*, pp. 3–21. New York: Basic Books, 1975.

_____ (1935). The manic defence. *Collected Papers: Through Paediatrics to Psycho-analysis,* pp. 129–144. New York: Basic Books, 1975.

_____ (1936). Appetite and emotional disorder. In *Collected Papers: Through Paediatrics to Psycho-analysis*, pp. 33–51. New York: Basic Books, 1975.

_____ (1939). Aggression and its roots. In *Deprivation and Delinquency*, pp. 84–99. London: Routledge, 1990.

_____ (1941). The observation of infants in a set situation. In *Collected Papers: Through Paediatrics to Psycho-Analysis*, pp. 52–69. New York: Basic Books, 1975.

_____ (1942). Child department consultations. In *Collected Papers: Through Paediatrics to Psycho-Analysis*, pp.70–84. New York: Basic Books, 1975.

_____ (1944). Ocular psychoneuroses of childhood. In *Collected Papers: Through Paediatrics to Psycho-Analysis*, pp. 85–90. New York: Basic Books, 1975.

———— (1945a). Primitive emotional development. In *Collected Papers: Through Paediatrics to Psycho-analysis*, pp. 145–156. New York: Basic Books, 1975.

———— (1945b). Thinking and the unconscious. In *Home Is Where We Start From: Essays by a Psychoanalyst*, ed. C. Winnicott, R. Shepherd, and M. Davis, pp. 90–100. New York: W. W. Norton, 1986.

———— (1947). Hate in the countertransference. In *Collected Papers: Through Paediatrics to Psycho-analysis*, pp. 194–203. New York: Basic Books, 1975.

———— (1948a). Primary introduction to external reality. Unpublished Manuscript. Winnicott Correspondence. Courtesy of Archives of Psychiatry, New York Hospital–Cornell Medical Center.

———— (1948b). Paediatrics and psychiatry. In *Collected Papers: Through Paediatrics to Psycho-analysis*, pp. 157–173. New York: Basic Books, 1975.

———— (1949a). Mind and its relation to the psyche-soma. In *Collected Papers: Through Paediatrics to Psycho-analysis*, pp. 243–254. New York: Basic Books, 1975.

———— (1949b). Birth memories, birth trauma, and anxiety. In *Collected Papers: Through Paediatrics to Psycho-analysis*, pp. 174–193. New York: Basic Books, 1975.

———— (1950a). Growth and Development in Immaturity. In *The Family and Individual Development*, pp. 21–29. London: Routledge, 1989.

———— (1950b). Some thoughts on the meaning of the word "democracy." In *Home Is Where We Start From: Essays by a Psychoanalyst*, ed. C. Winnicott, R. Shepherd, and M. Davis, pp. 239–259. New York: W. W. Norton, 1986.

———— (1950–1955). Aggression in Relation to Emotional Development. In *Collected Papers: Through Paediatrics to Psycho-analysis*, pp. 204–218. New York: Basic Books, 1975.

———— (1952). Psychoses and child care. In *Collected Papers: Through Paediatrics to Psycho-analysis*, pp. 219–228. New York: Basic Books, 1975.

_____ (1953). Symptom tolerance in paediatrics: a case history. In *Collected Papers: Through Paediatrics to Psycho-analysis*, pp. 101–117. New York: Basic Books, 1975.

_____ (1954a). The depressive position in normal emotional development. In *Collected Papers: Through Paediatrics to Psycho-analysis*, pp. 262–277. New York: Basic Books, 1975.

_____ (1954b). Metapsychological and clinical aspects of regression within the psycho-analytical set-up. In *Collected Papers: Through Paediatrics to Psycho-analysis*, pp. 278–294. New York: Basic Books, 1975.

_____ (1954c). Withdrawal and regression. *The Maturational Process and the Facilitating Environment*, pp. 255–261. London: Hogarth, 1965.

_____ (1955). Group influences and the maladjusted child. In *The Family and Individual Development*, pp. 146–154. London: Routledge, 1989.

_____ (1956a). Primary maternal preoccupation. In *Collected Papers: Through Paediatrics to Psycho-analysis*, pp. 300–305. New York: Basic Books, 1975.

_____ (1956b). Paediatrics and childhood neurosis. In *Collected Papers: Through Paediatrics to Psycho-analysis*, pp. 316–321. New York: Basic Books, 1975.

_____ (1957a). The contribution of psycho-analysis to midwifery. In *The Family and Individual Development*, pp. 106–113. London: Routledge, 1989.

_____ (1957b). On the contribution of direct child observation to psycho-analysis. In *The Maturational Process and the Facilitating Environment*, pp. 109–114. London: Hogarth, 1965.

_____ (1957c). Integrative and disruptive factors in family life. In *The Family and Individual Development*, pp. 40–49. London: Routledge, 1989.

_____ (1957d). Excitement in the aetiology of coronary thrombosis. In *Psycho-Analytic Explorations*, ed. C. Winnicott, R. Shepherd, and M. Davis, pp. 34–38. Cambridge, MA: Harvard University Press, 1989.

_____ (1957e). The mother's contribution to society. In *Home Is Where We Start From: Essays by a Psychoanalyst*, ed. C. Winnicott, R. Shepherd, and M. Davis, pp. 123–127. New York: W. W. Norton, 1986.

_____ (1958a). The capacity to be alone. In *The Maturational Process and the Facilitating Environment*, pp. 29–36. London: Hogarth, 1965.

_____ (1958b). Child analysis in the latency period. In *The Maturational Process and the Facilitating Environment*, pp. 115–123. London: Hogarth, 1965.

_____ (1959–1964). Classification: is there a psycho-analytic contribution to psychiatric classification? In *The Maturational Process and the Facilitating Environment*, pp. 124–139. London: Hogarth, 1965.

_____ (1960a). Counter-transference. In *The Maturational Process and the Facilitating Environment*, pp. 158–165. London: Hogarth, 1965.

_____ (1960b). Joseph Sandler, comments on "On the Concept of the Superego." In *Psycho-Analytic Explorations*, ed. C. Winnicott, R. Shepherd, and M. Davis, pp. 465–473. Cambridge, MA: Harvard University Press, 1989.

_____ (1960c). On security. In *The Family and Individual Development*, pp. 30–33. London: Routledge, 1989.

_____ (1960d). The family and emotional maturity. In *The Family and Individual Development*, pp. 88–96. London: Routledge, 1989.

_____ (1960e). The effect of psychosis on family life. In *The Family and Individual Development*, pp. 61–78. London: Routledge, 1989.

_____ (1960f). Ego distortion in terms of true self and false self. In *The Maturational Process and the Facilitating Environment*, pp. 140–152. London: Hogarth, 1965.

_____ (1960g). The relationship of a mother to her baby at the beginning. In *The Family and Individual Development*, pp. 15–20. London: Routledge, 1989.

_____ (1960h). The theory of the parent–infant relationship.

In *The Maturational Process and the Facilitating Environment*, pp. 37–55. London: Hogarth, 1965.

―――― (1961a). Psychoanalysis and science: friends or relations. In *Home is Where We Start From: Essays by a Psychoanalyst*, ed. C. Winnicott, R. Shepherd, and M. Davis, pp. 13–18. New York: W. W. Norton, 1986.

―――― (1961b). Varieties of psychotherapy. In *Deprivation and Delinquency*, eds. C. Winnicott, R. Shepherd, and M. Davis, pp. 232–240. London: Routledge, 1990.

―――― (1961c). A personal view. *St. Mary's Hospital Gazette* 5:67, July-August.

―――― (1962a). Providing for the child in health and in crisis. In *The Maturational Process and the Facilitating Environment*, pp. 64–72. London: Hogarth, 1965.

―――― (1962b). Ego integration in child development. In *The Maturational Process and the Facilitating Environment*, pp. 56–63. London: Hogarth, 1965.

―――― (1962c). A personal view of the Kleinian contribution. In *The Maturational Process and the Facilitating Environment*, pp. 171–178. London: Hogarth, 1965.

―――― (1962d). The five year old. In *The Family and Individual Development*, pp. 34–39. London: Routledge, 1989.

―――― (1962f). The aims of psycho-analytical treatment. In *The Maturational Process and the Facilitating Environment*, pp. 166–170. London: Hogarth, 1965.

―――― (1963a). The development of the capacity for concern. In *The Maturational Process and the Facilitating Environment*, pp. 73–82. London: Hogarth, 1965.

―――― (1963b). Fear of breakdown. In *Psycho-Analytic Explorations*, ed. C. Winnicott, R. Shepherd, and M. Davis, pp. 87–95. Cambridge, MA: Harvard University Press, 1989.

―――― (1963c). Two notes on the use of silence. In *Psycho-Analytic Explorations*, ed. C. Winnicott, R. Shepherd, and M. Davis, pp. 81–86. Cambridge, MA: Harvard University Press, 1989.

_____ (1963d). Training for child psychiatry. In *The Maturational Process and the Facilitating Environment*, pp. 193–202. London: Hogarth, 1965.

_____ (1963e). Morals and education. In *The Maturational Process and the Facilitating Environment*, pp. 93–105. London: Hogarth, 1965.

_____ (1963f). From dependence towards independence in the development of the individual. In *The Maturational Process and the Facilitating Environment*, pp. 83–92. London: Hogarth, 1965.

_____ (1963g). Struggling through the doldrums. In *Deprivation and Delinquency*, ed. C. Winnicott, R. Shepherd, and M. Davis, pp. 145–155. London: Routledge, 1990.

_____ (1963h). Communicating and not communicating leading to a study of certain opposites. In *The Maturational Process and the Facilitating Environment*, pp. 179–192. London: Hogarth, 1965.

_____ (1964a). *The Child, the Family, and the Outside World*. Harmondsworth, England: Penguin.

_____ (1964b). C. G. Jung, a review of memories, dreams, reflections. In *Psycho-Analytic Explorations*, ed. C. Winnicott, R. Shepherd, and M. Davis, pp. 482–492. Cambridge, MA: Harvard University Press, 1989.

_____ (1964c). Youth will not sleep. In *Deprivation and Delinquency*, ed. C. Winnicott, R. Shepherd, and M. Davis, pp. 156–158. London: Routledge, 1990.

_____ (1964d). Psycho-somatic disorder. In *Psycho-Analytic Explorations*, ed. C. Winnicott, R. Shepherd, and M. Davis, pp. 103–114. Cambridge, MA: Harvard University Press.

_____ (1965a). Do progressive schools give too much freedom to the child? In *Deprivation and Delinquency*, ed. C. Winnicott, R. Shepherd, and M. Davis, pp. 209–219. London: Routledge, 1990.

_____ (1965b). The price of disregarding psychoanalytic research. In *Home Is Where We Start From: Essays by a Psychoanalyst*, ed. C. Winnicott, R. Shepherd, and

M. Davis, pp. 172–182. New York: W. W. Norton, 1986.

_____ (1965c). New light on children's thinking. In *Psycho-Analytic Explorations*, pp. 152–157. Cambridge, MA: Harvard University Press, 1989.

_____ (1966a). The child in the family group. In *Home Is Where We Start From: Essays by a Psychoanalyst*, ed. C. Winnicott, R. Shepherd, and M. Davis, pp. 128–141. New York: W. W. Norton, 1986.

_____ (1966b). The split-off male and female elements to be found in men and women. In *Psycho-Analytic Explorations*, ed. C. Winnicott, R. Shepherd, and M. Davis, pp. 169–188. Cambridge, MA: Harvard University Press, 1989.

_____ (1966c). The absence of a sense of guilt. In *Deprivation and Delinquency*, ed. C. Winnicott, R. Shepherd, and M. Davis, pp. 106–112. London: Routledge, 1990.

_____ (1966d). The ordinary devoted mother. In *Babies and their Mothers*, pp. 3–14. Reading, MA: Addison-Wesley, 1966.

_____ (1967a). The concept of a healthy individual. In *Home Is Where We Start From: Essays by a Psychoanalyst*, ed. C. Winnicott, R. Shepherd, and M. Davis, pp. 21–38. New York: W. W. Norton, 1986.

_____ (1967b). Postscript: D. W. W. on D. W. W. In *Psycho-Analytic Explorations*, ed. C. Winnicott, R. Shepherd, and M. Davis, pp. 569–582. Cambridge, MA: Harvard University Press, 1989.

_____ (1967c). Mirror-role of mother and family in child development. In *Playing and Reality*, pp. 130–138. New York: Penguin Books, 1971.

_____ (1967d). The concept of clinical regression compared with that of defence organisation. In *Psycho-Analytic Explorations*, ed. C. Winnicott, R. Shepherd, and M. Davis, pp. 193–199. Cambridge, MA: Harvard University Press, 1989.

_____ (1968a). The use of the word "use." In *Psycho-

Analytic Explorations, ed. C. Winnicott, R. Shepherd, and M. Davis, pp. 233–235. Cambridge, MA: Harvard University Press, 1989.

_____ (1968b). Sum, I am. In *Home Is Where We Start From: Essays by a Psychoanalyst*, ed. C. Winnicott, R. Shepherd, and M. Davis, pp. 55–64. New York: W. W. Norton, 1986.

_____ (1968c). The use of an object and relating through identifications. In *Psycho-Analytic Explorations*, ed. C. Winnicott, R. Shepherd, and M. Davis, pp. 218–227. Cambridge, MA: Harvard University Press, 1989.

_____ (1968d). Children learning. In *Home Is Where We Start From: Essays by a Psychoanalyst*, ed. C. Winnicott, R. Shepherd, and M. Davis, pp. 142–149. New York: W. W. Norton, 1986.

_____ (1968e). Communication between infant and mother, and between mother and infant, compared and contrasted. In *Babies and their Mothers,*, pp. 89–103. Reading, MA: Addison Wesley, 1987.

_____ (1969a). Physiotherapy and human relations. In *Psycho-Analytic Explorations*, ed. C. Winnicott, R. Shepherd, and M. Davis, pp. 561–568. Cambridge, MA: Harvard University Press, 1989.

_____ (1969b). James Strachey: obituary. In *Psycho-Analytic Explorations*, ed. C. Winnicott, R. Shepherd, and M. Davis, pp. 506–512. Cambridge, MA: Harvard University Press, 1989.

_____ (1970a). Cure. In *Home Is Where We Start From: Essays by a Psychoanalyst*, ed. C. Winnicott, R. Shepherd, and M. Davis, pp. 112–120. New York: W. W. Norton, 1986.

_____ (1970b). On the basis for self in body. In *Psycho-Analytic Explorations*, ed. C. Winnicott, R. Shepherd, and M. Davis, pp. 261–283. Cambridge, MA: Harvard University Press, 1989.

_____ (1970c). The place of the monarchy. In *Home Is Where We Start From: Essays by a Psychoanalyst*, ed. C.

Winnicott, R. Shepherd, and M. Davis, pp. 260–268. New York: W. W. Norton, 1986.

_____ (1970d). Individuation. In *Psycho-Analytic Explorations*, ed. C. Winnicott, R. Shepherd, and M. Davis, pp. 284–288. Cambridge, MA: Harvard University Press, 1989.

_____ (1970e). Living creatively. In *Home Is Where We Start From: Essays by a Psychoanalyst*, ed. C. Winnicott, R. Shepherd, and M. Davis, pp. 39–54. New York: W. W. Norton, 1986.

_____ (1971a). The location of cultural experience. In *Playing and Reality*, pp. 112–121. New York: Penguin.

_____ (1971b). Creativity and its origins. In *Playing and Reality*, pp. 76–100. New York: Penguin.

_____ (1971c). *Playing and Reality*. New York: Penguin.

_____ (1971d). Playing: creative activity and the search for the self. In *Playing and Reality*, pp. 62–75. New York: Penguin.

_____ (1971e). *Therapeutic Consultations in Child Psychiatry*, New York: Basic Books.

_____ (1972). *Holding and Interpretation*. New York: Grove.

_____ (1975). *Collected Papers: Through Paediatrics to Psycho-analysis*. New York: Basic Books.

_____ (1977). *The Piggle: An Account of the Psychoanalytic Treatment of a Little Girl*. Madison, CT: International Universities Press.

_____ (1979). *The Maturational Processes and the Facilitating Environment*. London: Hogarth.

_____ (1984). *Deprivation and Delinquency*. Ed. C. Winnicott, R. Shepard, and M. Davis. New York: Routledge.

_____ (1988). *Human Nature*. Ed. C. Bollas, M. Davis, and R. Shepherd. New York: Schocken.

_____ (1989). *Psycho-Analytic Explorations*. Ed. C. Winnicott, R. Shepherd, and M. Davis. Cambridge, MA: Harvard University Press.

Wordsworth, W. (1940–1949). *The Poetical Works of Wil-*

liam Wordsworth. Ed. E. de Selincourt and H. Dar-
bishire. Vol. 4. London: Oxford University Press.

Wordsworth, W. (1974). *The Prose Works of William
Wordsworth.* Ed. W. J. B. Owen and J. Worthington
Smyser. Vol. 1–3. London: Oxford University Press.

Wordsworth, W. (1987). The prelude. In *The Norton An-
thology of English Literature*, 5th edition, ed. M. H.
Abrams, pp. 1449–1528. New York: W. W. Norton.

Wright, K. (1991). *Vision and Separation: Between Mother
and Baby.* Northvale, NJ: Jason Aronson.

Credits

The author gratefully acknowledges permission to reprint the following:

Index